Katrin Meyer

The Link between Corporate Social and Corporate Financial Performance

An Empirical Investigation of Electric Utilities
- Before and During the Financial Market Crisis -

Dissertation zur Erlangung des Grades eines Doktors der Wirtschafts- und Sozialwissenschaften (Dr. rer. pol.) der Universität Hamburg, Fakultät Wirtschafts- und Sozialwissenschaften

Bibliografische Information der Deutschen Nationalbibliothek:
Die Deutsche Nationalbibliothek verzeichnet diese Publikation in der Deutschen Nationalbibliografie; detaillierte bibliografische Daten sind im Internet über http://dnb.dnb.de abrufbar.

© *2013 Katrin Meyer*

Herstellung und Verlag: BoD – Books on Demand, Norderstedt

ISBN: 978-3-7322-4576-5

The Link between Corporate Social and Corporate Financial Performance

Acknowledgements

This dissertation has been submitted to and accepted by the School of Business, Economics and Social Sciences at Hamburg University in June 2012. The status quo of the literature equates to the date of submission.

I wish to thank various people for their contribution to this project.

First and foremost I would like to thank my supervisor Prof. Dr. Alexander Bassen for his useful critiques, his enthusiastic encouragement and I am especially grateful for his patient guidance. I would also like to thank Prof. Dr. Zündorf, my second examiner for supporting me. Moreover, I would like to thank the team of Prof.Dr. Bassen for the great support, especially Dr. Houdou Basse Mama.

Second, my grateful thanks are extended to Joachim Schlange, who inspired me to investigate the case of Corporate Responsibility from a scientific point of view.

Third, I would like to thank oekom research and Thomson Financial for providing me the data for the empirical analysis.

I would also like to thank all participants of the survey. More than 200 analysts and investors took the time to respond to the questionnaire.

Finally, my special thanks should be given to Ursula Meyer, Iris Henne, Felise Maennig-Fortmann, Hans Jaich, Fabian Pont and Coco Bourin.

Table of Contents

List of Tables VIII
List of Figures X
Abbreviations XII
1 Introduction 1
　1.1 Relevance of the Topic 1
　1.2 Literature Review 3
　　1.2.1 Introduction - more than 40 years of CSP/CFP research 3
　　1.2.2 Direction of the link between CSP and CFP 5
　　1.2.3 Methodology of the Studies 8
　　1.2.4 Measuring Corporate Social Performance 11
　　1.2.5 Measuring Corporate Financial Performance 14
　　1.2.6 CSP and Risk 15
　　1.2.7 CSP and the Financial Crisis 17
　　1.2.8 Results from Meta-Analytical Research 19
　　1.2.9 Conclusion 22
　1.3 Aim of the Research 23
　1.4 Structure of the Research 23
2 Foundation of Corporate Social Responsibility and the Electric Utility Industry 27
　2.1 The Concept of Corporate Social Responsibility 27
　　2.1.1 Stakeholder Theory 27
　　2.1.2 Differentiation to related Concepts 31
　　　2.1.2.1 Corporate Social Responsibility 31
　　　2.1.2.2 Corporate Citizenship 34
　　　2.1.2.3 Corporate Governance 37
　　　2.1.2.4 Environmental, Social and Governance Issues . 40
　　　2.1.2.5 Sustainable Development 41
　　　2.1.2.6 Triple Bottom Line 43
　　　2.1.2.7 Corporate Responsibility 45
　　2.1.3 The Framework of Corporate Social Responsibility 47

2.2 The Utility Industry 51
  2.2.1 Industry Background 52
    2.2.1.1 Liberalization, Unbundling and Market
            Regulation 55
    2.2.1.2 Challenges, Key Drivers and Business Risks ... 57
  2.2.2 Corporate Social Responsibility Topics in the Utility
        Industry 60
    2.2.2.1 Mapping the Main Stakeholder Groups 61
    2.2.2.2 Major Environmental and Social Concerns 64
3 Theoretical Foundation 67
  3.1 Theory-based approaches to CSR 67
    3.1.1 Instrumental Theories 68
    3.1.2 Political Theories 70
    3.1.3 Integrative Theories 71
    3.1.4 Ethical Theories 73
    3.1.5 Conclusion 74
  3.2 Neoclassical Economics 76
    3.2.1 Origination 77
    3.2.2 Assumptions 79
    3.2.3 Critical Assessment of Neoclassical Economics 81
    3.2.4 The Neoclassical Paradigm and CSR 83
      3.2.4.1 Albert Carr - Business as a Poker Game 84
      3.2.4.2 Milton Friedman – Constraint Profit-Maximizing
              View 85
      3.2.4.3 Theodore Levitt – Functionalist Fundamentalist
              Position 88
      3.2.4.4 Elaine Sternberg – Distributive Justice and
              Ordinary Decency 89
      3.2.4.5 David Henderson – CSR as a Threat to the
              Market Economy 90
    3.2.5 Summary 92
  3.3 Resource-based View 93
    3.3.1 Origination 94
    3.3.2 Definitions and Assumptions 97

3.3.2.1 Definition of the Term Resource 98
3.3.2.2 Definition of Sustainable Competitive Advantage
.... 100
3.3.2.3 Assumptions 102
3.3.3 Critical Assessment of Resource-based View 104
3.3.4 Resource-based View and Corporate Social
   Responsibility 107
   3.3.4.1 Tangible and Intangible Resources 107
   3.3.4.2 Environmental Performance 109
   3.3.4.3 CSR Typologies 113
   3.3.4.4 CSR, Crises and Risk Management 118
3.3.5 Summary 124
4 Research Framework 128
 4.1 Introduction 128
 4.2 Survey Framework 132
  4.2.1 Integrating the Perspective of Investment
   Professionals 132
  4.2.2 Operationalizing Strategic and Non-Strategic CSP 135
 4.3 Modeling the Relationship between Corporate Social
  Responsibility, Firm Performance and Risk for the
  Empirical Analyses 139
  4.3.1 Introduction 139
  4.3.2 Constructing and Operationalizing CSP 139
  4.3.3 Constructing CFP 143
   4.3.3.1 Operationalizing CFP 144
   4.3.3.2 Measurable Effects of CSP on CFP 145
  4.3.4 Constructing Risk 148
   4.3.4.1 Operationalizing Risk 148
   4.3.4.2 Relation between CSP and Risk 150
  4.3.5 Further Influencing Factors 154
   4.3.5.1 The Lagged Effect Between CSP and CFP 154
   4.3.5.2 The Influence of the Market Structure 154
 4.4 Hypotheses and Research Framework 156

5 Empirical Analyses 159
  5.1 Sample Description 160
    5.1.1 Survey Sample... 160
      5.1.1.1 Structure of the Survey 161
      5.1.1.2 Survey Methodology and Participant Selection
      163
      5.1.1.3 Response Rate... 168
    5.1.2 Sample for CSP/CFP Analysis 169
      5.1.2.1 Oekom CSP Data 169
      5.1.2.2 CFP and Risk Data.. 173
    5.1.3 Sample for Electric Utilities 176
    5.1.4 Discussion and Limitations 178
  5.2 Descriptive Statistics and Bivariate Analysis................. 180
    5.2.1 Results of the Survey.. 180
      5.2.1.1 Results of the Survey – Introduction 181
      5.2.1.2 Results of the Survey – Main Part 185
      5.2.1.3 Results of the Survey – Additional Questions 195
      5.2.1.4 Conclusion of Survey Results......................... 197
      5.2.1.5 Factor Analysis – Constructing Strategic and
        Non-Strategic CSR... 198
    5.2.2 CSP/CFP Descriptive Data.................................... 202
      5.2.2.1 Factor Analysis – Strategic and Non-Strategic
        CSP... 202
      5.2.2.2 Correlation Matrix 209
      5.2.2.3 Conclusion 214
  5.3 Cross-sectional Regression Analysis 215
    5.3.1 OLS Models.. 216
    5.3.2 Results 219
      5.3.2.1 Model 1 to Model 4 for 2004.......................... 220
      5.3.2.2 Summary of Results for the 2004 Models 228
      5.3.2.3 Model 1 to Model 4 for 2008.......................... 231
      5.3.2.4 Summary of Results for the 2008 Models 238
  5.4 Discussion of OLS Models 240

    5.4.1 Testing Normal Distribution and Homoscedasticity 240
    5.4.2 Testing the Single Items of Strategic and Non-strategic CSP 243
    5.4.3 Summary of OLS-Models 255
6 Conclusion 259
    6.1 Survey Results.. 260
    6.2 Strategic versus Non-strategic CSR-resources 263
    6.3 CSP, Risk and the Insurance effect during the crisis 266
    6.4 Limitations 269
    6.5 Implications for Future Research and Management 272
7 Annex 276
    7.1 Summary and Assessment of Critiques to the RBV 276
    7.2 Survey Questionnaire 2009 277
8 Bibliography 283

List of Tables

Table 1:	Theoretical Framework in regard to the direction of the CSP/CFP link	6
Table 2:	Concept, Instruments and Actions of Corporate Citizenship	4
Table 3:	Summary of Terms in regard to Content, Novelty, Scientific Acceptance and Internationality	48
Table 4:	Generation by Energy Source: Total Electric Utilities	53
Table 5:	Classification of CSR Theories	75
Table 6:	A Natural-Resource-Based View: Conceptual Framework	111
Table 7:	CSR Typologies of Strategic and Non-Strategic CSR	126
Table 8:	Quantification of Strategic and Non-Strategic CSR	136
Table 9:	Comparison KLD and Oekom Rating	142
Table 10:	Overview Hypothesis: Expected results between CSP-typologies and CFP	146
Table 11:	Overview Hypothesis: Expected results between CSP composite rating and CFP	147
Table 12:	Overview Hypothesis: Expected results between CSP and firm risk (beta coefficient)	151
Table 13:	Selection criteria analysts	165
Table 14:	Selection criteria Investors	166
Table 15:	Total number of participants	167
Table 16:	Respondents to the Survey	168
Table 17:	Translation of the Oekom Rating Scheme into a Numeric Scheme	173
Table 18:	List of CFP and Risk Data.	175
Table 19:	Electric Utility List of the Oekom Rating for the CSP/CFP-Analysis	177

Table 20:	Association with CSR Investors (2005 and 2009). 182
Table 21:	Association with CSR Analysts (2005 and 2009).. 183
Table 22:	Differences between analysts and investors rating for all CSR components.. 186
Table 23:	Differences between Analysts and Investors perception for the single CSR items 187
Table 24:	Mean Values and Significance Economic Responsibility... ...189
Table 25:	Mean Values and Significance Environmental Management (2005 and 2009) 190
Table 26:	Mean Values and Significance Energy (2005 and 2009) 192
Table 27:	Mean Values and Significance Climate (2005 and 2009) 193
Table 28:	Mean Value and Significance Social Responsibility (2005 and 2009) 194
Table 29:	Mean Values and Significance Corporate Citizenship and Stakeholder management (2005 and 2009)...... 195
Table 30:	Extra Premium for good CSP 196
Table 31:	How will the financial crisis affect CSR?............... 196
Table 32:	Grouping into strategic, coerced and altruistic CSR 199
Table 33:	Factor Analysis and Reliability of Strategic, Coerced and Altruistic CSR 201
Table 34:	Translating the Oekom 2004 CSP-measures into strategic and non-strategic CSP 204
Table 35:	Translating the Oekom 2008 CSP-measures into strategic and non-strategic CSP 205
Table 36:	Factor Analysis and Reliability Testing of Strategic and Non-Strategic CSP 207
Table 37:	Consistency for Cronbach's alpha.......................... 208
Table 38:	Correlation-Matrix for 2004 (CSP) and 2005 (CFP) 209

Table 39:	Correlation Matrix for 2008 (CSP) and 2009 (CFP)	212
Table 40:	Summary of Regression Models and Equations (OLS) before and during the crisis	217
Table 41:	Regression Model 1: MTBV 2005 with CSP 2004	220
Table 42:	Regression Model 2: ROE 2005 with CSP 2004	222
Table 43:	Regression Model 3: ROA 2005 with CSP 2004	223
Table 44:	Regression Model 4: Beta 2005 with CSP 2004	226
Table 45:	Summary of Results of the OLS Regression Models for 2004	230
Table 46:	Regression Model 1: MTBV 2009 with CSP 2008	233
Table 47:	Regression Model 2: ROE 2009 with CSP 2008	234
Table 48:	Regression Model 3: ROA 2009 with CSP 2008	235
Table 49:	Regression Model 4: Beta 2009 with CSP 2008	237
Table 50:	Summary of Results of the OLS Regression Models for 2008	239
Table 51:	Correlation-Matrix 2004 Strategic CSP versus single CSP-measures	245
Table 52:	Regression Model Strategic CSP versus Staff Relations 2004	246
Table 53:	Correlation-Matrix 2004 Non-strategic CSP versus single CSP-measures	247
Table 54:	Regression Model Non-Strategic CSP versus single items 2004	248
Table 55:	Correlation-Matrix 2008 Strategic CSP versus single CSP-measures	251
Table 56:	Regression Model Strategic CSP versus single items 2008	253
Table 57:	Correlation Matrix 2008 Non-strategic CSP versus single CSP-measures	254
Table 58:	Regression Model Non-strategic CSP versus single items 2008	255
Table 59:	Summary of Results of the OLS-Models	256

List of Figures

Figure 1:	Stakeholder Network	29
Figure 2:	Definition of Corporate Social Responsibility	50
Figure 3:	Five Dimensions of the "old" Electricity Value Chain	54
Figure 4:	Stakeholder Groups of Electric Utilities	61
Figure 5:	Materiality Matrix of Centrica	65
Figure 6:	The Framework of the Resource-based View	103
Figure 7:	Research Framework	157
Figure 8:	Structure of the Questionnaire	161
Figure 9:	The relation between the survey and the CSP/CFP-link analysis.	162
Figure 10:	Histogram Beta_05/ Relations with External Stakeholders_04	241
Figure 11:	P-P Diagram Beta_05/ Relations with External Stakeholders_04	242
Figure 12:	Scatter Plot Beta_05/ Relations with External Stakeholders_04	242

Abbreviations

CAPM	Capital Asset Pricing Model
CFP	Corporate Financial Performance
CEP	Council on Economic Priorities
CR	Corporate Responsibility
CSP	Corporate Social Performance
CSR	Corporate Social Responsibility
EBITDA	earnings before interest, taxes, depreciation, and amortization
EU	European Union
GRI	Global Reporting Initiative
KLD	Kinder, Lydenberg and Domini
NGO	Non Governmental Organization
MTBV	Market to Book Value
OLS	Ordinary Least Square
ROA	Return on Assets
ROE	Return on Equity
RBV	Resource-based view
SCA	Sustainable Competitive Advantage
SCP	Structure-conduct-performance-hypothesis
SRI	Socially Responsible Investment
VRIN-criteria	value, rareness, imperfectly imitable, non- substitutable
WBCSD	World Business Council for Sustainable Development
WTO	World Trade Organization

1 Introduction

1.1 Relevance of the Topic

Through the dynamics of economic changes it is expected from companies to fulfill the demands of stakeholders, not only shareholders (Crowther/ Rayman-Bacchus, 2004, 3; McIntosh et al. 2003, 15; Smith 2003, 54). Integrating stakeholder demands into the process of corporate decision-making and taking responsibilities that go beyond complying with existing law is called *corporate social responsibility* (CSR). (e.g. Bassen/ Meyer/ Schlange, 2006)

The motivation to act responsibly is not always an ethical motivation but more and more market driven, as stakeholders, or e.g. non-governmental organizations (NGO), raise critical issues and, creating negative profiles in the public, consequently influence the behavior of consumers. But also other stakeholder groups, like employees and community groups, drive various topics and force companies to act in a responsible manner (e.g., McWilliams/ Siegel/ Wright, 2006).

Especially shareholders play an increasingly active roll in these processes. Institutional investors, for example, more often demand information of the company, going beyond the sheer financial performance indicators, as they want to reduce their risk or seek investment opportunities. On the one hand, CSR issues, or not complying with CSR expectations, lead to a high-risk exposure that might impact a company's license to operate. The most apparent risk of irresponsible corporate behavior is the risk of losing reputation. "Incidents caused by irresponsible behavior can damage the trust and the loyalty of stakeholders towards a company" (Bassen/ Meyer/ Schlange, 2006, p.8). Such a behavior often leads to consumer boycott. On the other hand, a company that engages in CSR can be an attractive investment, because engaging in CSR is also a signal for good management and therefore lower risks (e.g. Waddock/ Graves, 1997). Accordingly, engaging in CSR is not only risk mitigation; it can also be used as a method for value creation, e.g. by attracting investors through responsible behavior. Especially long-term orientated institutional investors tend to reject companies with a poor CSR performance (e.g. Cox/ Brammer/ Millington, 2004). Irresponsible behavior seems to impact a company's performance negatively. But how is a company's performance affected by a loss of trust in the whole system through irresponsible behavior? The financial crisis is an example of irresponsible behavior, not on the corporate level but a loss in trust in the whole financial system.

The financial crisis, which is dated from 2007 to 2010, starting with the subprime mortgage crisis in the U.S., left a huge footprint in the world economy. There are various reasons that led to the crisis, like high-risk mortgage loans, mortgage fraud and inaccurate credit ratings. The crisis is mainly a consequence of irresponsible behavior (Boettke/ Luther, 2010). Irrespective of its causes, it is likely that the financial crisis has an impact on CSR. The potential impact of this crisis on CSR has not been researched so far. It is not clear in which way this irresponsible behavior influences the CSR performance of a company.

To summarize, irresponsible corporate behavior can cause unexpected risks, whereas responsible behavior has the capacity to lower risks and increase opportunities. However, in which way responsible as well as irresponsible behavior is linked to financial performance is not clear. Previous empirical research on the question of whether *corporate social performance*[1] (CSP) is linked to *corporate financial performance*[2] (CFP) and in which way it affects the risk measures of a company has delivered mixed results. Also the interrelation between CSP and CFP during times of crises has not yet been researched in-depth. The following section discusses previous research about the relationship between CSP and CFP and company risk.

1.2 Literature Review

1.2.1 Introduction - more than 40 years of CSP/CFP research

The question of the link between CSP and CFP has been the focus of several different empirical studies. Research in this field has already been published in the early seventies (e.g. Moskowitz, 1972; Bragdon/ Marlin, 1972). Historically, this time marks the starting point of more than 40 years of empirical CSP/CFP research. In the Moskowitz as well as in the Bragdon and Marlin study a positive relation between CSP and CFP was found, but the CSP measuring methods were until then not well developed. So the following years, especially the 80's, were characterized by the search for the right CSP measure (e.g. Arlow, 1982; Cochran/ Wood, 1984; Ullmann 1985; Aupperle/ Hatfield/ Carroll, 1985; McGuire/ Sundgren, Schneeweis 1988). In the 90's CSP/CFP research developed especially in the area of more fine-

---

[1] According to Wood: *Corporate social performance revisited*, (1991) CSP is "a business organization's configuration of principles of social responsibility, processes of social responsiveness, and policies, programs, and observable outcomes as they relate to the firm's societal relationships."
[2] CFP is measured with various accounting and/or market-based measures; 1.2.5 Measuring Corporate Financial Performance

grained measurement methods for CSP, e.g., by using data of specialized rating agencies like KLD and furthermore by developing profound theoretical frameworks for analyzing the CSP/CFP-relation (e.g. McGuire/ Schneeweis/ Branch, 1990; Griffin, 1997; McWilliams/ Siegel, 1997; Russo & Fouts, 1997; Waddock/ Graves, 1997). The decade starting the new millennium "became preoccupied with the Enron Era of scandals" (Carroll/ Shabana, 2010, p.88). This era is dominated by the search for the business case of CSR and also characterized by using complex methods to empirically investigate the CSP/CFP-link (e.g. Waddock/ Graves, 2000; Walsh/ Weber, 2003; Schreck, 2009; Carroll/ Shabana, 2010). Summarizing the results of the above-mentioned decades of CSP/CFP research it can be concluded that they are mixed. The single studies do not provide a clear insight into this relation, the results vary according to the methodologies used to apply the techniques to measure CSP and as well CFP.

In the following, the different approaches to CSP/CFP research are introduced. First of all, the different directions of the link are matter of discussion (Chapter 1.2.2 Direction of the link between CSP and CFP). The methodologies used to investigate the CSP/CFP link vary and, depending on the used methodology, lead to different results. Therefore, the key is to introduce the different methodologies to understand the complexity of CSP/CFP research (Chapter 1.2.3 Methodology of the Studies). Further, the measurement of CSP and as well CFP is crucial and may influence the results of the research. Therefore this topic will be discussed in Chapter 1.2.4 (Measuring Corporate Social Performance) and in Chapter 1.2.5 (Measuring Corporate Financial Performance). As discussed in Chapter 1.1 (Relevance of the Topic), CSP and risk are assumed to be interrelated. Accordingly, the literature about this interrelation will be discussed as part of the literature review (Chapter 1.2.6 CSP and Risk). The last aspect that may influence the CSP/CFP relation are the recent events of the financial market crisis. Literature investigating if and in which way the crisis has influenced CSP will be analyzed in Chapter 1.2.7 (CSP and the Financial Crisis). The results of meta-analytical research summarize the key findings of 40 years of CSP and CFP research best, and they give an outlook as to how further research should be directed (Chapter 1.2.8 Results from Meta-Analytical Research). This section closes with a short conclusion, which already indicates the direction of the underlying research (Chapter 1.2.9 Conclusion).

It is not the aim of the following section to integrate each paper that has been published in 40 years of CFP/CFP research. The section rather aims at presenting the most influential and path-breaking research to each topic.

1.2.2 Direction of the link between CSP and CFP

The direction of the link is the key question in CSP/CFP research. Does CSR pays off, or is it the other way around, where CSP leads to a negative financial performance, or is it neither nor? Preston and O'Bannon (1997) developed a typology to picture the possible relationship between CSP and CFP. The table below summarizes the possible outcomes of CSP/CFP research in a theoretical framework. This framework will be used in the following to discuss the potential directions of the CSP/CFP link.

Direction of the link between CSP and CFP

Causal Sequence	Positive link	Negative link
Social performance leads to financial performance	Social impact hypothesis	Trade-off hypothesis
Financial performance leads to social performance	Available funding hyothesis	Managerial opportunism hypothesis
Social performance and financial performance are synergetic	Positive synergy	Negative synergy

Table 1: Theoretical Framework in regard to the direction of the CSP/CFP link (Preston/ O'Bannon, 1997)

When theoretical framing the CSP/CFP relation, basically three directions are possible: either that CSP leads to CFP or that CFP leads to CSP, lastly the CSP and CFP are synergistic. These general directions and relationships can either be positively or negatively linked (Preston, O'Bannon, 1997).

Most of the literature, however, assumes a positive CSP/CFP relation, so that good CSP leads to a better CSP, or in other words, the social impact hypothesis is expected. This kind of relationship is often found in aggregated studies with broad measures of CSP and CFP (e.g. Rennings/ Schröder / Ziegler, 2003; Ziegler et al., 2002).

Waddock et al. (1997) found evidence for the available funding hypothesis or slack resource theory. In this theory it is argued that better financial performance enables a company to invest more (slack) resources (e.g. financial) in CSR. Also McGuire et al. (1988) found empirical evidence for this theory. It could be shown that a firm's prior performance is closely related to CSP, which supports the idea that higher CFP leads to higher CSP.

According to the trade-off hypothesis a negative relationship is theorized. The main argument behind it is that investment in CSR results in upfront costs, which is likely to reduce the profitability of a company and therefore has a negative effect on CFP. This also reflects Friedman's neoclassical argument that it is the responsibility of a businessman to increase its profits. Evidence for this hypothesis is first found e.g. by Vance (1975). The results of this empirical study showed that good CSP was associated with declining stock prices relative to market average.

A further hypothesis with a negative relation is called managerial opportunism. This hypothesis assumes that short-term orientated behavior of managers leads to a negative CSP. Preston et al. (1997) theorize:

> [If] financial performance is strong, managers may attempt to crash in by reducing social expenditure in order to take advantage of the opportunity to increase their own short-term private gains. Conversely, when financial performance weakens, managers may attempt to offset and perhaps appear to justify their disappointing results by engaging in conspicuous social programs. (p. 423)

In the case of the positive synergy hypothesis or the "virtuous circle" (Waddock et al., 1997), CSP is theorized to stem from good management by addressing stakeholder expectations, which enhances characteristics like competitive advantage and reputation. In the case of the virtuous circle, CSP and CFP are in that way interrelated, as they are mutually dependent. The circle starts with good CSP, which leads to higher profits, which in turn can again be invested in even better CSP.

A further possible relationship, not explicitly named by Preston and O'Bannon, is the neutral relationship. Especially McWilliams and Siegel (2000) argued that a relationship between social and financial measures exists by chance, since there are too many variables that influence the relationship. They demonstrate that many studies suffer from specification errors and may be poorly designed. The authors conclude that the existing econometric estimates of the impact of CSP on CFP are biased and that there is the need for more complex models to construct the CSP/CFP relationship.[3]

The illustration of the possible links of the CSP to CFP demonstrate the complexity of this research field and it also shows that the link may depend to a high degree on the methodology used. In the following paragraph the various methodologies that have been approached so far will be discussed.

1.2.3 Methodology of the Studies

The methodology of CSP/CFP research can be divided into basically four groups: portfolio studies, event studies, case studies and multivariate regression analyses (Wagner/ Schaltegger, 2003). In the following, the different methodologies are presented

---

[3] This paragraph is based on the paper: Bassen/ Meyer/ Schlange (2006): The Influence of Corporate Responsibility on the Cost of Capital, SSRN. This paper was developed as part of the underlying thesis.

and discussed, especially in regard to the outcome the studies produce.

Portfolio studies (e.g. Derwall/. Guenster/ Bauer/ Koedijk, 2005) usually compare the performance of above average CSR performers against below average performers. Portfolio studies are mainly used in SRI research to investigate if an ethical portfolio leads to the expected output. Diltz (1995) e.g. constructed a portfolio by using different CSR performance indicators and correlated them with the daily return. Using this methodology, Diltz found evidence that environmental performance led to a better stock performance. However, not all measures could approve these results. One of the latest publications using portfolio studies deals with the economic virtues of SRI and CSR (Derwall, 2007). Derwall (2007) used SRI stock portfolios with a superior return/risk profile and analyzed them with special regard to firm value and the cost of capital. This main result of this study is: "integrating SRI criteria into portfolio construction does not negatively affect investment performance" (Derwall, 2007, p.258).

While portfolio studies offer some direct implications for institutional investors interested in SRI, their findings are rarely applicable on a firm-level. Moreover the results are only retrospective and depend very much on the time period, the risk adjustment, and the reweighting of the portfolio. There are not many studies using this methodology and it even became less popular in recent years. Closely related to portfolio studies are event studies.

Event studies focus on the short-term effect on capital markets after responsible or irresponsible corporate actions (e.g. Blacconiere/ Northcut, 1997; Rao, 1996). It is an empirical study of prices of an asset just before and after some event, like environmental or social incidents. A classical example is that of Rao (1996), who examined the performance of companies after reported pollution events. The performance after such an event was significantly below the companies' expected returns.

The main critique of event studies is that they are seen inadequate if it is the only way to examine the relationship between CSP and CFP. They just provide estimates of the short-term impact on shareholders and not on other stakeholders. Another critique is that event study findings are very sensitive to even small changes in research design (McWilliams/ Siegel, 2000).

In most of the literature, multivariate regression analysis is used (Cochran and Wood, 1984; McGuire et al., 1988; Rennings/ Schröder/ Ziegler, 2003; Cox et al., 2004), which examines the longer-term relationship between CSP and CFP. In these studies, a multitude of CSP and CFP measures are used, with mixed results. Some studies find clear evidence for a positive CSP/CFP relation, others not (Chapter 1.2.8 Results from Meta-Analytical Research).

The main critique of this methodology is that it often lacks in profound theoretical underpinnings for the expected link.

Lastly, case studies are a fourth methodological approach to investigate the CSP/CFP link. They are based on a single company and aim at promoting CSR. The main advantage is that they provide more in-depth analyses of the links between CSP and CFP but defy any industry-wide generalizations.[4]

---

[4] The prior paragraph is based on the paper: Bassen/ Meyer/ Schlange (2006): The Influence of Corporate Responsibility on the Cost of Capital, SSRN. This paper was developed as part of the underlying thesis.

What all the researches conducted in this field have in common is that the measurement of social and environmental performance is often poor, mainly because of the instruments used to measure CSP. These measures can generally be classified into one-dimensional and multidimensional and will be discussed in the following chapter.

1.2.4 Measuring Corporate Social Performance

As already pointed out, CSP can either be measured via one-dimensional or multi-dimensional measures. In the following these two types are introduced.

One-dimensional studies just focus on one specific dimension of corporate responsibility. In most of the cases they refer to the social responsibility of companies. One of the earliest studies trying to figure out the relationship between corporate responsibility and economic success is by Moskowitz (1972). Using only one dimension to measure (social) responsibility, he admits:

> It is extremely difficult to construct standards by which a company's social performance can be accurately measured (…). After four years of closely monitoring businesses' social involvement, however, I have observed a number of company names cropping up time after time with regard to positive and constructive responses to social problems. (Moskowitz, 1971, p.71)

Moskowitz ranked 67 selected firms in terms of his predominantly subjective evaluation of their level of social responsibility. Especially in early studies the Moskowitz social responsibility rating is used. Although Moskowitz's developed criteria to measure social responsibility are used in further studies, this approach does not satisfy today's scientific standards.

There are also one-dimensional CSP approaches using only ecological measures. The data most often used to measure CSP are from the Council on Economic Priorities (CEP). The CEP publishes, for example, climate gas emission rankings of multinational enterprises. But especially in recent studies, multidimensional CSP measures are preferred.

Multidimensional CSP measures can either consist out of third-party assessments, e.g. the Kinder, Lydenberg and Domini (KLD) rating, or of company self-reported data. According to Wood (2010), in current research the most often multivariate measures are third-party CSP ratings, such as KLD, Viego or others. "These ratings are achieving great popularity as CSP measures, largely because they are third-party assessments of CSP and do not rely so heavily on company self-reports (…)." (Wood, 2010, p.65)

Probably one of the most ground-breaking studies at the time using the multidimensional KLD rating is the paper of Waddock/ Graves (1997). They address the measurement problem of CSP in the paper and reflect that the most appropriate way to measure CSP is using multidimensional measures, because CSP is a multidimensional construct. The complexity of CSP requires appropriate measures. "(…) Measurements of single dimensions provide too limited a perspective on how well a company is actually performing in the relevant social domains." (Waddock/ Graves, 1997, p.305) The results of the study using KLD as multidimensional measure support the slack resource theory that prior financial performance leads to a better CSP.

A recent CSP/CFP study discussing and also using multidimensional CSP measures was conducted by Schreck (2009). In this study the Oekom Corporate Responsibility Rating is used to empirically investigate the CSP/CFP relation. Schreck speaks out for using single CSP measures, aggregated by the multidimensional ratings, instead of searching for the universal CSP/CFP relation. "This would then lead to a more differentiated analysis (...)." (Schreck, 2009, p.31) In the conclusion, Schreck summarizes the results "that there is no empirical basis for the assumption of a generic CSP/CFP link" (Schreck, 2009, p.124). However, when using single CSP measures of the multidimensional Oekom rating, the results are more promising. Schreck finds, for example, evidence for the good management hypothesis, assuming that corporate responsibility stems from good management and enhances the firm's competitive advantage. Companies with a good CFP also show superior performance in corporate governance and environmental management & eco-efficiency.

These are just a few examples and results of studies using either single measures or multidimensional CSP measures. Chapter 1.2.8. (Results from Meta-Analytical Research) gives an overall picture of the current status of CSP/CFP research.

1.2.5 Measuring Corporate Financial Performance[5]

According to Margolis and Walsh (2003), researchers used approximately 70 different economic performance measures in 127 studies conducted between 1972 and 2000 with the aim to investigate the CSP/CFP link. These measures can generally be classified into two main categories: accounting-based and market-based indicators. A third category, the perceptual measures exist as well, but they won't be discussed in this context, as they play a minor role in CSP/CFP literature (Orlitzky/ Schmidt/ Rynes, 2003, p.408).

Compared to CSP, CFP is a broad concept. Moreover, the measurement of CFP is much more advanced and sophisticated than that of CSP. But still it brings about many controversies, especially when it comes to the debate over accounting and market-based measures.

Classical market-based measures or investor returns used in CSP/CFP literature are price per share or share price appreciation (Orlitzky, Schmidt and Rynes, 2003, p.408). In previous literature, market-based measures were more popular than accounting measures, with the argument that they assess the external efficiency of the firm and tend to be more objective and rather more forward-looking than accounting measures. They are assumed to reflect – under conditions of market efficiency – the best ability of the company to generate future economic benefits (McGuire,

---

[5] The following chapter (1.2.5. Measuring Corporate Financial Performance) is based on the paper: Bassen/ Meyer/ Schlange (2006): The Influence of Corporate Responsibility on the Cost of Capital, SSRN. This paper was developed as part of the underlying thesis.

Sundgren and Schneeweiss, 1988), and therefore were considered as the proper performance measure (Ullmann, 1985).

Accounting-based measures, such as return on assets (ROA) and return on equity (ROE) show the internal efficiency of a target corporation (Orlitzky, Schmidt and Rynes, 2003, p.408). A critical aspect of them is that they are short-term orientated in nature and "tap only historical aspects of performance" (Hillman/ Keim, 2001, p.129). In today's CSP/CFP literature it is unanimous consent that especially the long-term value of a firm is more accurately captured by market measures. But still, most studies use both, accounting and market-based measures, in order to provide comparability across studies.

1.2.6 CSP and Risk[6]

Previous research has mainly focused on the relationship between CSP and CFP and used risk measures predominantly as control variables in the studies (cf. Margolis/ Elfenbein/ Walsh, 2009). The results presume a strong relation between CSP and risk, though not many studies examined the CSP/CFP link from a mere risk perspective. However, this question is especially interesting when assuming that CSP might lower company risk and therefore lower the cost of capital (cf. Bassen/ Meyer/ Schlange, 2006). In the following, studies will be introduced that focus on this risk perspective while investigating the CSP/CFP link.

---

[6] The following chapter (1.2.6 CSP and Risk) is based on the paper: Bassen/ Meyer/ Schlange (2006): The Influence of Corporate Responsibility on the Cost of Capital, SSRN. This paper was developed as part of the underlying thesis.

The relationship between CSP and risk was first examined by Spicer (1978):

> Spicer used a sample of companies disposed to pollution and found that companies with better pollution control records tended to have higher profitability, lower total risks, lower systematic risk, and higher price-earning ratios. (Bassen/ Meyer/ Schlange, 2006, p.10)

McGuire (1988) and also Herremans/ Akathaporn,/ McInnes (1993) showed that CSP measures are closely connected with risk. Both studies could empirically prove that good CSP resulted in lower risks. In both studies, beta – the measure for systematic risk – was used.

Orlitzky and Benjamin (2001) conducted a meta-analysis on the link between CSP and risk measures. Based on previous empirical findings, they hypothesized that the higher a firm's CSP the lower its financial risk. They argued that previous research had been too much focused on the CSP/CFP link without taking into account the risk perspective, although true economic performance consists out of both, good financial performance and low-level financial risk (Orlitzky/ Benjamin, 2001). For their study, they analyzed 17 previous studies. Most of them used beta (systematic risk) as market risk measures or accounting risk measures, mainly estimated by the standard deviation of a firm's long term ROA or ROE (Orlitzky/ Benjamin, 2001, p.379). The results show that "the higher the a firm's corporate social performance the lower the financial risk incurred by the firm" (Orlitzky/ Benjamin, 2001, p.388). However, CSP is especially strongly related to measures of market risk (beta).

They summarize that "a firm that is socially responsible and responsive may be able to increase interpersonal trust between and among internal and external stakeholders, build social capital, lower transaction costs, and, therefore, ultimately reduce uncertainty about its financial performance" (Orlitzky/ Benjamin, 2001, p.391).

Other approaches are researching the CSP/risk link also from a cost of capital perspective, arguing that the lower the company risk, the lower the cost of capital. Bassen, Meyer and Schlange (2006) found evidence that CSP and risk are linked. In the study, risk was measured with beta and also the S&P credit rating were used as a proxy for default risk. The authors of the study come to the conclusion that "a complete lack of CSR engagement exposes a company to unnecessary high risk" (Bassen et al., 2006, p.1). However, in this study a single-industry approach was chosen, therefore these results are only applicable for the electric utilities industry. Bauer and Hann (2010) empirically tested for the cost of capital by using credit risk ratings. They tested in which way environmental management and credit risk implications for bond investors are related by using multivariate regression analysis (Bauer/ Hann, 2010). They concluded with their results that the "analysis shows that firms with environmental concerns pay a premium on the cost of debt financing and have lower credit ratings assigned to them" (Bauer/ Hann, 2010, p.24).

1.2.7 CSP and the Financial Crisis

There are a growing number of publications investigating the effects of the current financial crisis on CSR. One example is a book edited by Sun, Stewart and Pollard (2010). In this work, various authors address the question in which way the financial crisis influenced CSR. Issues like why CSR failed to prevent the global financial crisis and how the crisis may reframe CSR are discussed. This work can be valued as probably the most comprehensive collection of different perspectives on the topic of CSR and the financial crisis.

However, up to now not much literature has been published investigating the CSP/CFP relation under the circumstances of the financial crisis. This specific topic is up to now under researched. Basically two papers could be found that are dedicated to this topic from the CSP/CFP perspective.

The first paper, by Fernández-Feijóo Souto (2009), approaches this topic theoretically. The objective of this paper is to reflect on the consequences of the current economic and financial crisis on corporate social responsibility. In this paper CSR and the crisis are linked together. It is argued: "firms will be in a better position to overcome the turbulent situation of the current economic and financial crisis, using CSR as a business opportunity" (Fernández-Feijóo Souto, 2009, p.46). This hypothesis is in line with the assumption that CSR is an insurance-like protection during times of crisis.

Giannarakis and Theotokas (2011) did an empirical analysis of a sample of 112 companies on the question, if an economic downturn affects CSP. They found out that companies tend to increase their performance to regain the lost trust in business: "The results indicate increased CSR performance before and during the financial crisis except for the period 2009-2010" Giannarakis/ Theotokas, 2011, 6). This would imply that although companies are losing in shareholder value due to the worldwide downturn of the financial markets they further invest in CSR.

Because the crisis is too recent and still not totally overcome, it is problematic to draw conclusions out of empirical tests. Only first tendencies can be observed and trends described.

1.2.8 Results from Meta-Analytical Research

The meta-analyses that emerged in the early 2000's give a comprehensive overview of the results and obstacles of CSP/CFP research. These meta-analytical papers best reflect the status quo of CSP/CFP research. Since 2003 basically four meta-analytical studies on the relation between CSP and CFP have been published. The first meta-analysis published is the paper of Orlitzky, Schmidt and Rynes (2003); a further paper is the meta-analytical work of Margolis and Walsh (2003), which was published in the same year. These two papers can be seen as the most influential work in recent years.[7]

In the above-mentioned meta-analyses different methodological approaches are used. Orlitzky, Schmidt and Rynes (2003) combine studies on the linkage between CSP and CFP by using the technique of the psychometric meta-analysis, which is rigorous analysis, while Margolis and Walsh (2003) apply a simple "vote counting" technique to pool results. Due to dissimilar methodical approaches, the conclusions drawn by these authors differ.

---

[7] The following paragraphs about the meta-analysis of Orlitzky, Schmidt, Rynes (2003) and Margolis/ Walsh (2003) are based on the paper: Bassen/ Meyer/ Schlange (2006): The Influence of Corporate Responsibility on the Cost of Capital, SSRN. This paper was developed as part of the underlying thesis.

Margolis and Walsh (2003) present a detailed overview of the literature, with over 95 studies between 1971 and 2001, integrated in their analysis. The results deliver mixed results and no clear picture on the CSP/CFP relation. They identified 55 studies with a positive CSP/CFP relation. Whereas in 21 studies no linkage could be found, 7 studies delivered data presenting a negative relationship and 18 studies reported mixed results. A main critique of Margolis and Walsh is that the sources of data and the measures utilized by many studies are poor.

Orlitzky et al. (2003) conducted a meta-analysis of 52 studies and found an overall positive CSP/CFP link. In their analysis, CSP measures are higher correlated with accounting-based than with marked-based measures. Their findings suggest that social responsibility and, to a lesser extent, environmental responsibility is likely to pay off, because they found a clear positive relation between these measures and CFP. Moreover, they criticized the vote-counting technique used by Margolis and Walsh. It has been shown that this technique delivers statistical invalid results.

In 2005 a further meta-analysis was published by Allouche and Laroche (2005). They also criticize the poor statistical methods used in previous research like that of Margolis and Walsh (2003). They state, in regard to the used statistical methods, that only the paper of Orlitzy et al. (2003) "made valuable contributions" (Allouche et al., 2005, p.1). Because of new publications in the CSP/CFP research field they conducted a further meta-analysis using similar statistical methods. They identified 82 studies within a total 373 single observations and used multivariate regressions to analyze the CSP/CFP relation. However, despite the larger sample and methodologically more fine-grained statistical methods, Allouche et al. (2005) basically came up with results similar to Orlitzky et al. (2003). Summarizing, Allouche et al.

(2005) could find as well a positive relation between CSP and CFP measures. However they also found evidence that some CSP attributes, such as CSP reputation, have a greater affect on CSP than others, such as social disclosure. Having a closer look on their findings regarding the used control variable, it appears that firm size is a valuable control variable, whereas industry, risk and R&D do not have an affect on the CSP/CFP relation.

The most recent meta-analysis is that of Margolis, Elfenbein and Walsh (2009). In their study even more studies are integrated into the meta-analytical research and it is, therefore up to now, the most comprehensive meta-analysis integrating 251 studies. Although the statistical methods used differ from the latter studies, the results are in line with previous meta-analytical study results. Margolis et al. (2009) once again used the vote counting technique with the result, that 59% of the studies show no significant relation, 28% a positive and 2% a negative relation between CSP and CFP, and where 10% of the studies could not be included in the analysis. There seems to be evidence for a slightly positive relationship between CSP and CFP. Interestingly Margolis et al. (2009) also tested if the CSP/CFP relation has been stronger in the last decade, with the argument that companies have become strategically more sophisticated in addressing social concern and being socially responsible. However, the results of this analysis show an even weaker effect between CSP and CFP, which implies that the association between CSP and CFP has not increased over time (Margolis et al., 2009, p.25). In regard to their findings, they are the first scholars who pose the question whether researchers should further search for the CSP/CFP link, because they do not assume that further research will result in different findings. They basically see two options for future research. The first is "seeking more precision in analyzing the empirical connection between CSP and CFP" and the second is asking "alternative questions about CSP" (Margolis et al. 2009, p.28). The author of this paper decided to follow the first option, of conducting further research and identify conditions under which CSP and CFP are interrelated.

1.2.9 Conclusion

According to the literature review there is much evidence that there is a positive relation between CSP and CFP. CSP is mainly measured in a multidimensional way and the most popular method used is to analyze the CSP/CFP link is via regression analysis.

The risk perspective in this research field is especially interesting, because economic performance is both high return and low risk. But the relation between CSP and risk measures is until now under researched. So the question is how investment professionals, in this case investors and analysts, perceive CSR and if they prize it.

A further aspect is in which way the financial market crisis has influenced the CSP/CFP link. Until now there is not much research available on this topic. Only a few papers have been published so far, assuming that CSR functions like an insurance-like protection.

The reliability of the measures used for CSP and CFP is often criticized. The quantification of CSR is moderate and therefore it is difficult to prove a clear and direct relationship. Moreover, CSR depends on the industry a company operates in. Many studies fail to take account industry difference in their approaches. In this field, more research, theoretical as well as empirical, needs to be conducted to further fathom the complexity of the CSP/CFP relation.

1.3 Aim of the Research

It is the objective of this research to investigate the CSP/CFP/risk link before and during the financial market crisis, with a special focus on the question of how investment professionals value CSR.

Above all, this research investigates the business case of CSR. Mainly, this research is a classical approach to the field of CSP/CFP research, though it also includes the opinion of investment professionals. A further advancing aspect is that it investigates the CSP/CFP link before and during the crisis. The author shows a single industry approach, because each industry has its own specific CSR topics, which are not comparable.

Building on available literature, this research aims to advance the existing approaches of CSP/CFP research.

1.4 Structure of the Research

The paper is divided into six chapters, starting with the introduction in which the relevance of the topic is outlined. The literature review, which is also part of the first chapter, gives a first insight into the research field. It presents previous findings of CSP/CFP research but also the limitations of it. Based on the literature review, the basic aims of the research are outlined.

The second chapter is a foundation of the basic terms dealt with in the research. The terms of CSR are defined, which is essential because many different definitions and approaches to CSR circulate. Therefore, it is essential to define the concept of CSR especially in comparison to related concepts. Besides the classical CSP/CFP research, this paper is also focuses on the capital market perspective on CSR. Therefore the capital market mechanisms are introduced. In this part of the research the fundamentals of how to operationalize CFP are laid by introducing the concepts of risk and return, portfolio selection and the capital asset pricing model. This research investigates the CSP/CFP link with a single industry approach, focusing on electric utilities, and accordingly the industry will be presented in Chapter 2. First of all, the industry with its general topics of market regulation and liberalization and its main business risk are outlined. Secondly, the main CSR topics that the industry is facing currently and in the future are introduced.

The third chapter lays the theoretical foundation for the research. It is the aim of this chapter to first of all define the main CSR theories and determine which theories are mainly used in the field of CSP/CFP research. Based on these insights, the two underlying instrumental theories or approaches of neoclassical economics and resource-based view (RBV) are introduced. Using neoclassical economics theory, CSR is embedded into first of all mainstream economics and the doctrine of profit maximization. This perspective clearly focuses on an instrumental view of CSR. The second theory introduced is the RBV, which is the most common theoretical approach in analyzing the strategic use of CSR and in investigating the relation between CSP and CFP. According to the RBV framework, CSR is a resource and, through the effective control and manipulation of CSR as a resource, a company is capable of achieving a sustainable competitive advantage. Based on these two theories, the research framework is developed in Chapter 4.

The research framework lays out the concrete approach of the analysis. It starts with an introduction in which the two parts of the research are introduced, a survey with mainstream analysts and investors, and the CSP/CFP analysis. The following sections are structured accordingly. First, the framework for the survey is outlined, with a division of CSR into strategic, tactical and operational CSR. Secondly, the expected relation between CSP/CFP and risk measures is modeled. The modeled relationships finally end up in the hypotheses underlying this research.

Chapter 5 is all about the empirical analyses. It starts with a sample description. This part of the chapter is structured into 4 sections. In the first section the survey sample is introduced, followed by the sample description of the CSP and CFP data and also of the utility companies researched in this thesis. The sample description finishes with a discussion and the validation of the limitations regarding the sample.

The second part of Chapter 5 contains the descriptive statistics and the bivariate analysis. First of all, the survey results are presented and analyzed, followed by a factor analysis to aggregate specific CSP measures. The second part of this section is analyzing the CSP/CFP relation on a descriptive level, e.g. by using correlation analysis. The correlation analysis of the CSP and CFP data gives the first insight into this relation and is therefore the foundation for the following cross-sectional regression analysis.

The cross-sectional analysis is the core of Chapter 5, the empirical analysis. The assumed relations between CSP and CFP will be tested with OLS regressions, firstly for the years before the financial market crisis and secondly for the years during the financial market crisis.

Afterwards, the discussion of the results gives insights into the link between CSP and CFP in the electric utilities industry and gives first answers to the question in which way the financial market crisis has affected CSR. To get an even deeper understanding of the research topic, further statistical testing and analysis will be carried out as part of the discussion.

Chapter 6 is the final chapter, which aims at consolidating the results. First of all, the results of the central research question are presented and concluded. Then the contribution of the survey with investment professionals, the question which CSR resources contribute to financial performance, and finally in which way the crisis has affected CSR are discussed. Afterwards the limitations of this research are examined. The research ends with implications for future research and for management.

2 Foundation of Corporate Social Responsibility and the Electric Utility Industry

The following chapter gives an introduction into the basic concepts and terms dealt within this research. First of all the term *corporate social responsibility* will be introduced and defined. Afterwards the capital market mechanisms will be introduced with a focus on risk and return and its measurement. At last an overview of the electric utility industry is given, because the empirical data of this research are based on this industry.

2.1 The Concept of Corporate Social Responsibility

This section defines corporate social responsibility. The first part addresses the complex role of the various stakeholder groups that play an important role in understanding the recent CSR debate. CSR as a term and a concept will be analyzed and defined by a differentiation of related terms. At the end of this section a definition and a framework of CSR is given as a basis for this research.

2.1.1 Stakeholder Theory

Stakeholder theory is closely related to the concept of CSR. It is not, like the upcoming definitions, a synonym or related concept of CSR; it is rather a theoretical model expanding and explaining the concept of CSR. The idea of stakeholder theory can be seen as a subordinated concept explaining the mechanism leading to

CSR. For that reason, it is aim of this chapter to introduce the stakeholder theory and link it to the discussion of CSR.

The expression 'stakeholder' was first recorded in the 1960's by the Stanford Research Institute (Freeman/ McVea, 2001). However, the theoretical approach was mainly developed and brought forward by Freeman in the 1980's. The stakeholder theory starts by looking at various groups to which the corporation has a responsibility. The main starting point is the claim that corporations are not simply managed in the interests of their shareholders alone, but that there is a whole range of groups, the stakeholders, which have legitimate interest in the corporation as well (Freeman, 1984). Although there are a number of different definitions, Freeman's original definition (Freeman, 1984, p.46) is perhaps the most widely used: "A stakeholder in an organization is (…) any group or individual who can affect or is affected by the achievement of the organization's objectives." This definition raises the question of what exactly is meant with "affects" and "affected by".

Evan and Freeman (1993) suggest applying two simple principles. The first is the principle of corporate rights, which demands that the corporation has the obligation not to violate the rights of others. The second, the principle of corporate effect, saying that companies are responsible for the effects of their actions on others. In the light of these two basic principles the term 'stakeholder' can be defined in the following more precise way:

A stakeholder of a corporation is an individual or a group which either:

is harmed by, or benefits from, the corporation, or whose rights can be violated, or have to be respected, by the corporation. (Crane/ Matten, 2007)

This definition makes clear that the range of stakeholders differs from company to company, and even for the same company in different situations, tasks, or projects. Using this definition, then, it is not possible to identify a definitive group of relevant stakeholders for any given situation. Figure 1 (Stakeholder Network) roughly pictures the idea of the stakeholder concept. It shows various stakeholder groups with their influential and increasing pressure they put on companies to act responsibly. This figure is only one example of different forms of stakeholder activism and the mechanisms behind them.

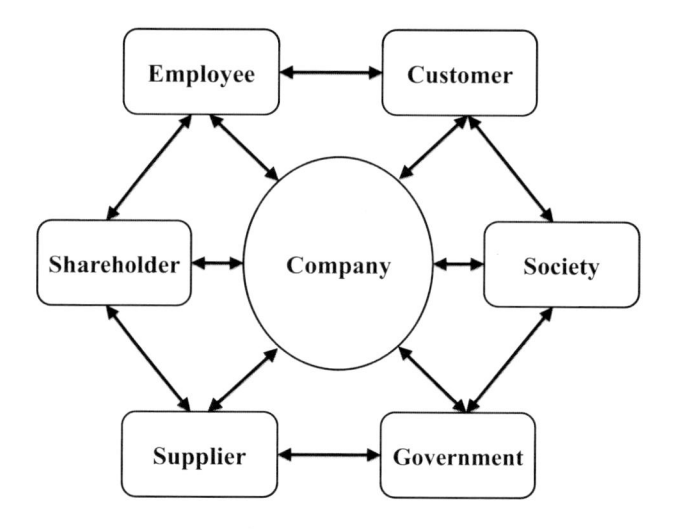

Figure 1: Stakeholder Network (Matten/ Crane, 2005, p.51)

In the center of the figure is the company, which is in constant interaction with various stakeholder groups, like employees, customers and shareholders. The stakeholders as well are in mutual contact with each other. The employees for example, as internal stakeholders, have special demands on the company, like an adequate salary, fair treatment, advanced training opportunities and others. It is the role of the company to fulfill these demands at least in part, otherwise a company may loose its license to operate. This is just one very simple example of the stakeholder mechanisms. These mechanisms are much more complex in real business life and they are getting even more complex e.g. by the increasing demands of customers, upcoming legislation, more active NGO's. These mechanisms of stakeholder influence may put an increasing pressure on corporations, which forces the management to act more responsibly. Summarizing, the central task of the stakeholder management is:

> to manage and integrate the relationships and interests of shareholders, employees, customers, suppliers, communities and other groups in a way that ensures the long-term success of the firm. A stakeholder approach emphasizes active management of the business environment, relationships and the promotion of shared interests. (Freeman/ McVea, 2001, p.10)

Stakeholder theory has become an essential part of CSR literature (Freeman/ McVea, 2001). In this thesis, the stakeholder approach serves as a subordinated framework or concept that is essential to understand the complexities of the CSR mechanisms. Therefore, stakeholder management will be an integral part of the CSR definition framework introduced in Chapter 2.1.3 The Framework of Corporate Social Responsibility.

2.1.2 Differentiation to related Concepts

There is much confusion about the definition of terms like: corporate social responsibility (CSR), corporate citizenship (CC), sustainability, corporate governance (CG), environmental social and governance (ESG) issues, corporate responsibility (CR) and triple bottom line (TBL) in practice as well as in theory. The following chapter analyses the different concepts by tackling them first of all from the historical perspective up to the current usage of the terms and their role in scientific research.

For this thesis the author is looking for a broad concept of responsible corporate behavior, which is also accepted in the scientific community and will probably also be used as such in the future. Therefore, each chapter ends with a short evaluation of the various terms to conclude which of the terms is appropriate for this research paper. Chapter 2.1.3 (The Framework of Corporate Social Responsibility) and Table 3 (Summary of Terms in regard to Content, Novelty, Scientific Acceptance and Internationality) summarize this evaluation.

2.1.2.1 Corporate Social Responsibility

The term CSR has its origin in the Anglo-Saxon countries. In these approaches the emphasis has historically been on the social responsibilities of company. The term has its beginnings with the development of enterprises in the 19th Century (WBCSD 1999, p.5; Smith 2003, p.52).

Traditionally in the United States, CSR has been defined much more in terms of a philanthropic and community based model.

The systematic reasoning about a conceptual framework for CSR started in the United States of America (USA) half a century ago. Bowen (1953) assumes in his publication *Social Responsibilities of the Businessman* that the social responsibility of the businessman needs to be linked to the expectations and values of the society.

Probably the most established and accepted framework of CSR is the 'four-part model of corporate social responsibility' as initially proposed by Carroll (Carroll, 1979). Carroll regards CSR as a multi-layered concept, which can be differentiated into four interrelated aspects – economic, legal, ethical and philanthropic responsibilities. Carroll offers the following definition:

> Corporate social responsibility encompasses the economic, legal, ethical and philanthropic exceptions placed on organizations by society at a given point in time. (Carroll, 1979, p.35)

In this United States-based CSR approach the linkage to environmental issues is not explicitly integrated. In this way the US approach is different to the European approach.

The focus of the European CSR movement is more the concept of 'sustainability' (see Chapter 2.1.1.4 Sustainability) (Bowie/ Werhane, 2005, p.105). The official publication on that subject by the European Union was developed for the Green Paper released in July 2001. It defines CSR as "a concept whereby companies integrate social and environmental concerns in their business operations and in their interaction with their stakeholders on a voluntary basis" (European Commission, 2001).

Also on supranational level CSR is an issue. The UN Global Compact defined CSR as "an approach to business that embodies transparency and ethical behavior, respect for stakeholder groups and a commitment to add economic, social and environmental value" (SustainAbility/ UN Global Compact, 2004, p.6).

A redefinition of CSR has recently been proposed by Freeman et al. (2006). He suggests a new approach to CSR called *company stakeholder responsibility* (CSR) as a term to express the responsibilities of a company towards its stakeholders. Therewith Freeman addresses the main problems of the term corporate social responsibility. First of all, he argues that corporate social responsibility is often about "seeming to do good works" with the implication that companies "need to do good works". But business is already social because capitalism is a system of social cooperation, "a system of working together to create value for each other (...)". So the 'social' of CSR is replaced by the word stakeholder, which suggests that the main goal of CSR is to create value for stakeholders. The replacement of corporate to company signals that all businesses need to be involved, no matter the size, the stage and other determinants of the business. This redefinition of the term CSR is fairly new and therefore is not established yet in theory and even less in practice. Although the CSR approach of Freeman is convincing, it hasn't been established yet in the scientific world because the term CSR is already associated and established with 'corporate social responsibility'. Therefore a redefinition is difficult to set up.

2.1.2.2 Corporate Citizenship

The term and concept *corporate citizenship* (CC) also originates in the Anglo-Saxon countries and deals with the role of the company as a 'good corporate citizen'. There are basically three different views and definitions of CC.

The first one, which is a very common understanding, especially in the European academic literature, describes CC as an aspect of CSR. According to this definition, CC is the external aspect of CSR, describing the engagement in the society by donations and sponsoring, *corporate volunteering* and others. This understanding is in line with the definition of the *Global Compact*. Referring to the Global Compact, CC involves: "(…) companies understanding that they are both public and private entities (...)" (McIntosh et al., 2003, p.50). According to Dubilzig/ Schaltegger (2005), CC is the attempt of a company to be perceived as "a good citizen of a society". This can be expressed by mainly two instruments, as introduced by Maaß/ Clemens (2002):

Corporate Citizenship

Concept	Instruments	Action
Corporate Volunteerung	Donations, Sponsoring, Foundations	Funds/ Cash Material expenses Services
Corporate Giving	Voluntary engagement of employees Secondment-programme	

Table 2: Concept, Instruments and Actions of Corporate Citizenship (according to Maaß/ Clemens, 2002)

The instruments can be divided into the concept of *corporate giving* and *corporate volunteering*. The possibility of actions is from one-time activities to long-term engagements, like e.g. sponsoring partnerships. The more intense an engagement is, the more time for planning and coordination is needed. Summarizing this approach, CC can be seen as an aspect of a more strategic subordinated concept, CSR.

In recent years a more extensive understanding of CC is growing. This extended view of CC is basically the same as that of CSR. Matten and Crane (2005) put forward an extended theoretical conceptualization of CC. In their provocative paper they first of all analyze the conventional views of CC, which are divided into the limited one, "the identification of CC as charitable donations" and the equivalent view, which is "a conflation of CC with existing conceptions of CSR". Finally they come up with a new extended definition of CC: "CC describes the role of the corporation in administering citizenship rights for individuals." This definition eliminates the notion that the corporation itself is a citizen but underlines that the corporation administers certain aspects of citizenship for other constituencies e.g. stakeholders. Waddock (2004) also addresses the fact of "parallel universes" when it comes to the terminology of corporate citizenship, corporate responsibility and related terms. Waddock sees "CC is manifested in the strategies and operating practices a company develops in operationalizing its relationships with and impacts on stakeholders and the natural environments". This definition is also extended and goes beyond the sheer sponsoring activities as it integrates the stakeholder perspective.

Another example for the forthcoming of using CC and CSR synonymously is the definition of the World Economic Forum saying:

It can be defined as the contribution a company makes to society through its core business activities, its social investment and philanthropy programmes, and its engagement in public policy. That contribution is determined by the manner in which a company manages its economic, social and environmental impacts and manages its relationships with different stakeholders, in particular shareholders, employees, customers, business partners, governments, communities and future generations. (World Economic Forum, 2002)

The third definition of CC is a theoretical democratic approach, in which the company is seen as an active citizen of society. This approach is in a way already integrated in the above-described ones, but in this concept it has a rather political notion. The company is not just being involved in society; it has the same rights and obligations as every citizen and therefore has the duty to be involved in society. In this definition, CC can be seen as a general discourse on corporate responsibility and if a company can and should have the same rights as a citizen.

Although there has been the attempt by some scholars to extend the concept of CC, it is still mainly associated with sponsoring and philanthropic activities of a company, especially in Europe. The first view of CC, in which CC is seen as an aspect of CSR, still seems to be the most common one. However, more and more researchers tend to re-interpret the original meaning to a more extended meaning closely related to CSR. Especially in Anglo-Saxon research, CC is an often-used expression.

Because of the still content-wise narrow scope of the term corporate citizenship, and the fact that it is not established as a broad concept in scientific literature, corporate citizenship as a broad term seems not appropriate for this thesis. It will only be used in the more narrow way of philanthropy.

2.1.2.3 Corporate Governance

Like some of the other concepts introduced before, *corporate governance* has a long history as well. It was first named and defined by Adam Smith in 1776:

> The directors of companies, being the managers rather of other people's money than of their own, it cannot well be expected that they should watch over it with the same anxious vigilance with which the partner in a private copartnery frequently watch over their own. [...] Negligence and profusion, therefore, must always prevail, more or less, in the management of the affairs of such a company. (p. 700)

However, since then a lot of different definitions turned up, mainly depending on the discipline in which they are used. Narrow definitions just deal with the relationship between managers and the capital market participants whereas broad definitions also take other stakeholders' perspectives into account.

An example for a more narrow definition is given by Shleifer/ Vishny (1997): "Corporate governance deals with the ways in which suppliers of finance to corporations assure themselves of getting a return on their investment."

A broader definition has been published by the World Bank:

> Corporate Governance is concerned with holding the balance between economic and social goals and between indi-

vidual and communal goals. The corporate governance framework is there to encourage the efficient use of resources and equally to require accountability for the stewardship of those resources. The aim is to align as nearly as possible the interests of individuals, corporations and society. (Sir Adrian Cadbury in 'Global Corporate Governance Forum', World Bank, 2000)

Another corresponding definition is the one by the Organization for Economic Cooperation and Development (2004):

Corporate governance is only part of the larger economic context in which firms operate that includes, for example, macroeconomic policies and the degree of competition in product and factor markets. The corporate governance framework also depends on the legal, tax, regulatory, and institutional environment. In addition, factors such as business ethics and corporate awareness of the environmental and societal interests of the communities in which a company operates can also have an impact on its reputation and its long-term success. (p.12)

Irrespectively of the different theoretical approaches and definitions of corporate governance given above, the topic has become very important for companies in the last decade. The reason for this is the high-profile collapses of a number of large firms like Enron[8]. In order to prevent such collapses and to enhance transparency and building up trust in companies, most governments,

---

[8] Enron: the Enron scandal was a financial scandal involving Enron Corporation and its accounting firm Arthur Anderson, which was revealed in late 2001. After a series of revelations involving irregular accounting procedures conducted throughout the 1990s, Enron was on the verge of bankruptcy by November of 2001.

starting with the United States, released laws, like the Sarbanes-Oxley Act (SOX), or soft laws and principles, like the German Corporate Governance Codex. All the laws, guidelines and rules published have some principles in common; they include honesty, trust and integrity and other soft factors to the organization. In the whole debate of CSR and other related terms, corporate governance is the only concept that became partially legally binding, at least in some countries and for listed corporations.[9]

Summarizing the different perspectives on CG on the lowest common denominator, it is a control instrument for company's transactions, consisting of a set of rules. These rules can either be mandatory, like regulations on accounting standards, or voluntary, like code of conducts. Either way, the company has to comply with these rules, especially if they are legally binding. Because of the increasing number of regulations and soft laws in this field, CG has become an important topic for companies and therefore as well for scholars. Because CG not only includes regulatory demands but can also include a set of voluntary rules, mainly value- and ethical-based codes of conduct, it is closely linked to CSR. Both concepts deal with the responsibility of a company.

Nevertheless, most of the research on CG is based on a more narrow perspective, interpreting CG as a set of rules to ensure transparent accounting principles (e.g. Daily/ Dalton, Cannella, 2003). Also in company practice this division is made; CG has the notion of fulfilling binding rules, like SOX, whereas CSR is used

---

[9] Although some aspects of what can be summarized under CSR, e.g. environmental standards, or labor laws, are also binding, the CSR concept as a whole is not binding. Therefore corporate governance is seen as the first legally binding concept in the field of responsible business.

for fulfilling stakeholder demands on a voluntary basis. Nevertheless, CG and CSR are closely linked and therefore CG is part of the CSR framework underlying this thesis.

2.1.2.4 Environmental, Social and Governance Issues

The above-mentioned corporate scandals such as Enron have rendered financial data untrustworthy and brought corporate governance issues on the agenda of investors. Environmental as well as social issues sparked interest in the financial community, such as the question in which way companies integrate the risk of climate change into their business. The term ESG (environmental social and governance issues) summarizes these developments of integrating the so-called non-financial factors in the decision-making process of analysts and investors (Center of Financial Market Integrity - CFA Institute, 2008).

According to the CFA, ESG are the issues "that investors are considering in the context of corporate behavior. Often these ESG issues have been considered nonfinancial or nonquantifiable in nature and have a medium to long-term time frame in their effect on a company" (Center of Financial Market Integrity - CFA Institute 2008, p.28).

A more precise, but in terms of content in line with the CFA definition, is one proposed by the law firm Freshfields Bruckhaus Deringer and the Enhanced Analytics Initiative for the UNEP FI (2005). It defines environmental, social, and governance issues "as having one or more of the following characteristics":

Are the focus of public concern (e.g. genetically modified organisms); are qualitative and not readily quantifiable in monetary terms (e.g. corporate governance, intellectual capital); reflect externalities not well captured by market mechanisms (e.g. environmental pollution); are often the focus of a tightening policy and regulatory framework (e.g. greenhouse gas emissions); or arise throughout the company's supply chain (e.g. labour issues at supplier factories). (p.18)

Bassen and Kovacs assert, "up to present there is no clear general understanding of this concept" (2008, p.184). ESG is a term mainly used in the field of responsible investment disclosure. Until now, the term could not make its way into the scientific community yet. Moreover it can be said that, although there seems to be a common understanding of what is meant with ESG in the financial community, the term is not precisely defined, nor does it appear that it is intended to be interpreted as an exclusive list. It is rather a concept, like Triple Bottom Line (Chapter 2.1.2.6), trying to redefine the model of CSR into the language of financial market participants. ESG does not yet fulfill the criteria for a use in scientific literature. Accordingly, ESG as a term and concept is not part of the CSR framework underlying this thesis.

2.1.2.5 Sustainable Development

From a historical perspective, the roots of the concept of sustainability can be found haunting in the early 17th century. Here, sustainability describes the best possible usage of growth of game while sustaining the base stock (Henning 1991, p.11). The German term for sustainability 'Nachhaltigkeit' was first used in academic literature in 1818 by Kasthofer in a work about forestry. In his work, Kasthofer analyzed the exposure of humans towards nature during the time of industrialization. During this time the energy demand increased dramatically with the consequence of deforestation without reforestation. He argued, in order to sustain the forest for energy use and to avoid negative side effects, such as erosion, that not more trees than nature could create should be lumbered (Kasthofer 1818, p.71). This is what he called sustainable forestry.

However, the concept of sustainable development became popular with the publication of the Brundtland report. In 1987 the United Nations Commission on Environment and Development (Brundtland Commission) drew attention to the fact that economic development often leads to deterioration, not an improvement, in the quality of people's lives. The Commission therefore called for "a form of sustainable development that meets the needs of the present without compromising the ability of future generations to meet their own needs" (United Nations, 1987).

Until now, this definition is the most frequently used and quoted one, but still not universally accepted. A major critique is that this definition is rather general and vague and, therefore, hardly applicable to real-world issues (Rauscher, 1996).

Referring to the definition of the Brundtland Commission, two key issues of sustainable development could be identified: (1) Development is not just about more profits and higher standards of living for a minority. It should be about making life better for everyone and (2) this should neither involve destroying or recklessly using up our natural resources, nor polluting the environment.

Currently the terms 'sustainability' and 'sustainable development' are somewhere between a serious concept for our future existence and a buzzword with little meaning, which makes it very difficult to come up with a clear definition. Lélé (1991) describes the term as a "catchphrase" especially embraced by non-governmental and governmental organizations used for policy-making activities. The author of this article also certifies a lack of consistency in its interpretation.

In contrast to CSR, 'sustainable development' has a stronger focus on environmental concerns, especially in scientific literature and on social or economic issues, than CSR for example has. Therefore, and also because the term is often used as a buzzword, sustainable development will not be used in the CSR framework of this thesis. However, the idea of sustainable development functions as a kind of umbrella for the whole topic of CSR, with the idea of meeting "the needs of the present without compromising the ability of future generations" (United Nations, 1987).

2.1.2.6 Triple Bottom Line

The definition of sustainability is closely related to the concept of the *Triple Bottom Line* (TBL). According to Elkington (2004), TBL has its history in the report "Our Common Future", published in 1987 by the World Commission on Environment and Development. The TBL can be defined conceptually as economic prosperity, environmental quality and social justice (Elkington, 2004). The term TBL is probably the newest concept in this field. It was first mentioned by Elkington (1994). On the question why he came up with this term he answered: "(…) in 1994 we had been looking for new language to express what we saw as an inevitable expansion of the environmental agenda that SustainAbility (founded in 1987) had mainly focused upon to that point." (Elkington, 2004, p.1)

The expansion of the environmental agenda is the social value a company adds. This means: "In the simplest terms, the TBL agenda focuses corporations not just on the economic value that they add, but also on the environmental and social value that they add – or destroy" (Elkington, 2004, p.3).

Referring to this definition, the TBL concept corresponds with the concept of sustainable development and also with CSR, because all of them integrate the three pillars: economic, environmental and social responsibility.

In these definitions the meaning of 'bottom line' has not yet been addressed. Bottom line is an economic expression mainly used in accounting; it is the line in a financial statement that shows the net income or loss.

The TBL concepts therefore expand the criteria traditionally used for measuring success, the financial measures, to economic, environmental and social measures. In other words, TBL is a concept demanding reporting that takes social and ecological measures into account besides the financial performance measurement. The concept of TBL is very successful and a growing number of major international corporations, such as BAA, BP, BT, DuPont, Ford, Novartis and others, acknowledge the need to address the 'triple bottom line'.

However, the concept of TBL could not make its way into the academic community. One example is an article by Norman/ MacDonald (2003), in which it is argued, "the Triple Bottom

Line is an unhelpful addition to current discussions of corporate social responsibility." They argue that the term sounds more promising than it is really is. The main critique is that the term suggests measuring the bottom line of social and environmental performance, which is first of all nothing new and secondly the TBL concept does not provide any help e.g. by providing a measuring standard or tools how to measure.

Summarizing, the popularity of this concept has its origin in its expression itself, because it uses the language of the financial community. Therefore the threshold of using it is lower in comparison to slightly esoteric terms like CSR.

But still, the term TBL does not add value to the research on CSR and is therefore not used and established in CSP/CFP studies. Accordingly, TBL will not be part of the CSR framework introduced in Chapter 2.1.3 (The Framework of Corporate Social Responsibility).

2.1.2.7 Corporate Responsibility

It is not clear when and where the term was first coined, but it is assumed that *corporate responsibility* (CR) is the continental European answer on corporate social responsibility, because the word 'social' is sometimes misleading, as it seems not to refer to e.g. environmental responsibility. Especially in German speaking countries the term CR is often used, for example by German heavyweight companies such as Bertelsmann, Linde and Siemens. Another, but rather non-academic parameter underlying the notion that CR is especially used in the German language is found in the online encyclopedia Wikipedia. A definition of CR is only given in German in which CR is claimed to be the advancement of CSR and is described as a comprehensive management approach, encompassing besides economic, environmental and social responsibility, also corporate governance, corporate citizenship, stakeholder management and the responsibility for the supply chain (*Wikipedia*, 2009). The term CR does not seem to add value to the discussion of CSR either, because the described aspects of CR can also be found in extended CSR definitions, like the ones given above.

Having a closer look on the way these companies use the expression, there seems to be no common understanding of CR in practice. An example from the website of Linde AG shows that the two terms CSR and CR can be used synonymously. "For us, corporate responsibility means adopting a responsible approach toward employees and natural resources, toward the funds entrusted to us, and toward the promotion of societal interests." (Linde, corporate website) Whereas, Siemens, for example, offers a broader view of CR, emphasizing CR as a strategic management task. "We view corporate responsibility as a strategic, management-driven task that integrates our business, environmental and citizenship activities to create sustained tangible and intangible value for our company and our stakeholders by ethically sound means." (Siemens, company website)

According to these definitions, the author can barely recognize the difference between a broader definition of CSR and the way CR is used. Moreover, the term CR is rarely used in academic literature. Here as well, an accurate definition could have not been established yet. Summarizing, CR is not a new concept but rather a further term in the jungle of CSR concepts. The term probably will not make its way into academic literature.

2.1.3 The Framework of Corporate Social Responsibility

In the previous section it became clear that the meaning of the term corporate social responsibility is described in multiple ways in literature and as well in practice. Up to know there is no clear definition of this term and different related concepts needed to be analyzed and discussed in order to base the following on a profound CSR definition.

The table below (Table 3: Summary of Terms in regard to Content, Novelty, Scientific Acceptance and Internationality) summarizes the results of the previous section. The used criteria for the analysis, which are content, historical use, scientific acceptance and internationality, clearly speak for the use of CSR as a term and concept.

Summary of terms in regard to content, novelty, scientific acceptance and internationality

	Content	History vs. Novelty	Scientific acceptance	Internatiotnality
Corporate Social Responsibility	covers mulitple aspects of responsible corporate behavior	a long history	very accepted	used worldwide
Corporate Citizenship	covers only a single part of responsible corporate bevavior	a long history	very accepted	used worldwide
Corporate Governance	refers preliminary to the part of fulfilling regulatory demands	a long history	very accepted, but in a different scientific context	used worldwide
Environmental Social and Goernance Issues	a concept redifining CSR into financial market language	a new concept	not used yet in scientific literature	used worldwide by the financial community
Sustainable Development	a broad cooncept, that functions like an umbrella for the whole discussion	a long history	accepted, but not used in the CSP/ CFP-discussion	used worldwide
Tirple Bottom Line	a concept redefining CSR into accounting language	a new concept	not established in CSP/ CFP-context	used worldwide, but with a focus in the US
Corporate Responsibility	covers multiple aspects of responsible corporate behavior	not a new concept, only a different term for CSR	not established	primarily used in German speaking countries

Table 3: Summary of Terms in regard to Content, Novelty, Scientific Acceptance and Internationality

Because there is not yet a generally accepted definition of the term CSR it is essential to define what is meant with CSR in this research. The use of CSR nowadays tries to harmonize the different streams and approaches, especially the environmental/sustainability stream and the corporate citizenship/ philanthropy stream. Today's approach to CSR also includes the stakeholder element. Referring to this idea, CSR can be defined as follows:

CSR is the responsibility a company has towards its stakeholders. This responsibility is a general responsibility, referring to all business activities a company has. It includes the economic, the social and the environmental responsibility a company might have.

This definition of CSR implies that CSR goes beyond voluntary engagement, as it also includes the legal obligations a company has, such as compliance issues.

Within the CSR framework there are different *CSR instruments* (like corporate citizenship, environmental engagement, etc.), which function as a toolbox and can be used to balance and fulfill stakeholder needs.

The following graph (Figure 2: Definition of Corporate Social Responsibility) summarizes the comprehensive interpretation of CSR for this research.

```
                    Stakeholder dialog / stakeholder management
    ┌─────────────────────────────────────────────────────────────┐
    ↓                                                             ↓
                    Corporate Social Responsibility
    ┌──────────────┐        ┌──────────────┐        ┌──────────────┐
    │  Corporate   │        │ Sustainability│       │  Corporate   │
    │  Governance  │        │              │        │  Citizenship │
    └──────────────┘        └──────────────┘        └──────────────┘
            ┌──────────────┬──────────────┬──────────────┐
            │  Economic    │ Environmental│    Social    │
            │responsibility│responsibility│responsibility│
            └──────────────┴──────────────┴──────────────┘
    ↑                                                             ↑
    └─────────────────────────────────────────────────────────────┘
                    Stakeholder dialog / stakeholder management
```

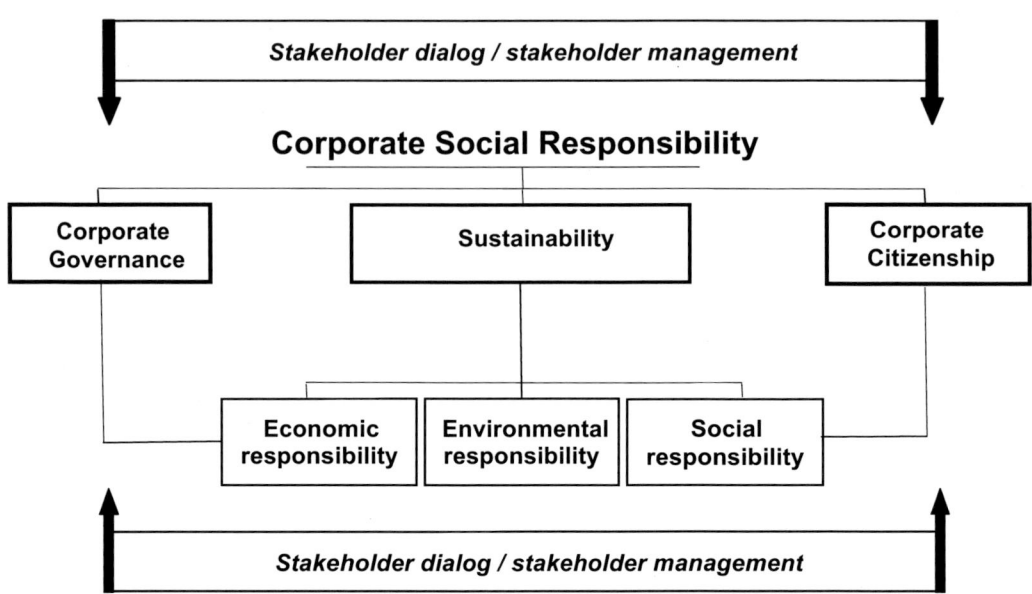

Figure 2: Definition of Corporate Social Responsibility (according to Schlange & Co., 2006)

To conclude, according to this definition the term CSR is about the general responsibility a company has towards its stakeholders, which comes very close to the definition of Freeman's "corporate stakeholder responsibility". It includes all responsibilities and obligations a company has. The responsibilities are defined by the stakeholder needs. It is the task of a company to find the right balance in fulfilling the diverse needs, as these needs are often conflicting. Moreover, it is essential to understand that there is not a "one size fits all" solution for companies, because CSR depends on the stakeholder needs and they vary, depending e.g. on the industry, the country and other factors.

2.2 The Utility Industry

Electricity is one of the most important forms of energy, nowadays influencing every aspect of daily life as well as shaping the industrial development in most countries. Electric energy is essential for the operation of modern technologies and systems. Therefore, it can be considered that electrical power has reached the status of a 'meta-technology' (Byrne/ Mun, 2003). Accordingly, the electric utility industry is one of the biggest industries worldwide. Moreover, the electricity demand will increase in the next decades. It is predicted that it will globally rise by 53% from 2008 to 2035 (*The New York Times*, 2011). These developments indicate that electric utilities play an important role for the future developments of economies. The industry is set under increasing pressure from various stakeholder groups to act responsible, especially because of the increasing demand.

According to the World Business Council for Sustainable Development (WBCSD), the most significant forces are "the need to meet or exceed regulatory requirements, conditions of operating licenses, participation in voluntary initiatives and stakeholder demands for increased transparency, accountability and responsibility" (Searcy/ McCartney/ Karapetrovic, 2006, p.136).

For these reasons and interdependencies of industry growth, stakeholder demands and sustainability forces, it is especially interesting to have a closer look at the CSP/CFP link of electric utilities. But first of all it is essential to understand the basic mechanisms, challenges and threats facing the industry. It is aim of this section to give these insights.

To get a profound overview of the industry it is essential to understand what shaped it in the last decades and what are the current and future issues shaping the industry. The industry background (Chapter 2.3.1) gives an historical overview of the electricity value chain, which is essential in order to understand what drives the industry nowadays. The industry background focuses further on the process of deregulation of the last decades and it also reflects the current status of the industry. Afterwards the CSR topics shaping the industry are discussed.

Evidently the utility market is diverse and very much depends on the country and region it is operating in. An analysis of these differences in various countries, e.g. in regard to the regulatory surroundings, is not the focus of this research. The upcoming industry analysis integrates the main topics and only if necessary it addresses differences in regard to regional characteristics.

2.2.1 Industry Background

Electricity has been generated for the purpose of powering human technologies for at least 120 years from various sources of energy. The first power plants were run on wood, while today the sector relies mainly on oil, natural gas, coal, and nuclear power and a small amount from hydrogen, solar, bio mass, wind and geothermal (renewables) sources. The table below shows the current energy mix of the world energy generation.

Generation by Energy Source: Total Electric Utilitties

	2009	**1999**
Coal	55,00%	55,70%
Fuel Oil	1,00%	2,70%
Natural Gas	14,70%	9,30%
Nuclear	18,60%	22,80%
Wind	0,50%	0,10%
Hydro	10,00%	9,30%
Other Renewables	0,20%	0,10%

Table 4: Generation by Energy Source: Total Electric Utilities (Edison Electric Institute, 2010, p.39)

Summarizing, a first specific of the electric utility industry is the fact that electricity is produced, or more correctly generated, in many ways, using different sources and also very different technologies.

Moreover, utilities are faced with specific physical characteristics, which shape the processes of the electricity flow. Although there are many technical solutions to store electricity, e.g. with batteries or pumped storage, the technologies face manifold constraints, such as high costs or low energy density (Electricity Storage Association, 2012). However, the storage enables the balance of supply and demand, which is important to effectively match supply and demand. But until now, it is almost not possible to store electric energy cost effectively; accordingly it has to be consumed immediately (Delmas/ Russo/ Montes-Sancho/ Tokat, 2009).

The electricity value chain consists of five dimensions: the fuel/ energy source, generation, transmission, distribution and the delivery/ supply (Figure 3).

Fuel/ Energy Source ⇨ Generation ⇨ Transmission ⇨ Distribution ⇨ Delivery

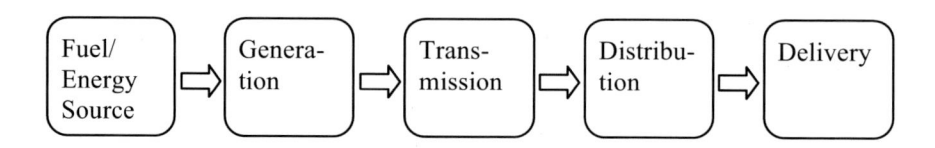

Figure 3: Five Dimensions of the "old" Electricity Value Chain (Energy Storage Council, 2007)

These 5 dimensions are also called "traditional" way, because it is the classical value chain of state-owned, regulated and unbundled utilities. But as a consequence of liberalizing the electric utility markets the vertical unbundling activities started (Atienza Serna, 2009). With the beginning of the early 1990s "a set of institutional reforms – including unbundling, privatization of ownership, and the introduction of competition into the generation sector – began to be promoted as a global solution to the problems of the electricity industry" (Byrne/ Mun, 2003, p.49).

Garcia and Fink (2009) see the unbundling process as key driver of this industry. Therefore, Chapter 2.2.1.1 (Liberalization, Unbundling and Market Regulation) addresses in more detail these processes that shaped the industry in the last decades and is still shaping them. In the following chapter (2.2.1.2 Challenges, Key Drivers and Business Risks) further key drivers and the main business risks are discussed. Afterwards the CSR topics affecting the utility industry and vice versa are introduced (Chapter 2.2.2 Corporate Social Responsibility Topics in the Utility Industry). The chapter closes with a summary.

2.2.1.1 Liberalization, Unbundling and Market Regulation

Independent of the level of development of a certain country, the trend towards liberalizing the energy market is reshaping the industry. Traditionally electric utilities operated in strictly regulated markets and were in most cases state-owned (Joskow, 2008). These mainly vertically integrated utilities often produced overcapacities. This became especially evident during the 80s and 90s, when electricity demand slowed down. Besides reducing the overcapacities, the liberalization seemed to be an appropriate method of gaining more efficiency (International Energy Agency/ OECD, 2005).

The general idea of liberalizing the energy markets is to "develop competitive electricity markets that fulfill the goals of real economic benefits" (International Energy Agency/ OECD, 2005, p.11). These assumptions are based on the postulate that the market economy is capable of optimal market allocation under free competition. When liberalizing the electricity markets technical, economic and political challenges need to be considered.

The first and central step of liberalization is to introduce competition in the formerly monopolistic industry by breaking down these monopolistic structures of vertically integrated utilities (International Energy Agency/ OECD, 2005, p.15). This is mainly achieved by unbundling the different segments of the electricity supply chain (Atienza Serna, 2009).

There are basically two different organizational models of unbundling. The first one is the transmission system order (TSO), in which a single company handles both, transmission and the operation of the system. The second one model is the independent order (ISO), in which system operator and transmission are also separated (Atienza Serna, 2009). The TSO model is mainly used in the European countries, whereas the ISO model is primarily used in the U.S. and also, for example, in South America. The differentiation is important because the various effects of these two models on the electricity market vary. In turns out that the ISO model "presents many advantages in terms of efficiency and security of supply", whereas the TSO model "is essential to preserve efficient functioning of the electricity market" (Atienza Serna, 2009, p.247).

The question in which way the deregulation affects performance was investigated by Delmas et al. (2009). They could empirically demonstrate that deregulation is not unidirectional. It has positive impacts, like higher environmental outcomes, and negative effects, like less efficiency. A further difficulty in liberalizing electricity markets is that competition is more difficult to achieve, mainly because "electricity generation is marked by high capital costs and constraints on building power plants" (Delmas et al., 2009, p.174). This limits the number of players.

Jaskow (2008) concludes that "creating well functioning competitive wholesale and retail markets for electricity is very challenging both technically and politically" (Jaskow, 2008, p.37). The following paragraph focuses on the challenges, the key drivers and the main business risk the industry is facing.

2.2.1.2 Challenges, Key Drivers and Business Risks

According to Nguyen (2008), Senior Advisor at the International Energy Agency, the top three challenges for the next decades are, energy security, energy investments and climate change (Nguyen, p.2008).

Energy security is about the availability of energy resources for consumption. The International Energy Agency (IEA), which was mainly established to increase energy security, defines it as: "the uninterrupted physical availability at a price which is affordable, while respecting environment concerns" (International Energy Agency, 1.5.2012). The challenge of energy security is mainly due to the already-mentioned worldwide rising demand for electricity, e.g. through the higher demand in transition economies like China, and the strong reliance on fossil fuels, such as coal, oil and gas (Nguyen, 2008). Accordingly it should be the aim of policy makers to, on one level, mitigate the short-term risk of unavailability and, on the second level, to approach the roots of energy insecurity, which are basically:

- Energy system disruptions linked to extreme weather conditions or accidents.
- Short-term balancing of demand and supply in the electricity market.
- Regulatory failures.
- Concentration of fossil fuel resources.
  (International Energy Agency/ OECD, 2007, p.12)

Improved energy investments can be seen as the most significant benefit of liberalization and at the same time it is the most serious challenge. The problem of investments is that many of the projects have very long lead times and carry financial liabilities for several decades. However, investments in the electricity generation and transmission are key for the successful development of sustainable electricity markets (International Energy Agency/ OECD, 2005).

The process of deregulation and therewith the creation of competitive electricity markets also changed the capital structure of utilities. "The onset of deregulation changed the investment climate completely. Deregulation was an exogenous event that changed a firm's long-term strategy for creating value for its shareholders." (Bulan/ Sanyal, 2008, p.2) There are basically four major issues that are shaping the industry in regard to energy investments in liberalized electricity markets:

1. The improvement of investment performance to ensure economic efficiency.
2. The affection of technology choices in a surrounding of liberalization and investment risk.
3. The way power generation investors are adapting to investment risks.
4. High price volatility and the pressure on governments to intervene. (Fraser, 2003)

The interactions between the market conditions, market investments, and the regulatory framework are diverse and very complex. Accordingly, these manifold interactions cannot be discussed in detail as part of this research. However, central to the topic of energy investments is the fact that the industry requires $ 4 trillion of investment between the years 2000 and 2030 (Fraser, 2003). But investing in electric utilities is associated with high risks; accordingly investors expect a high rerun when investing in this risky market. The main risk for the investor is still the future level of price (Fraser, 2003).

> While this risk affects all generating technologies, it does so in different ways. Technologies, which have a higher specific investment for capacity, even though they may have relatively low fuel costs (wind, nuclear) are more greatly affected by this risk because there is less they can do to respond. (p.28)

The uncertainty in regard to prices not only affects the technology invested in, but also projects with a long lead time, which is typical in the industry. A further factor associated with risk is the regulatory surrounding. Changes in the market rules, e.g. emission controls for specific technologies, put on opportunity costs (Fraser, 2008).

One of the major risks facing the power industry is the regulatory surrounding and the increase of regulatory demands due to climate change risks, the third major challenge facing the industry. Climate change is seen as the major problem facing the globe and a great challenge for the 21st century. "To remain competitive, today's utility must respond to the risks and opportunities from climate change (...)." (Ceres 2010, p.4)

The Kyoto protocol is just one example of regulation in this field. Because it is on a supranational level it is probably the most important for internationally operating electric utilities. Besides that, there are also many regulations on the European and national levels. The EU for example approved a climate and energy package in 2008 with concrete reduction targets for greenhouse gas emissions. This should be mainly achieved by strengthening and expanding the emission trading system, which is the EU's key tool for cutting emission with economic instruments (European Commission, 2008). Environmental regulations are enacted with a direct effect on the power industry, particularly with the focus on reducing greenhouse gas emission. The trend of increasing regulation continues. According to a survey by Pricewaterhouse-Coopers (PwC) with global utility leaders, it is assumed that regulation is even increasing and will be a major force shaping the sector (PwC, 2008).

Summarizing, these regulations and the various challenges, like cost of carbon emissions, the emerging of clean technologies, etc., bring with them a high uncertainty for investors, which will even grow in the future.

2.2.2 Corporate Social Responsibility Topics in the Utility Industry

The above-given industry background has already touched some CSR topics, like climate change and its impact on the power industry. In the following, the main stakeholders of the industry will be mapped in order to get a deeper understanding of the influencing factors that shape the industry. This part relies on scientific publications as well as on the corporate communication of electric utilities. The corporate communication of electric utilities gives an up to date perspective on the main stakeholder groups and its topics. Then the main CSR subjects are discussed, first the environmental and afterwards the social topics are introduced and discussed.

2.2.2.1 Mapping the Main Stakeholder Groups

Stakeholders are determining the long-term success of a company (Chapter 2.1.1 Stakeholder Theory); accordingly it is crucial to integrate their opinions into the corporate decision-making progress.

Having a closer look at what the utility companies see as their stakeholders, the picture quickly becomes clear (Figure 4: Stakeholder Groups of Electric Utilities).

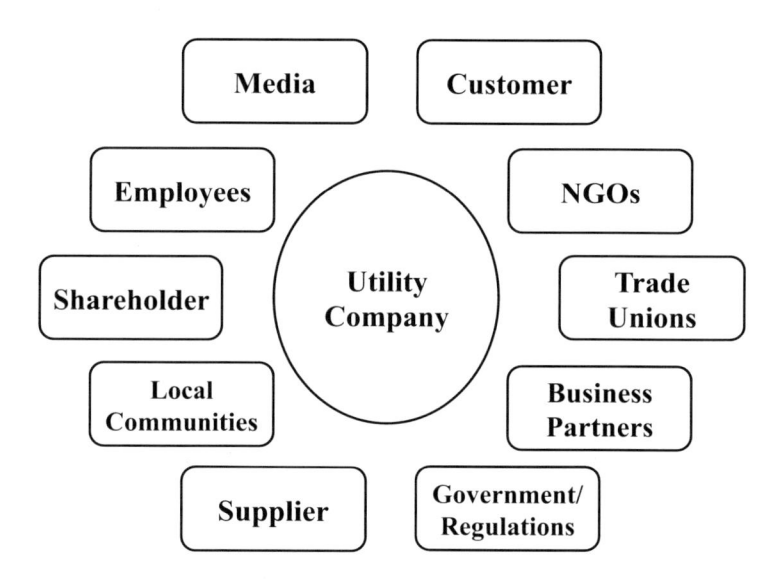

Figure 4: Stakeholder Groups of Electric Utilities (own graph, exemplary website content from EDF Energy, PG&E, National Grid and Centrica PLC, 10.04.2012)

For mapping the stakeholder groups of electric utilities, some of the biggest electric utilities were analyzed in regard to their stakeholder engagement. The graph above (Figure 4) is the result of this process, mapping the stakeholder groups a utility company is engaged in. It shows that a utility company engages with the usual set of stakeholders, like shareholders, employees, media, customers, NGOs, trade unions, business partners and suppliers. But especially for utility companies, the government and regulatory bodies are of importance as well, since the process of liberalization continues (as discussed in the previous chapter). Further, local communities are especially for utility companies, relevant because utilities strongly intervene partially into the communities, e.g. through infrastructure projects. When prioritizing the above-named stakeholder groups, utilities have mainly three key stakeholders, customers, employees and shareholders (e.g. Starace, 2009; EDF, 2012; Centrica, 2012).

Due to the ongoing process of liberalization, customers, industrial as well as retail, are becoming increasingly important for the industry. Until deregulation, customers "have been largely unaware of the costs and environmental implications associated with energy consumption and have been largely passive, captive recipients of a service passed on to them by the utility industry at a cost" (Starace, 2009, p.152). But nowadays in a more or less liberalized market, utilities have to take customer expectations into account, as they now have the freedom to choose not only the supplier but also the energy mix. In the liberalized markets it becomes more and more easy to compare different suppliers and change them, e.g. through web-based platforms that compare tariffs. The former passiveness is changing into "informed, conscious, responsible, and interactive clients, who will be increasingly empowered (...)" (Starace, 2009, p.153). With the ongoing process of deregulation, customers become a serious stakeholder group for utilities.

Like for most of the companies, employees have a major stake in the current and future success of a company. The same is for electric utilities. But due to the process of liberalization, the employees of electric utilities are especially important for the industry. It is the challenging task of the employees to support the process of change from regulated companies to companies operating in a free market. Accordingly, utilities have to take account for that when scouting and supporting employees. Centrica expresses the importance of their employees as follows: "Our employees are fundamental to our success as a business. We rely on them to deliver against our strategic objectives and must provide an environment in which everyone can flourish" (Centrica, 2012). Starace (2009) sees an upcoming massive change in the personnel structure of electric utilities. Training, career development and remuneration will increase, whereas job security will decrease.

As already discussed in the previous section, the utility is a very capital-intensive industry and in the upcoming years new capital is needed e.g. for huge projects, like upgrading the grid or the construction of new facilities. Fraser (2003) dropped the number of $ 4 trillion of investment needed between the years 2000 and 2030. Therefore, attracting new investors and satisfying current investors is a major task of utilities. National Grid, a major utility company, puts it this way: "Our aim is to ensure that the value of our business is reflected in our share price. We aim to make National Grid attractive to debt investors so that we can finance our operations as effectively as possible" (National Grid, 2012). It is the task of utility companies to deliver shareholder expectations, by showing credible growth paths, controlling volume and price risks, presenting sustainable solutions and in general by being a reliable partner (Starace, 2009).

2.2.2.2 Major Environmental and Social Concerns

On the one hand, it is the challenge of utilities to maximize profits and fulfill shareholder expectations and, on the other hand, the environmental and social concerns facing the industry must be fulfilled. For utilities it is crucial to find the right trade-off between profit maximization and environmental and social demands. In the following the major environmental and social concerns shaping the industry are presented and discussed.

The stakeholder graph above displays that utilities already integrate various stakeholder groups and their specific demands (Illustration 4: Stakeholder Groups of Electric Utilities). According to Starace (2009) this is vital, because:

> Companies (...) need to implement a corporate social responsibility model that takes account of the interests of society and of the companies' responsibility for the impact of all aspects of company activities, not only customers, employees, and shareholders, but also on communities and the environment. (p.154)

The materiality matrices of utility companies give a good orientation, the topics of which are, from the stakeholder perspective, of highest interest and concern. A materiality matrix is a tool, adapted from risk-analysis, which companies use to prioritize various stakeholder topics (*Accountability*, 2006). The graph below (Figure 5: Materiality Matrix of Centrica) is one example of a materiality matrix and stands exemplary for the utility industry.

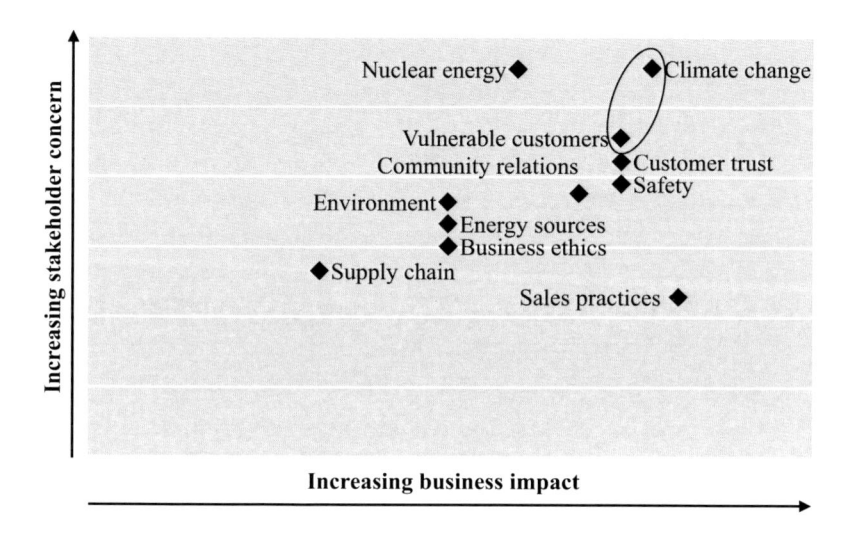

Figure 5: Materiality Matrix of Centrica (Centrica, 2012)

The matrix shows clearly that climate change is a major concern for the industry, from the stakeholder perspective and also with a high business impact. The highest ranked social concerns are vulnerable customers, but they are clearly prioritized below climate change.

The serious issue of climate change has already been discussed in Chapter 2.2.1.2 (Challenges, Key Drivers and Business Risks) as one of the major overall risks facing the industry. Therefore this topic will not be discussed further at this point. But summarizing, climate change and coping with the effects of it is the top issue for electric utilities. The energy supply is accountable for 25% of greenhouse gas emissions globally (IPCC, 2007). However, policy makers as well as electric utilities are already addressing this topic with different instruments. From the regulatory side, implementing environmental standards and emission trading schemes are only two examples to reduce greenhouse gas emissions. The utility companies themselves, for example, invest largely in renewable energy projects and programs to increase efficiency. But not only climate change is the driving factor behind the expansion of renewables. Also shortages and the price increase in conventional energy sources are driving these developments. However, the process is still at the very beginning (Vahrenholt, 2009).

Societal issues are not as evident in the power industry as environmental issues are. However, a key issue is the responsibility of insuring the health and safety of the employees in the three operating segments of generation, transmission and distribution. Besides that, Oekom (2008) figured out the following key issues: (1) security of supply for all sections of the population, and (2) fair commercial practices, which can also be summarized under the topic of vulnerable customers, like in the Centrica materiality matrix (Centrica, 2012).

Regarding the security of supply, utilities are obliged to monitor and maintain the networks and guarantee a steady supply. In many countries the transmission grids are not well-maintained and the networks are sometimes overstrained, so that a breakdown is nothing unusual, especially in emerging markets like China, but also in the western world like in the U.S.A. A further topic in this field is to offer a basic supply for all customers, e.g. by offering continuous supply with affordable prices (Oekom, 2008).

3 Theoretical Foundation

In the field of CSR research, numerous theories and approaches can be identified. It is aim of this section to first of all define the main CSR theories and then to analyze which of the theories are used in CSP/CFP research. For the aggregation of the hypotheses it is necessary to base them on substantial theories. These theories will be explained in depth in the second part of this section.

3.1 Theory-based approaches to CSR

The most common systematization of CSR theories and related approaches is the following classification into four groups: instrumental, political, integrative and ethical theories. Instrumental theories are those in which the corporations' only purpose is to increase profits, whereas integrative theories focus on the satisfaction of societal demands. Political theories concern themselves with the power of corporations in society and a responsible use of this power; whereas ethical theories are based on ethical responsibilities of corporations to society (Garriga/ Melé, 2004). A further classification has been proposed by Waddock (2008) in form of a concept tree. Waddock uses the metaphor of a tree to, on the hand, describe the evolution of CSR and, on the other hand, to picture the interrelation of different concepts and approaches. However, the concept tree is in contrast to the classification of Garriga and Melé (2004), an approach that is based more on definitions and less on a theoretical classification. Accordingly, the concept of Garriga/ Melé (2004), which is based on the four aspects of social systems by Parsons, is more appropriate for a theoretical framework than the concept tree of Waddock (2008). In the following sections, this theoretical framework proposed by Garriga and Melé (2004) will be discussed in more detail.

3.1.1 Instrumental Theories

As the term 'instrumental' already indicates, in this field of theories the corporation is only seen as an instrument for wealth creation: Accordingly CSR is only acceptable if it is in line with this aim (Garriga, et al., 2004, p.51).

The dictum of wealth creation is very shareholder orientated, having its origin in neoclassical economics. The prospects of the shareholder, as the owner of a company, must be fulfilled. If it is in the interest of the shareholder to engage in CSR, or if CSR leads to profit-maximization, the engagement is desired, but if not, it is an undesired engagement. CSR stays a means to an end, or in other words, it is only an instrument for wealth creation. The same applies to stakeholder management. Stakeholder interests should only be integrated if they contribute to the maxim of profit maximization.

Within the field of CSP/CFP research, most of the studies are based on instrumental and integrative theories, trying to find an economic reasoning between the relation of CSP and CFP (Chapter 1.2 Literature Review).

Depending on the economic objective, Garriga and Melé (2004) identified three main groups of instrumental theories:

1. Maximization of shareholder value

According to this approach, maximizing shareholder value is the one and only reason for investing in CSR. The company invests in CSR as a general corporate decision focused on wealth creation. The agency theory is the main approach to explain the corporate decision-making with reference to shareholder value maximization. This approach is in line with neoclassical economics, which is discussed in Chapter 3.2 (Neoclassical Economics) with Friedman (1970) as its most famous advocate.

2. Strategic goal of achieving competitive advantage

This approach deals with the question of how to allocate and use resources to achieve competitive advantages through CSR. This instrumental approach is represented by the resource-based view (RBV). The RBV is a discipline of strategic management and it explains how a company can gain competitive advantages by determining the available strategic resources, such as CSR. In Chapter 3.3 (Resource-based View) this theory will be presented and used as a basis for the research framework of the underlying study.

3. Cause-related marketing

Cause-related marketing is defined as "the confluence of perspectives from several specialized areas of inquiry such as marketing for nonprofit organizations, the promotion mix, corporate philanthropy, corporate social responsibility (...)" (Varadarajan/ Menon, 1988, p.58). The aim of cause-related marketing is to increase profits, or to build trust by engaging in CSR. It is theorized that CSR can lead to a higher reputation by case-related marketing. This is a very narrow perspective, only focusing on the effects of marketing. This concept is not appropriate for this research, as it only focuses on the effects of marketing and is therefore not capable of framing the complex interactions between CSP and CFP.

3.1.2 Political Theories

Political theories focus on the interaction between business and society, while taking into account the power and responsibility of companies towards the society (Garriga et al., 2004). Moreover, they distinguish between *corporate constitutionalism, integrative social contract theory,* and *corporate citizenship.*

Corporate constitutionalism refers to Davis (1960). In his article, Davis argues that business is a social institution and therefore must use its power in a responsible way for societal welfare. But at the some time he rejects the idea of total responsibility of the business. The power of a business is defined by different constituency groups, which "restrict organizational power in the same way that a governmental institution does" (Davis 1967, p.68). The constituency groups channel the corporate power and as a consequence this theory is called 'corporate constitutionalism' (Garriga et al. 2004, p.56).

Integrative social contract theory was introduced by Donaldson (1982). It explains business from social contract theory, assuming "that a sort of implicit social contract between business and society exists" (Garriga et al., 2004, p.56). This perspective on the relation between business and politics is rather philosophical as the term 'social contract theory' already indicates. It is seldom used in the debate on the relation between CSP and CFP.

Another theoretical perspective in the CSP/CFP research grouped into political theories is that of corporate citizenship. The term 'citizenship' is taken from political science (Garriga et al. 2004, p.57). In Chapter 2.1.2.2 (Corporate Citizenship), the term with its various notions has already been discussed with the conclusion that there is not the one and only definition of it.

Political theories focus on the political interaction of a company with society and do not theorize the topic of wealth creation and profit maximization like instrumental theories do. However, the aspect of profit maximization is central when investigating the CSP/CFP link. The fundamentals of measuring CFP are closely linked to instrumental theories. Thus political theories are not the appropriate base for the underlying CSP/CFP research.

3.1.3 Integrative Theories

The basic assumption behind integrative theories is that business depends on society. Or in other words, without society business would not exist and therefore, business has a responsibility towards society and should interact with it to fulfill social demands (Garriga et al., 2004).

> Basically, the theories of this group are focused on the detection and scanning of, and response to, the social demands that achieve social legitimacy, greater social acceptance and prestige. (p.57)

Garriga et al. identified three approaches on how business can respond to societal demands, or what they call social responsiveness.

The first one is *issue management*, which arose in the 70s. Issue management research is influenced by strategic and international management and deals with the question of how a business can implement processes by which it can identify and react to social and political issues.

The second approach, the *principles of public responsibility*, which has its origin in public policy research, aims to define the scope of responsibilities. Preston and Post are the main advocates of this approach. In their studies they investigate the involvement of the firm in its social environment. From their point of view it is legitimate for business to be involved in public policy processes (Preston et. al., 1975).

The third approach categorized under integrative theories is *stakeholder management*. The term stakeholder and its theoretical meanings for CSR research has already been discussed and analyzed in Chapter 2.1.1 (Stakeholder Theory). Like all integrative theories, the stakeholder approach as well deals with the relation of business and society. The purpose of the stakeholder concept, originally outlined by Freeman (1984), is "to construct an approach to management which takes the external environment into account in a systematic and routine way" (Freeman, 1984, p.247). Accordingly, stakeholder management aims at integrating stakeholder demands into the decision-making processes of business, for example by establishing stakeholder dialogs (Freeman, 1984; Evan/ Freeman, 1993; Crane/ Matten, 2007). Through interacting with the stakeholders, the stakeholder approach is trying to achieve social legitimacy.

Integrative theories are besides instrumental theories the most often used theories in CSP/CFP research. However, they investigate primarily the business – society relation and search for legitimacy. They do not focus on the question if and to what extent CSP may pay off, as instrumental theories do. For this research, instrumental theories are taken into account but will not be part of the theoretical framework.

3.1.4 Ethical Theories

Ethical theories are grounded on value-based concepts. In these theories, businesses should engage in CSR because of the ethical obligation they have. Garriga and Melé (2004) distinguish between four different types of theories.

The first one is the normative stakeholder theory. Garriga/ Melé argue that stakeholder theory in its basic assumptions is grounded in ethical theory (2004, 61). Freeman and Evans already pointed out that "managers bear a fiduciary duty relationship to stakeholders" (1993, p.56). Donaldson and Preston (1995) formulated the normative core of stakeholder theory even more precisely. They based stakeholder theory on two major ideas: (1) stakeholders are persons or groups with legitimate interests in procedural and/ or substantive aspects of corporate activity and (2) the interests of all stakeholders are of intrinsic value

A further type of ethical theory is called *universal rights*, in which basically human rights and other rights are seen as universal. The authors assert that in recent years some universal-rights-based approaches for CSR have been proposed (Garriga/ Melé 2004, p.61). The most popular one is the UN Global Compact, which established ten principles, of which six are based on human rights, three on environmental responsibility, and one anti-corruption participle. The UN Global Compact itself calls these principles "universally accepted" (UN Global Compact, 14.8.2009).

The third approach of value-based theories is the concept of sustainable development. This concept has already been introduced in chapter 2.1.2.5 (Sustainable Development). It is a normative approach, which focuses on ethical responsibilities on macro as well as on business level. Sustainable development calls for meeting "the needs of the present without compromising the ability of future generations to meet their own needs" (United Nations, 1987).

Rooted in Aristotelian tradition is the common good approach. The common good of society is the referential value of CSR. "This approach maintains that business, as with any other social group or individual in society, has to contribute to the common good, because it is part of society." (Garriga/ Melé 2004, p.62)

Ethical theories do not search for an economic reasoning nor do they search for a general legitimacy to engage in CSR activities. But when researching the CSP/CFP link the economic reasoning is central. Hence ethical theories are not the appropriate basis for this research.

3.1.5 Conclusion

The above given insights into the different theories dealing with CSR demonstrate how manifold the CSR research field is. Garriga and Melé (2004) were the first to analyze the various theories and came up with this first classification of CSR theories.

The table below (Table 5: Classification of CSR Theories) summarizes the classification into instrumental, integrative, political and ethical CSR theories. The variety and diversity of approaches makes a clear choice for one theory difficult, as it is obvious that it can barely reflect and fulfill the complexity of the CSR research field. However, in scientific research it is also important to focus on a specific topic within the research field. This conflict is also immanent to the field of CSR research. It is not possible to fulfill all aspects of CSR research, as it is too manifold. Therefore it must be the aim to select the theory most appropriate for meeting the needs of the research question.

As already summarized at the end of each theoretical approach, the instrumental theories seem to be the most appropriate theories to investigate the CSP/CFP link, because they focus on achieving economic objectives and wealth creation, which is also a central question of this research. In table 5 (Classification of CSR Theories) the two instrumental theories utilized in this research to frame the CSP/CFP link are highlighted; this is first of all 'maximization of shareholder value' or in other words neoclassical economics and secondly 'strategic goal achieving' represented with RBV.

Classification of CSR Theories

Instrumental Theories	Political Theories	Integrative Theories	Ethical Theories
Maximization of shareholder value (Neoclassical Economics)	Corporate Constitutionalism	Issue management	Normative stakeholder theory
Strategic goal of achieving competitive advantage (Resource-based View)	Integrative Social Contract Theory	Principles of public responsibility	Universal rights
Cause-related marketing	Corporate Citizenship'	Stakeholder management	Sustainable Development Common good approach

Table 5: Classification of CSR Theories (own graph according to Garriga/ Melé, 2004)

In the following paragraphs the two theoretical approaches, neoclassical economics and RBV are introduced and discussed in order to build a research framework and design the hypotheses grounded on these substantial economic theories (cf. Chapter 4: Research Framework).

3.2 Neoclassical Economics

The neoclassical paradigm is about the profit-maximizing firm in the interest of the shareholder. At first view CSR, which is about the responsibilities a company has towards its stakeholders, and neoclassical economics have not much to do with each other. The advocates of neoclassical economics also argue against CSR. In the following, the main arguments of neoclassical economists against CSR are presented.

Although CSR is en vogue in these days and nearly every company listed on the stock markets is actively involved in CSR activities, practitioners as well as researchers question the mainly normative notion of CSR. In a special report on CSR in *The Economist* (January 19th, 2008) it is written, although CSR clearly has arrived, it is still "worth pausing to consider some of the arguments of those who question the whole point" (*The Economist*, 2008, p.8). Especially in these days of the CSR, hypercritical voices are raised more often and a lot of economists are attacking the idea of CSR.

Sternberg for example points out, "What using business resources for non business purposes actually is, is theft, an unjustified appropriation of owner's property" (1994, 42). There are three main objections against CSR, which can be summarized as follows: "that it encroaches on what should be the proper business of government; that CSR is a sideshow; and that it involves playing with other people's money" (*The Economist*, 2008, p.8).

These arguments are not new and have their origin in the neoclassical paradigm. Especially the last argument that CSR is nothing else than playing with other people's money might be the oldest and probably the most often used argument from critical scholars. One of the most famous advocates using this argument is the neoclassical economist Milton Friedman, saying in his article: "The social responsibility of business is to increase its profits" (Friedman, 1970).

In the following paragraph the neoclassical view is introduced to underline these arguments. They are especially interesting, because mainstream economics is largely neoclassical in its assumptions. First of all a prefatory overview of neoclassical economics is given (3.2.1 Origination, 3.2.2 Assumptions, 3.2.3 Critical Assessment of Neoclassical Economics), followed by an insight into the argumentation of neoclassical economists and their view on CSR (3.2.4 The Neoclassical Paradigm and CSR).

3.2.1 Origination

Neoclassic is the enhancement of classical theory. The main alteration between classical and neoclassical theory is the transition from objective to subjective value doctrine (*Gablers Volkswirtschaftslexikon*, 1996, 759ff.). Classical theorists like Adam Smith (1723-1790) or David Ricardo (1772-1823) laid the foundation with the idea of free markets that regulate themselves.

They developed a theory of value to investigate the dynamics of economies. However, the classical approach reached its boundaries and different theorists, especially in the UK and the U.S. in the late nineteenth century, after 'the Marginal Revolution[10] developed the neoclassical theory of money, interest and prices (Blaug, 1996, p.613; Rutherford, 1992, p.321)

The term 'neoclassical economics' was first used by Thorstein Velben (1900) to characterize Marshall and Marshallian economics (Colander, 2002, 131). Accordingly the term 'neoclassical economics' refers content-wise to the theories summarized under Marshallian economics. Because the term 'neoclassical' is more common it will be used in this research, but it represents the theories of Marshallian neoclassical economics. The basic view of neoclassical economics is "that an economy's equilibrium will occur after a disturbance because of a tâtonnement process with flexible wages and prices" (Rutherford, 1992, p.321). To say it with Weintraub (2002), an economics professor at Duke University:

> Buyers attempt to maximize their gains from getting goods, and they do this by increasing their purchases of a good until what they gain from an extra unit is just balanced by what they have to give up to obtain it. In this way they maximize "utility" — the satisfaction associated with the consumption of goods and services. (Weintraub, 2002)

---

[10] Marginalism: "An economic method, central to neoclassical economics, much used since 1870 in economics. In most cases, it compares an incremental change in one variable with such a change in another. (…) It assumes automatic movement to equilibrium and ignores institutional impediments." (Rutherford, 1992, p.284)

Marshall, Edgeworth, Pareto, Wicksell and Walras were the first and as well most prominent theorists contributing to economic theory around the economy's equilibrium. Neoclassical economics builds on marginal analysis and it still dominates economics today (Rutherford, 1992, p.321). It is also called metatheory because it is a set of implicit rules for constructing economic theory and its "fundamental assumptions are not open to discussion (…)" (Weintraub, 2002).

In the following paragraph the main assumptions of this theoretic stream will be introduced and discussed.

3.2.2 Assumptions

Having a closer look on the history and development of neoclassical economics, the term and its content is described in many ways. So far sixteen different 'schools' of neoclassical economics, divided into two main areas, the Anglo-American and the continental schools can be constituted. (Fonseca, 2010)

All these schools have five basic assumptions in common:

1. Rationality
2. Utility maximization
3. Partial supply and demand equilibrium
4. Perfect information
5. Free competition (Shotter, 2006, p.8 ff.)

Theories based on, or guided by, these assumptions are neoclassical theories.

Rationality means that consumers act rationally in the way that they balance all information, their future needs, and their pleasures optimally to achieve the best possible results (Shotter, 2006). The rational choice assumption is still a dominant paradigm in microeconomics. However, the assumption is also questioned with the argument that economic agents are not able to understand the world fully. Simon (1959) termed these constraints in rationality "bounded rationality". The term is used to designate rational choice that takes into account the cognitive limitations of both knowledge and cognitive capacity (Simon, 1959). The concept of bounded rationality is, for example, central in behavioral economics.

The utility maximization assumption is central to neoclassical economics. It is assumed that individuals seek to maximize utility or, in other words, individuals are aiming at making themselves as happy as possible. It is further assumed that the more goods an individual consumes, the less marginal (additional) utility he or she receives from additional quantities. "The marginal utility of a thing to anyone diminishes with every increase in the amount of it he already has" (Marshall, 1920, p.93). The utility maximization assumption is also transferred to firms. They are aiming at maximizing profits.

Fundamental to neoclassical economics is the assumption of the equilibrium of markets. Equilibrium is regarded as the 'balance of forces'. In this particular case it is referred to as the balance of demand and supply (Milgate, 1987). The interplay of supply on the one hand and demand on the other hand determines the prices of the market for a specific good. Market equilibrium is reached if supply and demand are equal.

A further integral part of neoclassical economics is the availability of perfect information (Marshall, 1920, p.341). Marshall assumed that every market participant who has "a perfect knowledge of the circumstances of the market expects the equilibrium price to be established" (Shotter, 2006, p.15).

The idea of free competition is that the markets regulate themselves through it, because through free competition supply and demand will be regulated naturally. It is assumed that the "market performs more efficiently if the commodities are well-specified and if buyers and sellers are fully informed of their properties and prices" (Stigler, 1987, p.53). To ensure free competition, the government should reduce its interventions to a minimum.

From the basic assumptions of neoclassical economics comes a wide range of theories about various areas of economic activity. The central paradigm of neoclassical theory is that of profit maximization. The aim of profit maximization is seen as the engine of business. However, neoclassical economics has been often criticized. The main critiques are presented in the following section (3.2.3 Critical Assessment of Neoclassical Economics).

3.2.3 Critical Assessment of Neoclassical Economics

The reasons for a critical view on neoclassical economics are manifold and as old as the paradigm itself. The most common critiques refer to the assumptions of neoclassical economics. It is said that they do not represent the reality. In the following the arguments of the fundamental critique in regard to the assumptions of rationality and utility maximization is presented. Afterwards a more general view on neoclassical economics and its role in today's economy after the financial market crisis, is given.

In regard to the rationality assumption it is argued that individuals are not able to reflect and understand the world fully and are as well unable to process all available data. Therefore individuals are only able to exercise a bounded rationality; they can only deal with a limited amount of information at a time (Simon, 1959). This means that individuals are not capable of making fully rational choices. Every decision in economics consists of the rational element in choice, emphasized by economics and non-rational elements. The perfect knowledge never exists, which means that all economic activity implies risk. Simon (1959) questions as well the assumption of utility maximization. He argues that decision-makers will not always aim on achieving the maximum return; they rather aim at a satisfying level (Simon, 1959). It is obvious that that there is a gap between neoclassical economics and reality.

Especially nowadays after the financial market crisis, neoclassical economics and its assumptions are under harsh critique. On the annual meeting of the American Economic Association in January 2010, one of the most important conferences for economists, the basics of today's economics, which are rooted in neoclassical economics, were questioned at its core. Through the financial market crisis, economic theory with its former models and theories were questioned fundamentally. Neoclassical economics promoted a faith in the market that it could not hold. Many economists assume that from this crisis a new democratic capitalist system will emerge, though its character is difficult to predict (Stiglitz, 2010).

The situation today is that, on the one hand, the world economy is still relying on the neoclassical paradigm but, on the other hand, it became evident that the assumptions of neoclassical theory do not represent reality. The postulates of efficient markets, rationality and market equilibrium are most critical. Economists of today call for a new theory that balances the shortcomings of neoclassical economics. Although these shortcoming are not new, there is up to now no theoretical alternative to the neoclassical paradigm. It is still the dominant paradigm in theory and as well as in practice. Although the criticism of neoclassical economics is profound and legitimate, the central paradigm of it, which is profit maximization, is still the engine of the market economy. Accordingly, the eligibility of applying it in this research is still given. In the following paragraph, different perspectives on CSR from a neoclassical perspective are introduced.

3.2.4 The Neoclassical Paradigm and CSR

This section introduces the main voices of scholars with a neoclassical view on CSR. This section is structured chronologically. It starts with Theodore Levitt (1958), who takes a functional position, followed by Albert Carr (1968), who views business as a poker game. Probably the most famous advocate arguing against CSR is Milton Friedman (1970). Elaine Sternberg (1999) defines two basics principles, which she calls 'distributive justice' and 'ordinary decency', and David Henderson (2001) sees in CSR a threat to the market.

3.2.4.1 Albert Carr - Business as a Poker Game

According to G. Lantos the most extreme position on CSR was taken by Albert Carr, which he calls "the pure profit maximizing view" (Lantos, 2001, p.12).

Carr (1968) maintains that the only purpose of business is to turn a product into profit. He argues further that we probably live in the most competitive societies and business is our main area of competition, which has been ritualized into a game of strategy. He compares the nature of business with poker. "While both have a large element of chance, in the long run the winner is the man who plays with steady skills" (1968, p.144). In poker as in business, anything goes within the accepted rules of the game. The government and the courts set the rules through laws and regulations. Carr also distinguishes between personal ethics and business ethics, saying: "The essential point, I said, is that the ethics of business are games ethics, different from the ethics of religion" (p.143). Violating ethical standards of society are common in business and are not necessarily violations of business principles. The business ethics standards permit e.g. misstatements and concealment of pertinent facts, lying about age and personal interests; that is what Carr calls bluffing and what he is saying is part of the game. As a business game player one has to play by the rules, otherwise one will not be successful. However, Carr also admits that integrity and honesty play an important role for a good reputation and thus for success in the long run, but that is still part of the game. Because "from time to time every businessman, like every poker player, is offered a choice between certain loss and bluffing within the legal rules of the game. If he is not reassigned to losing, if he wants to rise in his company and industry, then in such a crisis he will bluff and bluff hard" (Carr, 1968, p.153).

Summarizing, Carr's only standard of social responsibility above economics is obedience to the law (Lantos, 2001, p.12). But he also admits that soft factors like integrity play an important role in the game as they lead to a good reputation. Accordingly, CSR can also be part of the game, but only if it is linked to profit maximization.

The analogy taken by Carr of business as a poker game is criticized by a lot of commentators. "Whereas games are isolated from the rest of our lives, business is an integral part of society" (Lantos, 2001, p.12). Lantos argues further that, contrary to the pure profit-maximizing view, there is nothing special about business that somehow sets it apart from our ordinary ethical obligations. One cannot separate business life from the personal life.

3.2.4.2 Milton Friedman – Constraint Profit-Maximizing View

Also derived from the neoclassical economics is the mainly profit-based position of Milton Friedman. Lantos labeled it as the 'constrained profit-maximizing view', because in contrary to Carr, Friedman expects business, besides maximizing shareholder wealth and obeying the law, of being ethical (Lantos, 2001, p,11).

But to start at the very beginning, in 1970 *The New York Times* published an article by the well-known economist, and according to *The Economist*, "the most influential economist of the second half of the 20th century", Milton Friedman (*The Economist*,

2006). The *New York Times* article of 1970 with the title "The Social Responsibility of Business is to Increase its Profits" was a reaction to the climate of business in the 1960's, a period characterized as the "New Industrial State" by Galbraith (1969), arguing that the United States are no longer a free enterprise society but a structured state controlled by the largest companies. The goal of these companies is not the betterment of society but immortality through an uninterrupted stream of earnings. During this time large companies were managed by elites with little interest in shareholder return but started to get interested in corporate philanthropy. The article of Milton Friedman was a response to these developments. Friedman himself probably didn't expect such a response to his article because it is a very short offhand written article not using academic language but rather written in newspaper style. But it turned out that, almost 40 years later, this article is still in the focus of discussion and analysis when it comes to the discussion of the business case of CSR. In regard to the article's purpose, to comment on businessman behavior and not to write an academic article, the language is sometimes a little harsh, which should not be taken into account while interpreting the content.

The title "The Social Responsibility of Business is to Increase its Profits" summarizes already the main argument of Friedman, which is economic in nature. The article starts with a philosophical argument against corporate social responsibility, saying that only individuals can have responsibilities.

What does it mean to say that "business" has responsibilities? Only people can have responsibilities. A corporation is an artificial person and in this sense may have artificial responsibilities, but "business" as a whole cannot be said to have responsibilities, even in this vague sense. (Friedman, 1970)

This statement that only individuals can have a responsibility, is a fundamental axiom of Anglo-Saxon history and it goes back to philosophers like David Hume, an 18th century Scottish philosopher who was a friend of Adam Smith. Hume advocated a moral theory based on the freedom of the human will and its relation to the individual's character. This view of ethics is based on an individualistic society. Nowadays, in continental Europe and in other cultures like Japan collectivism, the communitarian ethic is predominant, in which the priority given to a group, e.g. a corporation, is prevalent. It is obvious that the philosophical argument of Friedman is not solid and consequently has been criticized by many scholars, especially by business ethicists.

The second argument of Friedman is more profound than the latter. This argument represents the traditional shareholder perspective or the neoclassical view. Friedman outlines that in a free economy:

> There is one and only one social responsibility of business – to use its resources and engage in activities designed to increase its profits so long as it stays within the rules of the game, which is to say, engages in open and free competition without deception or fraud." (Friedman, 1970)

This quote summarizes the neoclassical view and assumptions that Friedman's arguments are based on.

He argues further that making business managers responsible on the one hand to business owners for reaching profit objectives and at the same time to society for enhancing societal welfare represents a conflict of interest that has the potential to cause the demise of business. The businessman is nothing more than an agent for the shareholder, so the only duty the businessman has is to act on the behalf of the shareholder. "In either case, the key point is that, in his capacity as a corporate executive, the manager is the agent of the individuals who own the corporation or establish the eleemosynary institution, and his primary responsibility is to them." (Friedman, 1970)

If a businessman is spending money for social purposes he is spending the money of the shareholder, but the only responsibility he has is to increase the profit of the shareholder. Solving social problems should be the part of the government and is not the role of business. But contrary to Carr, Friedman expects ethical responsibilities of the manager because he calls for a "free competition without deception or fraud". Therefore Lantos titles Friedman's perspective the constraint profit-maximizing view (Lantos, 2001, p.12).

3.2.4.3 Theodore Levitt – Functionalist Fundamentalist Position

During the 1950's, while CSR became more popular in science and practice, Levitt was one of the first who raised a critical voice against CSR. In his paper: "The danger of social responsibility" (1958), Levitt examined the risks of engaging in CSR. Levitt discovered that corporations expand their activities into governmental areas. From Levitt's point of view it is the responsibility of the government to provide for the general welfare. According to Levitt the motivation of corporations of investing in welfare activities is less a social notion but it is "to prolong the lifetime of the business".

From his point of view, providing for the general welfare is the responsibility of government and a business is not a charitable organization and therefore he claims that business should stay out of politics (1960, p.45). The only legitimate function of business is profit making. He argues that a company which is engaged in CSR, or in his words, "involvement in party politics and endless good works" (1960, p.51) is inefficient, because it is distracting the business from is purpose of profit-maximization.

To summarize, according to Levitt, the only function of a corporation remains the axiom of profit-maximization. It is not the purpose of business to do good. His arguments are therefore rooted in neoclassical theory.

3.2.4.4 Elaine Sternberg – Distributive Justice and Ordinary Decency

Sternberg, a scholar in philosophy and former investment banker also takes a neoclassical perspective on CSR. From her point of view, the purpose of business is not to do good but rather to maximize the long term value of the organization for the shareholders. Nevertheless, business can also be ethical but only if it contributes to the business objectives of maximizing value (Sternberg, 1999, 39ff.).

In her article "The stakeholder concept: A mistaken doctrine", she defines ethical business as follows: "(…) business is ethical when it maximizes long-term owner value subject to distributive justice and ordinary decency". (Sternberg, 1999, p.40) The expressions 'distributive justice' and 'ordinary decency' are the factors that make business ethical.

Sternberg clearly distinguishes 'ordinary decency' from 'being nice'. She argues that the long-term view of business requires confidence and trust in the future. Business must be "conducted with honesty, fairness and the absence of physical violation (…). Collectively, these constraints embody what may be called 'ordinary decency'" (Sternberg, 1999, p.39).

'Distributive justice', is the distribution of organizational rewards according to the organizational objectives. To say it in simple words "those who do most for the organization deserve most from the organization" (Sternberg, 1999, p.40). If both factors, 'ordinary decency' and distributive justice', are integrated into business it is ethical.

To conclude, Sternberg's view of business is neoclassical in its assumptions. The most important fact, which distinguishes business from everything else, is that the purpose of it is to maximize its value over the long run by selling goods and services. This does not mean that business cannot be socially responsible, but these actions of socially responsible business are only acceptable if they help in maximizing the long-term value. "If, however, a socially 'responsible act' does not contribute to the business objective, then it's wrong – ethically as well as financially – for a business to perform it." (Sternberg, 1999, p.40).

3.2.4.5 David Henderson – CSR as a Threat to the Market Economy

In the paper "Misguided Virtue: False Notions of Corporate Responsibility" (2001) Henderson ascertains that the subject of CSR, or in other words, "the proper conduct of business enterprises" is old as capitalism itself. But in recent years the concept of CSR developed to what he calls "a radical doctrine", because it embodies a wider concept of the role of private business.

The modern view of CSR expects business to take a leading role in making 'the world a better place'. Business should behave like a corporate citizen, and act upon the objectives of sustainable development, with the three dimensions of economic, environmental and social responsibility. Companies should further set goals, measure the performance of these goals and lastly they should be made accountable (Henderson, 2001, p.1).

Henderson argues that the pressure to act according to these demands comes mainly from public interest groups or NGO's, which are often hostile towards the market economy. Surprisingly, companies are not acting against this threat of the market economy; they even comply with these so-called 'society needs'. The effects on the market economy are manifold. One example of negative effects by CSR activism is damaged labor markets, because regulations made in the name of CSR undermine the freedom of contract and thus deprive people of opportunities.

However, Henderson sees the greatest potential of harm in the name of CSR, when governments or businesses try to regulate the world as a whole, by introducing international standards. Many businesses from all over the world agreed to comply with standards set, for example by the 'Global Compact', although circumstances are widely different across countries. Henderson summarizes this phenomenon as 'global governance' - the sharing of responsibility by businesses, government and selected NGO's. Through the phenomenon of global governance, businesses and NGO's receive rights that should be exclusively for governments, although they are not elected and are not politically accountable.

Henderson sees CSR is a new form of collectivism. He summarizes that the main problem of adopting CSR is the reduction of competition and economic freedom, the cornerstones of a functioning market economy. Therefore CSR is undermining the market economy in its foundation (Henderson, 2001).

3.2.5 Summary

The arguments against CSR mainly focus on the economic function of business, to maximize profits and not to solve social problems. All scholars who raised a voice against CSR do not criticize ethical corporate behavior in general, but from their point of view the first duty of a company is to maximize its profits.

Carr takes the most extreme position, he compares business with a poker game, in which bluffing is acceptable if it leads to profit maximization. He may have formulated his view in an extreme manner, but from Friedmans' point of view bluffing would not be acceptable in business. For Friedman responsible behavior is part of business. However, he also sees the only responsibility of a manager in maximizing the shareholder value. Levitt sees the danger in CSR mainly in the fact that business takes the responsibility of governments. It is not the function of business to perform good deeds and contribute to the social welfare. Sternberg's view is also under the premise of the neoclassical paradigm. From her point of view business should only engage in CSR if it helps to maximize profits. Henderson sees CSR is a new form of collectivism. From his point of view CSR is like a corset, which he calls 'global governance', which misleads business and results in a reduction of competition and economic freedom, which are the cornerstones of a functioning market economy.

All these perspectives mainly have one major argument against CSR, which is that of profit maximization. If CSR does not lead to profit maximization there is no point in doing it. CSR is only acceptable if it increases profits. However, the doctrine of profit-maximization is not a contradiction to CSR; it criticizes engaging in CSR for its own sake.

Starting from the neoclassical paradigm, this research tries to investigate which areas of CSR engagement may lead to profit maximization and are rewarded or penalized by the financial market.

3.3 Resource-based View

This chapter deals with the resource-based management approach, respectively the resource-based view (RBV). The RBV is a strategic management tool and deals with the topic of gaining sustainable competitive advantages for a company, by considering internal and external orientations (as introduced in Chapter 3.1.1 Instrumental Theories).

"The RBV has become one of the most influential and cited theories in the history of management theorizing." (Kraaijenbrink/ Spender, Groem, 2010, p.350) In their thesis, the relation between CSR, CFP, and risk is analyzed from the perspective of the RBV.

In the following sections, the RBV is introduced by first of all giving insights into the origin of it, followed by the assumptions made by this theoretical approach and a critical assessment. The last section explains CSR as a resource by introducing different theoretical and empirical researches investigating the link between CSP and CFP.

3.3.1 Origination

In this section the RBV is presented as a theory grounded in strategic management. First of all a distinction between market-based approaches of strategic management and the RBV are made. Secondly the historical evolution of RBV is discussed.

Traditionally strategic management theories have been dominated by market-based approaches, such as the Structure-Conduct-Performance-Hypothesis (SCP). According to this hypothesis the growth of a company is very much dependent on its strategic adaption to external factors (e.g. Edwards/ Allen/ Shaik, 2006).

The SCP and other market-based approaches take a market-oriented view of economics and business, in which the management puts emphasis on the external environment of the company. According to Davies (2005, p.37) market-based approaches were predominant in the 1980s. In these approaches it is assumed that the organization's success depends on its competitive environment, whereas the organization itself is of minor importance. Therefore, the management focuses on the requirements of the market by analyzing the competitors and the customers' needs.

Like the market-based view, the RBV is as well an approach of strategic management. Both approaches have certain similarities, as they deal with the topic of gaining sustainable competitive advantages for a company, by considering internal and external orientations, but with a different emphasis.

As Paladino et al. (1998, p.1782) state: "The market orientation of the firm examines the customer, the competitor and organizational resources (implicitly) respectively. The RBV, on the other hand, appears to reverse the order, analyzing organizational resources first, followed by the competitors and customers (implicitly)".

In contrast to the market-based view, the resource-based management approach puts emphasis on the internal factors of a company and explains the success of a company with the differences in the availability of its resources.

The resource-based view was established in the early 1990's as a consequence to the one-sided perspective of strategic management so far, with a focus on only external factors. In 1991 the *Journal of Management* published an article by Barney (1991), positioned relative to the SCP paradigm in economics and analyzing the link between firm resources and sustained competitive advantages. This article is seen as the path-breaking publication from which the RBV moved to mainstream (Barney, Wright, Ketchen, 2001, p.626). In the following paragraphs the historical development of the RBV is introduced.

According to Macharzina (1999, p. 56ff.) the issue of the resource-based approach has already been broached in the economic theories of David Ricardo, who argues that the restricted availability of resources is the reason for unequally distributed returns of companies.

Instrumental to the developments of the RBV is the publication of Penrose in 1959 (Kor/ Mahoney, 2004). The book *The Theory of the Growth of the Firm* (1959) by Penrose applies to be the foundation for the modern resource-based view of the firm. With her publication Penrose has directly and indirectly influenced the RBV (Kor/ Mahoney, 2004).

Penrose's aim was to develop a comprehensive theory of the growth of the firm. This theory should "explain several qualitatively different kinds of growth and must take account not only for the sequence of changes created by firm's own activities but also of the effect of changes that are external to the firm and lie beyond its control" (Penrose, 1959, p.4).

Penrose contributions "go significantly beyond the phenomenon of the growth of firms.", Penrose rather provides "a theory of effective management of firms' resources, productive opportunities, and diversification strategy" (Kor/ Mahoney, 2004, p.184). It is the first publication in which the relation between resources, capabilities and competitive advantage is theorized and therefore this work delivers the basic principles of the RBV.

Although not directly linked to the Penrose book, Wernerfelt (1984, p.171) translated the economic ideas of Penrose into the company strategies. He argued that resources are the potential causes for competitive advantages. This article is referred to as the initial point of the RBV as a theoretical concept for strategic management.

In terms of content closely linked to the article by Wernerfelt but not referred to, Barney (1986a, 1986b) laid the foundation for a framework of the RBV by introducing the concept of sustained competitive advantage and analyzing strategic market factors. Moreover, the initial management framework of the RBV was introduced by Barney in 1991. With this the basic criteria, today known as the VRIN-criteria (valuable, rare, in-imitable, non-substitutable), to evaluate resources were introduced. Since then the RBV evolved to an influential framework for understanding strategic management (Barney, 2001).

Summarizing the basic assumptions of the RBV, companies can be seen as a bundle of material and immaterial resources. They generate profits through their different qualitative factors, endowment, and position. This different efficiency and effectiveness in the usage of resources is caused by the varying historical development of the companies and gives the corporation a specific character. The resources that a company has to its disposal embody the basis for competitive advantage, which is the root of above-average profits of a firm (Bamberger/ Wrona, 1996).

In the following paragraph the assumptions of the RBV will be introduced by mainly referring to Barney's path-breaking concept of resources and competitive advantage.

3.3.2 Definitions and Assumptions

Considering the evolution of the RBV illustrated above, the basic definitions and assumptions of this theoretical approach will be analyzed in the following. This section especially focuses on the refined approach introduced by Barney (1991). The definitions of the term *resource* and *sustainable competitive advantage* are central for the RBV. Therefore these terms are first of all defined and the basic ideas behind the terms introduced (3.3.2.1 Definition of the Term Resource, 3.3.2.2 Definition of Sustainable Competitive Advantage).

Secondly the main assumptions are introduced (3.3.2.3 Assumptions).

3.3.2.1 Definition of the Term Resource

Up to now, no commonly accepted definition of the term *resource* could be developed among theorists. In this chapter, different definitions of the term 'resource' are presented and discussed, with the aim of finding an appropriate definition to be used as a basis in this research.

A suitable and probably most often found definition in the corresponding literature stems from Barney, who defines resources as "all assets, capabilities, organizational processes, firm attributes, information, knowledge, etc." (Barney, 1991, p.101). This reveals that a resource can be initially anything a company has at its disposal. Hence, also classifications of resources differ among theorists. Bamberger and Wrona (1996) argue that a variety of classifications regarding resources can be found in the corresponding literature. They can be classified according to their origin into internal and external resources. The authors explain that all internal material or immaterial goods, systems and processes can be defined as internal resources. Hence, external resources are those that a company has to obtain from the market due to a lack of know-how or financial assets (Bamberger/ Wrona, 1996, p.145).

Further differences in the categorization of resources among theorists are illustrated by Mäkinen and Seppänen (2006, p.3). Wernerfelt (1984) e.g. categorized resources into seven different types; other authors like Hall (1992) emphasize only on non-tangible resources. These facts amplify that "(…) the work identifying, listing and categorizing resources in the corresponding literature is still far from complete" (Priem et al., 2001, as cited in Mäkinen & Seppänen, 2006, p.3). In the following, the most recent definitions of RBV literature are presented.

Davies (2005, p.37) distinguishes between tangible and intangible resources as well as capabilities. Examples for the latter can be skills or culture. However, the borders between capabilities and intangible resources are not clear, because capabilities can also be the knowledge about the right application of resources.

Branco & Rodrigues (2006) explain: "Resources are the means through which firms accomplish the activities they are engaged in to convert inputs into outputs (…)" (Branco/ Rodrigues, 2006, p.116) and categorize resources into tangible and intangible resources, where tangible resources include physical and financial assets and intangible resources can be, for instance, know-how of employees, corporate culture and reputation. This definition is content-wise in-line with the early definition of Barney (1991) cited above. This demonstrates that, although RBV developed, scholars come back to the basic definition of 'resources'.

Accordingly, the almost classic and very basic definition given by Barney (2001) is used in this research, although there have been many attempts to define, redefine and to develop typologies for the term 'resource'. Resources are defined as "tangible and intangible assets firms use to conceive of and implement their strategies" (Barney, 2001, p.138). Central to this definition is first of all the distinction between tangible and intangible resources and the reference to strategies. In this context strategies are closely linked to firm performance and competitive advantage, because "strategy is a firm's theory of how it can gain superior performance in the markets within which it operates" (Barney, 2001, p.14). In this regard, competitive advantage means that a firm is implementing strategies to gain this superior performance. In the following section, the term (sustainable) competitive advantage, as a central term of RBV is defined in more detail.

3.3.2.2 Definition of Sustainable Competitive Advantage

The RBV focuses on achieving a sustainable competitive advantage (SCA) and explains the SCA of some firms over others. The concept of competitive advantage has been dealt with in management literature since the 1980s. Early literature on SCA goes even back to 1937. Alderson (1937), as cited by Hoffmann (2000), hinted that a fundamental aspect of competitive adaption is the specialization of suppliers to meet variations in buyer demands. Hoffman (2000) quotes two authors, Hall (1980) and Henderson (1983), who stress as well the need for firms to develop advantages in relation to its competitors in order to survive. The concept of SCA is central to the RBV. In the following a short overview into the definition of SCA is given.

The term SCA was introduced by Porter (1985). Although no definition was given, Porter discussed two strategies (low-cost and differentiation) to gain SCA. Surprisingly in most of the RBV literature there is no formal definition of SCA, although it is central to it. Most likely this is because the term seems to be self-explanatory for most of the scholars and moreover the conditions and sources under which the SCA is reached are more important. However, in the field of CSR research it is important to mention that, although the term 'sustainable' is part of the concept of SCA, it has not necessarily something to do with the concept of sustainability as discussed in Chapter (2.1.2.5 Sustainable Development) but rather with being competitive as a company in the long run. This competitiveness may be gained by using CSR resources, but this is not essential.

Probably closest to an explicit definition of SCA is that from Barney (1991):

> A firm is said to have a competitive advantage when it is implementing a value-creating strategy not simultaneously being implemented by any current or potential competitors. A firm is said to have a sustained competitive advantage when it is implementing a value-creating strategy not simultaneously being implemented by any current or potential competitors and when these other firms are unable to duplicate the benefits of this strategy. (p.102)

First of all this means that SCA is reached by a value-creating strategy, which is not implemented by others. This citation contains further two basic assumption of the RBV, that it should not be implemented simultaneously and that the competitor should not be able to duplicate these resources. So it is less the question of what SCA is, but more the question how it can be reached. The assumptions underlying the RBV are leading to the answer of how to reach SCA.

In the following section the assumptions and its consequences for the RBV are introduced.

3.3.2.3 Assumptions

The assumptions of the RBV are similar to the assumptions of neoclassical economics (Chapter 3.2.2 Assumptions), which are that firms are profit-maximizing entities and that human economic behavior is rational. This is not surprising, as the RBV has its foundation in neoclassical theory. However, unique to RBV are the following two assumptions:

1. Resource heterogeneity: competing firms may possess different bundles of resources.
2. Resources immobility: these resource differences may persist.

(Barney, 2001, p.141)

Barney (2001) remarks that these assumptions may exist, but not necessarily all firms possess these resources.

Resource heterogeneity means that firms have varying capabilities or, put in other words, firms have different resources (Peteraf, 1993). The idea of resource heterogeneity incorporates two attributes of a firm's resources: scarcity or rareness and non-substitutability (Barney, 1991). A firm's resource is rare when the demand for a resource is greater than the supply. Non-substitutable resources are those that cannot be, as the term suggests, substituted by other resources.

Immobility suggests that "some resources, some of the time, may be inelastic in supply, that is, more of a particular resource is not forthcoming even though demand for that resource is greater than its supply" (Barney, 2001, p.141).

Or in other words, immobility of resources means is the inability of firms "to obtain resources from other firms" (Madhani, 2010).

Barney (1991) summarized his thoughts and findings into a framework, which is shown in the figure below. The assumptions that resources are heterogeneous and immobile are given. The so-called 'VRIN criteria' (value, rareness, imperfectly imitable and non-substitutable) should give an orientation if resources may lead to a sustained competitive advantage. If resources fulfill the VRIN criteria it is likely that the firm gains sustained competitive advantage.

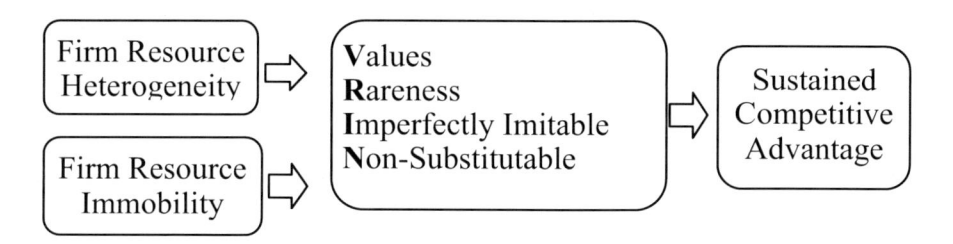

```
┌─────────────────┐
│ Firm Resource   │⇒  ┌──────────────────────┐     ┌──────────────┐
│ Heterogeneity   │   │ Values               │     │ Sustained    │
└─────────────────┘   │ Rareness             │⇒    │ Competitive  │
┌─────────────────┐   │ Imperfectly Imitable │     │ Advantage    │
│ Firm Resource   │⇒  │ Non-Substitutable    │     └──────────────┘
│ Immobility      │   └──────────────────────┘
└─────────────────┘
```

Figure 6: The Framework of the Resource-based View (Barney, 1991, p.113)

Based on these assumptions, many propositions following the logic of the RBV have been developed and as well empirically tested. In Chapter 3.3.4 (Resource-based View and Corporate Social Responsibility) the propositions in regard to CSR research will be introduced. Prior to that, a critical assessment of resource-based theory is given.

3.3.3 Critical Assessment of Resource-based View

Like every popular theoretical framework, the RBV is also subject to criticism that focuses on the shortcomings of it. These critiques are important to evaluate in order to advance this fundamental approach of strategic management. The section starts with a general critique, firstly in regard to the assumption of rationality and secondly the missing empirical support for the RBV. Then the conceptual shortcomings are discussed before a comprehensive overview of the main critiques is given.

The most basic criticism of the RBV is that it relies on the inconsistent assumptions of bounded rationality (Tywoniak, 2007). "On the one hand managers make boundedly rational decisions leading to resource heterogeneity, but at the same time RBV conceptualizes markets at equilibrium a situation where firms optimize, thus assuming substantive rationality" (Tywoniak, 2007, p.4). Besides this inconsistency of rationality, the general critique that choices cannot be rational is also relevant for the RBV. This critique is in line with the critique of neoclassical economics (Chapter 3.2.3 Critical Assessment of Neoclassical Economics).

Although the RBV is a widely accepted theory of strategic management, until now no empirical support for its basic principles could be found (Newbert, 2007). For example, the principles leading to SCA, described in the VRIN criteria (Figure 6: The Framework of the Resource-based View) are not empirically proven yet (Paladino et al., 1998). The first attempt to find empirical support for the RBV was conducted by Barney and Arikan (2001). However, due to technical shortcomings in the framing and sampling technique, they failed to support the RBV empirically. Newbert concludes that "given the nature of Barney and

Arikan's (2001) framing and sampling technique, and because no other assessment of the RBV literature has yet been conducted, the actual level of empirical support for the RBV remains uncertain" (Newbert, 2007, p.122). Therefore, Newbert (2007) tested for the actual level of empirical support for the RBV, with the result that the RBV "has received only modest support" (Newbert, 2007, p.121). Accordingly, the problem of no empirical support is more or less unsolved up to now.

The RBV is also in critique for its conceptual shortcomings. In 2001 Priem and Butler started a discussion about these conceptual shortcomings of the RBV in the *Academy of Management Review*. The first critique of Priem and Butler is that the RBV lacks subsequent definitional work, which is essential to formalize any concept as theory (Priem/ Butler, 2001, p.24). They argue that the RBV is not yet a theory of value creation, because it is circular. They argue that competitive advantage is defined as a value-creating strategy that is based on value as a resource among others. In simple terms, the input to create value is value. For Priem and Butler (2001), this argumentation of value offered by Barney (1991) is invalid in terms of theory building. In addition, the static approach of the RBV limits the use of it (Priem, 2001, p. 499).

Probably the most comprehensive overview of critiques and counter-arguments has been written by Kraaijenbrink, Spender and Groen (2010). They reviewed and assessed the principal critiques of the RBV and categorized them into 8 categories.

> Critique 1: The RBV has no managerial implications
> Critique 2: The RBV implies infinite regress
> Critique 3: The RBV's applicability is too limited
> Critique 4: SCA is not achievable
> Critique 5: The RBV is not a theory of the firm
> Critique 6: VRIN is neither necessary nor sufficient for SCA
> Critique 7: The value of a resource is too indeterminate to provide for a useful theory
> Critique 8: The definition of resource is unworkable

According to the assessment of Kraaijenbrink et al. (2010), the RBV can withstand most of the critiques, but the following critiques cannot be dismissed: "The indeterminate nature of two concepts fundamental to the RBV – resource and value – and RBV's narrow explanation of a firm's SCA" (Kraaijenbrink et al., 2010, p.359). They argue that the RBV orientates too much on the rationality of neoclassical economics, which is limiting its potential of becoming a theory of sustainable competitive advantage. Appendix 7.1 (Summary and Assessment of Critiques to the RBV) summarizes the assessment of Kraaijenbrink's et al. (2010) critiques of the RBV.

Summarizing, although the critiques are in some areas fundamental, the RBV and its advocates could withstand these critiques. RBV is still an established theory of strategic management, which is not static but rather evolves dynamically.

3.3.4 Resource-based View and Corporate Social Responsibility

In the field of CSR research the RBV is already a well-established theoretical framework used to explain CSR as a resource to gain competitive advantage. In a resource-based context, McWilliams et al. (2006, p.3) argue that the effective use of CSR as a resource is by a company that is capable of achieving SCA. In the following, an introduction to the dynamics of tangible and intangible CSR resources is given (3.3.4.1 Tangible and Intangible Resources) as a central distinction in the RBV. Afterwards, different perspectives from the RBV on the question if and in which way CSP and CFP are related are discussed. This section starts with an insight into the research of environmental performance from the perspective of the RBV (3.3.4.2 Environmental Performance). A fairly new aspect integrated in recent CSP/CFP research is constructing CSR as a multidimensional measure. This research distinguishes between different types and motives for CSR, which are introduced in Chapter 3.3.4.3 (CSR Typologies). Lastly, approaches explaining the CSP/CFP link during crises, and as a tool for risk management from the RBV, are presented and discussed (3.3.4.4 CSR, Crises and Risk Management), followed by a summary (3.3.5 Summary).

3.3.4.1 Tangible and Intangible Resources

As discussed in Chapter 3.3.2 (Definitions and Assumptions), the distinction between tangible and intangible resources is central to the RBV. Tangible resources include physical and financial assets and intangible resources can be, for instance, know-how of employees, corporate culture, experience and reputation (Branco/

Rodrigues, 2006). Following this distinction, the question is, which CSR resources are either tangible or intangible, which is discussed in the following.

Tangible resources are the resources that involve costs, e.g. through cost from investments in environmentally friendly technology (Hart, 1995). But they also involve costs for communication on CSR, e.g. through special CSR reports, and the communication with stakeholders, e.g. through dialogs, which require manpower and often the support of specialized consultants. These investments do tie up capital and influence the financial resources negatively (Kramer, 2009).

However, tangible resources or, in other words, financial resources can also be positively influenced through CSR engagement. Hart (1995) e.g. argues that through the investment in environmentally friendly technologies, or just through savings of natural resources like water and energy, operating costs can be reduced. This potential influence of tangible resources, especially in regard to environmental performance leading to SCA, is further discussed in Chapter 3.3.4.2 (Environmental Performance). A further aspect is the potential of cost avoidance or financial benefits through CSR engagement through investments (Branco/ Rodrigues, 2006). However, this has been a long discussed issue (cp. Chapter 1.2.1 Introduction - more than 40 years of CSP/CFP research), with mixed results in regard to the pay-offs.

In regard to the VRIN criteria, the nature of tangible resources is that they are easy to imitate and most often not rare. Therefore it is more difficult to reach SCA through them (Kramer, 2009). Accordingly, especially the intangible resources are the basis to reach SCA (Barney, 1991; Wernerfelt, 1984).

Intangible resources are by their nature more likely to fulfill the 'VRIN criteria' (value, rareness, imperfectly imitable and non-substitutable) and lead to SCA. In this context, Branco and Rodrigues (2006) explain that tangible resources are relatively easily imitable or substitutable, whereas intangible resources play a crucial role because they meet the criteria like inimitability and non-substitution. Their argument behind this is: "Intangible resources and capabilities are accumulated over time and cannot be acquired on tradable factor markets" (Branco/ Rodrigues, 2006, p.117).

Branco & Rodrigues (2006, p.126) see reputation reached by CSR engagement as the most important intangible asset that provides SCA (Branco/ Rodrigues, 2006). Other researchers argue that CSR as a whole is an intangible asset, because through CSR resources are more effectively used (e.g. Hillman/ Keim, 2001; Orlitzky et al., 2003).

From this discussion of tangible versus intangible CSR resources it can be concluded that especially the intangible resources will lead to a competitive advantage. In the following, different studies applying the RBV to investigate the CSP/CFP link are discussed.

3.3.4.2 Environmental Performance

In this section two perspectives on environmental performance from the RBV are discussed. As already mentioned, the first theoretical paper that applied the RBV framework to investigate CSR was by Hart (1995). Russo and Fouts (1997) also argue that environmental investments can outperform financially. Both are mainly focusing on tangible resources.

Hart (1995) proposes a natural-resource-based perspective of the firm and argues that it is likely that "strategy and competitive advantage in the coming years will be rooted in capabilities that facilitate environmentally sustainable economic activity" (Hart, 1995, p.991). Starting from this assumption, Hart introduced the natural-resource-based view, which is a conceptual framework for incorporating the challenges of the natural environment into strategic management. This framework is composed of three interconnected strategies: pollution prevention, product stewardship and sustainable development. Implementing theses key drivers would mean investing in tangible as well as in intangible resources. Hart identified these strategic capabilities as key drivers for firms to gain sustainable competitive advantage (Hart, 1995, p.992 ff.). The table below summarizes the basic ideas of Hart's framework. For each of the three strategic capabilities he identified the environmental driving force behind it, the key resource, and the potential competitive advantage a firm can gain by applying these strategies. The driving force behind the strategic capability of pollution prevention is e.g. minimizing the emissions, which is reached by continuous improvement (key resource), which, according to Hart, leads to lower costs and competitive advantage.

Strategic Capability	Environmental Driving Force	Key Resource	Competitive Advantage
Pollution Prevention	Minimize emissions, effluents & waste	Continuous improvement	Lower costs
Product Stewardship	Minimize life-cycle cost of products	Stakeholder integration	Preempt competitors
Sustainable Development	Minimize environmental burden of firm growth and development	Shared vision	Future position

Table 6: A Natural-Resource-Based View: Conceptual Framework (Hart, 1995, p.992)

Summarizing, the work of Hart was path breaking in applying the RBV to CSR research, although he only focused on environmental resources. However, Hart was the first scholar who asserted that environmental responsibility could constitute a resource or a capability that leads to a sustained competitive advantage (McWilliams/ Siegel/ Wright, 2006). Although this paper provided a theoretical framework that needed to be tested, Hart set the foundation for further research in CSR from a resource-based perspective. Russo and Fouts (1997) took this theoretical approach one step further by testing the prepositions made by Hart (1995).

Referring to Hart (1995) and drawing from the RBV, Russo and Fouts (1997) hypothesize that "high levels of environmental performance will be associated with enhanced profitability" (Russo/ Fouts, 1997, p.540). They argue that, if a firm goes beyond compliance in regard to environmental issues, e.g. investing in preventive technologies, there is under certain circumstances the possibility to outperform financially. The resource-based prediction would be: if companies are able to deploy physical assets in a way that competitors are not able to imitate easily, it is likely that they can gain competitive advantage. These preventive technologies (tangible resources) can influence the firm, e.g. through gaining efficiency in production, and it is also a method of risk prevention. Implementing environmental technologies beyond compliance also influences the corporate culture and human resources, so that e.g. top candidates might be easier to attract (Russo/Fouts, 1997). Translating this thought, Russo and Fouts assume that, through implementing tangible resources, also intangible resource will be implemented at the same time. In regard to intangible resources, Russo and Fouts (1997) identified tow factors supporting their hypothesis. "The first is, that a reputation for leadership in environmental affairs will increase sales among customers who are sensitive to such issues" (Russo/ Fouts, 1997, p.539). The second is "the ability to influence public policies in ways that confer a competitive advantage" (Russo/ Fouts, 1997, 540). Russo et al. call this ability, or intangible resource, political acumen. In terms of RBV these political skills are the resources to manage external constituencies.

For testing this hypothesis Russo et al. used firm level data from 447 companies covering all industries. However, the data from utilities were removed because their returns are subject to statutory limits. The dependent variable was ROA and the environmental rating used described the independent variable in the model. The results of empirically testing the model "are providing solid support" for the hypothesis (Russo/ Fouts, 1997, p.548).

In this paper it could be verified the fist time that firms with higher environmental performance had superior financial performance. Secondly, it was shown, "that the resource-based view of the firm can be applied fruitfully to corporate social responsibility issues" (Russo/ Fouts, 1997, p.551).

Summarizing, the two papers were the first investigating the link between environmental performance and CFP using the RBV as the theoretical background. The conclusion that can be drawn is, firstly, that the RBV is an appropriate theoretical theory to investigate this relationship, and secondly, that environmental performance, gained through tangible and also intangible resources, can lead to competitive advantage. However, since these studies have been published the research in this field evolved tremendously. In recent research, CSR is more and more seen as a multidimensional concept, which needs to be taken into account in research.

3.3.4.3 CSR Typologies

In recent years, theorists started to investigate CSP from a more sophisticated perspective by developing different typologies of CSR engagement and deducing strategic implications for firms. In 2001, Hillman and Keim, for example, called for a "more fine-grained approach" (2001, p.134) to study CSP and CFP and already offered an empirical investigation of such an approach. Investigating the CSP/CFP link by applying different CSR typologies is referred to as a significant theoretical breakthrough in this research area (McWilliams/ Siegel/ Wright, 2006). The following three studies (Baron, 2001; Hillman/ Keim, 2001; Husted/ Salazar, 2006) and their impact on the CSP/CFP literature are introduced in chronological order.

One of the first papers in which the multidimensional nature of CSR was taken into account was written by Baron (2001). In this paper a theory of private politics, CSR, and integrated strategy was developed, in which a distinction between two types of CSR, altruistic and strategic, was made. The theoretical deduction of this approach starts with a critique of previous CSP/CFP literature, because up to now these approaches leave the motivation of the social performance open (Baron, 2001, p.10). From Baron's point of view "their study can best be viewed as supporting the notion that good financial performance allows firms to redistribute from shareholders to others." Baron therefore advocates for a different view and assessment of CSP, because CSR behavior can have different motivations, which are not yet mapped in the used CSP measures. This shortfall of previous literature is illustrated in an example in which three firms reduce their toxic emissions. "Yet, one firm may do so because of altruistic preferences, a second because it faces an external threat by an international activist group, and a third because doing so will increase the demand for its products" (Baron, 2001, p.11).

Baron (2001) defines CSR as strategic if it is used to refer to a profit-maximizing strategy. "Strategic CSR is thus another component of a market strategy intended to capture value" (Baron, 2001, p.17). Investing in CSR without the purpose of profit maximizing is referred to as altruistic CSR. For Baron the motivation is decisive in examining the relation between CSP and CFP, because the motivation determines the effects on the market. CSP is always redistribution from economic stakeholders to others. By modeling various sequences of firm's behavior to mainly consumer boycotts, Baron (2001) examines the CSP/CFP link. Baron concludes that "a positive correlation is consistent with profit maximization and altruism". However "the relation should be stronger for profit-maximizing firms and weaker for altruistic firms" (Baron, 2001, p.40). This model implies that firms should seize any opportunity for strategic CSR to gain competitive advantage and improve profits. This theoretical model developed by Baron evolved the classical CSP/CFP research by distinguishing different motives for CSR. However, empirically testing this model is challenging, because the motives of firms engaging in CSR are not easy to assess.

A further approach of investigating the link between CSP and CFP from the RBV, by using different CSR typologies, was introduced by Hillman and Keim (2001). In this paper, the link between CSP and CFP is firstly deduced from the RBV and secondly tested empirically. Therefore this paper is probably the first in which the multidimensional aspects of CSP are tested empirically. Hillman and Keim (2001) argue that "the relationship between social performance and financial performance may be better understood by separating social performance into two components: stakeholder management and social issue participation" (Hillman/ Keim, 2001, p.126).

Stakeholder management is referred to as "building better relations with primary stakeholders like employees, customers, suppliers, and communities", whereas social issue participation is not related to the firm's direct relationship with primary stakeholders. Common forms of social issue participation may include, refusing to sell to the military, avoiding business in countries accused of human rights violation, etc. (Hillman/ Keim, 2001, p.126ff.). According to the RBV and the VRIN criteria, "resources that may lead to competitive advantage include socially complex and causally ambiguous resources, such as reputation, corporate culture, long-term relationships with suppliers and customers, and knowledge assets" (Barney, 1986; Leonard, 1995, Teece, 1998; In: Hillman/ Keim, 2001, 127). Accordingly long-term relations with primary stakeholders (stakeholder management) can lead to valuable, intangible competencies and therefore can lead to SCA. Integrated in these preliminary thoughts is already the question of causality, that CSP comes first and CFP second. Grounded on these theoretical thoughts, Hillman and Keim (2001) deduce two hypotheses. The first is, that "stakeholder management is positively associated with shareholder value creation" and secondly, "stakeholder management leads to improved shareholder value creation", which refers to the causality question of the CSP/CFP discussion (Hillman/ Keim, 2001, p.128). It is further argued that social issue participation has the opposite effect of stakeholder management. Social issue participation, seen as "a broader view of CSR engagement" does not provide a basis for value creation, because it is in most of the cases imitable and readily duplicated, e.g. the choice of a company not to engage in 'sin' industries. Accordingly, social issue participation, as a form of CSR does not fulfill the VRIN criteria and therefore cannot provide the basis for gaining competitive advantage (Hillman/ Keim, 2001, p.128ff.). Thus, Hillman and Keim propose the following two hypotheses: "Social issue participation is negatively related to shareholder value creation" and "leads to a decreased shareholder value creation" (Hillman/ Keim, 2001, p.129).

Using correlation and regression analysis the two hypotheses have been tested. CFP is measured with the market-based measure *market value-added*, because "it has the ability to capture the future value of income streams more appropriately" (Hillman/ Keim, 2001, p.130). To measure CSP, the commonly used Kinder, Lydenburg, Domini (KLD) index was used. Each KLD item was then screened based on their direct (stakeholder management) or indirect (social issue participation) relation to primary stakeholders. The results indicate a positive relationship between shareholder value, measured with market value-added, and stakeholder management, and a negative relationship with social issue participation. In regard to causality, there is an indication for the hypothesis that the direction of the link is from CSP to CFP.

This study showed firstly the usefulness of the RBV in investigating the CSP/CFP link and secondly it showed that the disaggregation of CSR into strategic (stakeholder management) and non-strategic or altruistic CSR (social issue participation) withstands first empirical tests, with stakeholder management or strategic CSR leading through a SCA. This study further demonstrates that CSP is multidimensional and that disaggregation is necessary to better understand the relationships studied.

The most recent theoretical research investigating the CSP/CFP link with a multidimensional perspective on CSR is that of Husted and Salazar (2006). It is the declared aim of the authors 'to take Friedman seriously' by "examining the conditions under which profit maximization and social performance are congruent" (Husted/ Salazar, 2006, p.76). They argue that there is a trade-off between profits and social performance. Profits and social performance cannot be maximized at the same time. It is aim of the research, to determine the conditions under which CSP leads to a better CFP. These conditions are analyzed by looking at three different types of CSR: the firm as altruist, as coerced egoist and as strategist (Husted/ Salazar, 2006).

Altruistic CSR refers to the case in which firms engage in CSR without expecting any benefits like increase of profits. Coerced egoism is defined as the CSR activity of a firm only when it is forced to engage e.g. through regulation, whereas strategic CSR is used by firms to maximize profits. The authors use cost-benefit analysis to determine the optimal level of CSR in each of the cases. Their model suggests, "it is to the advantage of the firm to act in a strategic manner, rather than react to a coercive (...) environment" (Husted/ Salazar, 2006, p.86). They conclude that previous research investigating the CSP/CFP link might have been misguided, because the multidimensional nature of CSR was not factored in. In regard to testing these prepositions empirically, it will be challenging to "sort out altruistic and strategic motivation", especially because firms have a portfolio of CSR projects, some of them strategic and others non-strategic.

To conclude, the multidimensional nature of CSR must be taken into account in CSP/CFP research. CSR cannot be seen and analyzed as a one-sided phenomenon. In fact, the distinction between strategic and non-strategic CSR opens promising advancements in the field of CSP/CFP research, which needs to be deepened. However, up to now there is no clear definition of what strategic and non-strategic CSR is and much less any reliable measurement methods of strategic and non-strategic CSR. It is the challenge of researchers to advance these preliminary and also path-breaking studies into a comprehensive research concept.

3.3.4.4 CSR, Crises and Risk Management

A further aspect relevant for the underlying research is the question of the influence of crises and if CSR functions as a form of risk management during and after crises. This is especially interesting because, if a company may not outperform through CSR, like other CSP/CFP literature proposed, it is still possible that CSR has the capacity to function as an insurance-like buffer. In the following two papers (Schnietz/ Epstein, 2005; Godfrey/ Merrill/ Hansen, 2009), analyses of the CSP/risk link from the RBV are presented.

Schnietz and Epstein (2005) empirically investigated the financial value of reputation during a crisis. Arguing that previous research on the link between CSP and CFP could not lead to clear results, because these studies relied on the study of positive events, they posed the research question, in which way negative events are related to the CSP/CFP link (Schnietz/ Epstein, 2005). They tested "whether a reputation for social responsibility acts as a 'reservoir of goodwill' during corporate crises" (Schnietz/ Epstein, 2005, p.327). In their model the hypotheses are positioned within resource-based theory, "treating corporate reputation as an intangible economic asset that contributes to a firm's sustainable competitive advantage" (Schnietz/ Epstein, 2005, p.329). Schnietz et al. (2005) argue in line with Russo and Fouts (1997) and Hillman and Keim (2001) that reputation as an intangible asset facilitates stakeholder management. Stakeholder management relies on complex and long-term relationships and is therefore difficult to imitate, which enhances the ability of firms to outperform. They theorized, relying on previous theoretical research, that "there also may be financial value in a reputation for corporate social responsibility during a crisis" (Schnietz/ Epstein, 2005, p.329). During crises, it is assumed that CSR decreases firm-specific risk and volatility. This theoretical reasoning has its roots in transaction cost theory, arguing: "Firms that focus not only on explicit contractual claims, but also on implicit claims, will realize higher market valuations" (Schnietz/ Epstein, 2005, p.331, secundum Cornell/ Shapiro (1987)). Firms with a higher reputation through CSR are less likely the target of future boycotts because they were able to build up a reservoir of goodwill. According to this argumentation, a firm's level of CSR must be related not only to the value of a company but also to lower levels of risk, particularly market measures of risks (Schnietz/ Epstein, 2005, p.331).

To test these hypotheses empirically Schnietz and Epstein (2005) applied event study methodology. The crisis-laden event they employed for the test was the failed 1999 World Trade Organization (WTO) ministerial meeting in Seattle. The reasons for failure were twofold, firstly an internal conflict between developed and developing countries regarding the goals, and secondly, massive demonstrations against environmentally harming and label abusing practices by multinationals (Schnietz/ Epstein, 2005, p.328). Here for the first time the issue of CSR was broached in public. Schnietz and Epstein (2005) posed the question of how investors reacted to this development and if investors treat firms with a reputation for CSR differently than firms without such a reputation.

As a sample they used the Fortune 500 list from 1999 and divided it into firms with and without reputation in CSR, using the Domini Social Index provided by KLD Research. The results were mainly consistent with the hypotheses. Moreover, the returns of the portfolio of 1999 Fortune 500 firms with a reputation for CSR did not decline significantly, but the portfolio of firms without a reputation for CSR declined significantly. These results give first evidence that CSR can act as a 'reservoir of goodwill' during crises. The main finding of this empirical work is that "a reputation for social responsibility yielded tangible financial benefit during the crisis of the Seattle meeting" (Schnietz/ Epstein, 2005, p.341). Especially interesting for the underlying research is the fact that industries facing the greatest crises, i.e. those companies in environmentally damaging and labor-abusing industries such as electric utilities, can gain the greatest benefit if they have a reputation for CSR.

The main limitation is of this research is that the results given apply only to this specific event. There is more research needed if the same or similar reactions can be observed during other crises. Moreover the question why investors penalized or rewarded firms stayed open (Schnietz/ Epstein, 2005, p.342). It is assumed that investors reward firms with a good reputation for CSR because they face a lower level of risks. However, the research does not give further insights into this question.

The risk-management hypothesis, saying that companies reduce their risk through CSR and are therefore valued higher by investors, has also been investigated by Godfrey, Merrill and Hansen (2009). Although they do not explicitly ground their research on the RBV, their theoretical framework fits into the RBV argumentation and they also refer to RBV literature.

Their key question is if shareholders gain when a firms strategy includes CSR (Godfrey/ Merrill/ Hansen, 2009, p.426). This question is also central to the previous CSP/CFP literature. In line with the CSP/CFP research stream, they investigate in particular "when participation in some types of CSR activities creates a form of goodwill or moral capital for the firm that acts as 'insurance-like' protection when negative events occur that preserves shareholder value (CFP)" (Godfrey et al., 2009, p.426). Though Godfrey et al. integrate a further aspect into their research, "namely, that CSR activities can provide an insurance mechanism to preserve — rather than generate — CFP" (Godfrey et al., 2009, p.426). Through this research approach they want to reply to previous shortcomings of the CSP/CFP research field, which mainly are: a lack of theoretical explanation or rather broad theoretical rationales, monolithic measures of CSP, and the focus on industry- or economy-wide events (Godfrey et al., 2009, p.426).

Based on these shortcomings, Godfrey et al. (2009) developed first of all a model explaining the CSP/CFP link. In regard to the relationship between CSR and shareholder value, they theorized that CSR, as an intangible asset, is a form of a insurance-like protection reducing risk. They further argue that this risk reduction adds value to shareholders. Furthermore, firms receive positive attributions or moral capital when they signal that they are not completely self-interested. However, the CSR activity must fulfill two features in order to be noteworthy: the activity must be of public knowledge and it must be substantial enough to be judged as credible (Godfrey et al., 2009, p.428). Godfrey et al. (2009) also adapt the argumentation of Schnietz and Epstein (2005) that during crises "punishments (based on negative events) will be more severe when bad acts are committed by bad actors" (Godfrey et al., 2009, p.428). Accordingly they posit "that CSR activity will signal to investors the presence of moral capital that may temper potential sanctions." (Godfrey et al., 2009, p.429). They also differentiate between different types stakeholder like Hillman and Keim (2001), between primary and secondary stakeholders. CSR engagement with primary is referred to as 'technical CSR', whereas the relation to secondary stakeholders is called 'institutional CSR'. They hypothesize: "In the context of a negative event, the shareholder value-loss mitigating property of CSR engagement is greater for institutional CSR activities than for technical CSR activities" (Godfrey et al., 2009, p.429). The modeling of CSR into a set of different heterogeneous firm actions and afterwards grouping them into technical and institutional CSR is in line with the RBV. One can argue that institutional CSR is more likely to fulfill the VRIN criteria, as they are not easy to imitate and they are rare in contrast to technical CSR. Accordingly, institutional CSR, as defined by Godfrey et al. (2009), is probably more capable of producing SCA. However, as already mentioned, Godfrey et al. (2009) do not focus on the RBV perspective in their paper.

Using CSR as independent variable and the change in shareholder value as dependent variable, Godfrey et al. applied the methodology of event study on a sample of 160 firms.

The key finding is that there is an overall support for the risk management hypothesis. "Participation in CSR activities does seem to yield insurance-like protection to a number of firms (…)." (Godfrey et al., 2009, p.441) From the authors point of view, CSR stands merely "as a proxy for quality management" (Godfrey et al., 2009, p.440). An even more interesting result is that the engagement in technical CSR (primary stakeholders) benefited only large firms, while engagement in institutional CSR (secondary stakeholders) benefited all groups. This outcome is also in line with the RBV argumentation that through institutional CSR it is more likely to gain SCA. This is a contradiction to the findings of Hillman and Keim (2001), who found out that social issue participation (non-strategic CSR) is negatively related to shareholder value creation. However, in the two papers different proxies for CSR were used.

Summarizing, the results of Godfrey et al. (2009) show first, that the monolithic construction of CSR fails to capture significant effects, and secondly, that there is more research needed to further investigate the different effects of single and grouped CSR measures. The RBV provides a profound theoretical framework to study the possible effects.

3.3.5 Summary

The section above gives an overview of the RBV in general and its application in CSP/CFP research.

Central to the RBV is the argument that a firm can gain a sustainable competitive advantage by effectively using its resources. Resources can be nearly everything, from assets, to capabilities, to processes and knowledge. (Barney, 1991) These resources can be either tangible or intangible in nature. Both forms of resources can lead to SCA. The 'VRIN criteria' function as an orientation tool. If resources fulfill the VRIN-criteria, of value, rareness, imperfectly imitable and non-substitutable, it is likely that the firm gains SCA.

The RBV is the most common theoretical approach in analyzing the strategic use of CSR and in investigating the relation between CSP and CFP. According to the RBV framework, CSR is seen as a resource and through the effective control and manipulation of this resource a company is capable of achieving SCA. In the context of the RBV and CSR, Branco and Rodrigues (2006) explain that tangible resources are relatively easily imitable or substitutable, whereas intangible resources play a crucial role, because they meet the VRIN criteria like inimitably and non-substitution. Therefore, especially the intangible CSR resources are the resources that should be developed to gain sustainable competitive advantage.

Hart (1995) was the first who developed a model to investigate the CSP/CFP relationship from the RBV, focusing on environmental performance and primarily tangible resources. Hart identified three key drivers (pollution prevention, product stewardship and sustainable development) for firms to gain sustainable competitive advantage (Hart, 1995, p.992 ff.) and developed a framework on the basis of these key drivers. Russo and Fouts (1997) tested the prepositions of Hart (1995) and hypothesized that "high levels of environmental performance will be associated with enhanced profitability" (Russo/ Fouts, 1997, p.540). Their results show that environmental performance can lead to competitive advantages. These two researches were path breaking during this time, because it was the first time the RBV was applied to CSR research and further it could be shown that there is a trade-off in form of higher financial outputs for CSR. However, the limitations of the two papers are also evident: firstly they only focus on environmental performance and mainly on tangible resources and secondly the measurement of the environmental performance is one-dimensional.

In previous years more fine-grained approaches in the field of CSP/CFP research emerged, taking into account the multidimensional nature of CSR. On the basis of the RBV, a distinction between basically strategic and non-strategic resources can be identified to be the main distinction (e.g. Baron, 2001; Hillman/Keim 2001; Husted/ Salazar, 2006). However, the distinction between strategic and non-strategic is not consistent and neither clearly defined as such. But the following table (Table 7: CSR Typologies of Strategic and Non-Strategic CSR) is a first attempt to categorize the different studies into strategic and non-strategic CSR. The table displays that the CSR-resources labeled with strategic CSR do fulfill the VRIN criteria, whereas the non-strategic or, for Baron (2001) and Husted/ Salazar (2006), altruistic CSR do not match the VRIN criteria.

CSR Typologies of Strategic and Non-Strategic CSR

	CSR typologies	Strategic vs. Non-Strategic CSR	Fulfillment of VRIN-criteria
Baron (2001)	Strategic CSR = profit maximizing	Strategic	yes
	Altrustic CSR = not expecting benefits	Non-strategic	partially
Hilman/ Keim (2001)	stakeholder management = building better relations with primary stakeholder	Strategic	yes
	social issue participation = is not referred to the firm's direct relationship with primary stakeholders = altruistic/ philanthropic CSR	Non-strategic	no
Husted/ Salazar (2006)	Altrusitic = CSR engagement without expecting benefits	Non-strategic	no
	coerced egoist = forced CSR activities like regulation	Non (coereced)	partially
	Strategist = the use of CSR to generate profits	Strategic	yes

Table 7: CSR Typologies of Strategic and Non-Strategic CSR (authors own illustration)

They conclude that the strategic use of CSR can lead to a sustainable competitive advantage, whereas the non-strategic use or altruistic CSR has negative effects on the financial performance of firms. The main advancement of these three studies is the fact they are all taking the multidimensional nature of CSR into account: According to McWilliams, Siegel and Wright (2006) this is referred to as a significant theoretical breakthrough in this research area. However, the fact that the used typologies are not consistent and the measurement methods are still poor is a clear limitation of the studies. Hillman and Keim (2001) suggest that future research should extend the decoupling of CSP and "further explore the differences between the dimensions (...)" (Hillman/ Keim, 2001, p.136)

A further aspect in the CSP/CFP literature investigated, and based on the RBV, is the question if CSR functions as a form of risk management during crises, which corresponds with the risk management hypothesis. Schnietz and Epstein (2005) assumed that investors reward firms with a good reputation for CSR because they face a lower level of risk. They found evidence that CSR can act as a 'reservoir of goodwill' during crises. Godfrey et al. (2009) hypothesized that CSR is a form of an insurance-like protection reducing risk and this risk reduction adds value to shareholders. Their key findings show that there is an overall support for the risk management hypothesis. Summarizing, there is first evidence that CSR seems to have the function of an insurance-like protection to a number of firms (Godfrey et al., 2009, p.440ff). Both studies use event study to investigate the risk management hypothesis. This methodology only focuses on one specific event and it is therefore not possible to generalize the results to other events. Moreover, the measurement methods of the used CSR typologies are not consistent and therefore lack the possibility of comparison.

It is aim of this research to investigate the CSP/CFP link from a profit-maximizing perspective (neoclassical economics) and by taking the multidimensional nature of CSP into account, which can be strategically used (RBV). In the following chapter (Chapter 4 Research Framework) the research framework, based on neoclassical economics and RBV is introduced.

4 Research Framework

When investigating the relation between CSP, CFP and risk, the neoclassical paradigm and the RBV complement each other. From the neoclassical perspective, investing in CSR is only acceptable if it is linked to profit maximization. The RBV describes which CSR resources can lead to a sustainable competitive advantage and in the next step to profit maximization. It explains CSR as a firm resource, which can be used to generate profit. The central research question for the underlying thesis is, which CSR resources can be utilized to generate profits, with a special focus on analysts' and investors' perceptions of this link. To analyze this question a framework is developed on the foundation of neoclassical economics and the RBV. It is the aim of this framework to model the relation between CSP, CFP and risk.

4.1 Introduction

Taking the shortcomings and critiques of previous studies on the relation between CSP and CFP into account (Chapter 1 and 3), this study investigates the CSP/CFP link with an improved approach. In the following, the basic assumptions underlying this research are introduced.

The main assumption made in this research based on instrumental theories (Chapter 3.1.1 Instrumental Theories) is that CSR can, under certain conditions, lead to profit maximization. In the following, the conditions under which CSR can lead to profit maximization, or eventually a loss in profit, are defined according to the theoretical foundations outlined in the previous chapter.

There are basically four observations, based on the theoretical background, which will be the cornerstones of this research:

- CSP is determining CFP → CSP is the independent variable
- CSP is multidimensional → no generic link between CSP and CFP
- CSP is dependent on the industry
- CSP is determined by stakeholders

In the following, these cornerstones will be constituted shortly.

Having a closer look at the history of quantitative CSP/CFP research, most of the studies use CSP as the independent and CFP as a dependent variable. Garcia-Castro et al. (2009) for example analyzed 127 studies investigating the CSP/CFP link from which 109 treat CSP as an independent and CFP as a dependent variable. (Garcia-Castro et al., 2009, 107) As a basic assumption, this research as well treats CSP as an independent variable and CFP as a dependent variable. It is assumed that CSP is determining CFP. Arguing from the RBV, CSR resources can lead to a competitive advantage (Chapter 1.2 Literature Review). Accordingly, it is hypothesized that CSP variables will influence or determine the CFP measures.

The question if there is a generic link between CSP and CFP delivered mixed results (Chapter 1.2 Literature Review). Although most of the studies found a positive link between CSP and CFP (e.g. Waddock/ Grave, 1997; Orlitzky et al. (2003)), others found a negative relation (e.g. Aupperle et al. (1985); McWilliams/ Siegel (2000)). Therefore, recent studies tend to integrate the multidimensional nature of CSP. Especially studies based on the RBV differentiate between strategic and non-strategic CSR engagement. (Baron, 2001; Hillman/ Keim, 2001; Husted/ Salazar, 2006) This study also attempts to take the multidimensional nature of CSP into account by differentiating between strategic and non-strategic CSP.

The third cornerstone of this research is the based on the fact that studies focusing on several industries at the same time also tend to deliver mixed results. CSR engagement is very industry-related and a comparison between industries is therefore difficult where the result can be misleading (Chapter 1.2 Literature Review). Accordingly, it is the aim of the underlying research to investigating the link between CSP and CFP from a narrow perspective by using a single-industry approach. The industry investigated in this research is the electric utility industry, which is especially affected by the process of liberalization and the challenges to react on climate change (Chapter 2.2 The Utility Industry).

The fourth determining factor for this research is influenced by the fact that CSR engagement is dependent on the stakeholder groups. CSP is determined especially by the key stakeholders, which are customers, employees and shareholders for the electric utility industry (Chapter 2.2.2.1 Mapping the Main Stakeholder Groups). However, due to the process of liberalization and the fact that the industry is very capital-intensive, this study primarily focuses on the most important stakeholder group, the investment professionals, represented by analysts and investors. A further aspect why this research focuses on investment professionals is that the study is based on instrumental theories, focusing on profit-maximization. It is assumed that the profit-maximizing perspective will best be reflected by investment professionals.

The perspective of the investment professionals will be integrated by an ex ante survey, before the CCSP/CFP link is analyzed via regression analysis. Accordingly, this research is divided into two parts:

1. Survey of mainstream analysts and investors

The survey examines how analysts and investors value certain CSR criteria and in which way they are integrating them into their investment decision before and during the financial market crisis (Chapter 4.2 Survey Framework). The survey further is the foundation for dividing CSP into different dimensions (Chapter 4.2.2 Operationalizing Strategic and Non-Strategic CSP) in order to take the multidimensional nature of CSP into account.

2. Quantitative analysis of the link between CSP, CFP and risk

Within this part of the research, the relation between the different CSP dimensions (according to the survey results), CFP and risk will be analyzed.

In the following sections, the research framework will be developed and introduced, starting with the survey and its objective in the research context (Chapter 4.2 Survey Framework). Afterwards, the relation between CSP, CFP and risk will be modeled, including the methods used to operationalize these measures (Chapter 4.3 Modeling the Relationship between Corporate Social Responsibility, Firm Performance and Risk for the Empirical Analyses). Finally, the hypotheses underlying this research are formulated and the final research framework is introduced (Chapter 4.4 Hypotheses and Research Framework).

4.2 Survey Framework

It is the objective of the underlying research to analyze the CSP/CFP link before and during the financial market crisis, with a special focus on the question of how investment professionals, as one of the most important stakeholder groups, value CSR. The survey is also used as a technique to take the multi-dimensional nature of CSR into account, by using the survey results to construct the CSP dimension in terms of strategic and non-strategic CSP according to the RBV. The following section gives reasoning to why the perspective of investment professionals is especially interesting (Chapter 4.2.1 Integrating the Perspective of Investment Professionals) and secondly, presents the idea and methods of operationalizing strategic and non-strategic CSP via a survey (Chapter 4.2.2 Operationalizing Strategic and Non-Strategic CSP).

4.2.1 Integrating the Perspective of Investment Professionals

Investment professionals are major stakeholders, especially of listed companies. Precisely, analysts and investors, as capital market participants, value companies by developing and using their ratings. The capital markets are seen as a seismograph for future economic developments, consequently they have the quality to picture future risks and opportunities (Heise, 2011). In the following, the general role of investors and analysts is explained and afterwards the reasons why investment professionals are especially interesting for this research are given.

Investors play a key role. An investor is anyone, from individuals to institutions, making an investment with the aim of maximizing profit. The money they invest in the market can be seen as the lubricant for the functioning of the capital market. This means that the movements and directions of the capital market are influenced by the investment decisions of investors, e.g. the industry, the product, and the company they are investing in. The majority of the volume invested in the market comes from so-called institutional investors, such as investment companies, mutual funds, investment banks and others (e.g. Achleitner 2001, Ryan 2007, Womack/ Zhang 2003).

Typically, the basis for an investment decision is laid by a profound research prepared by analysts. It is the task of an analyst to provide information as to who is buying and selling, with the aim of decreasing the information asymmetries between buyer and seller and thereby lowering the cost of capital (Diamond/ Verrecchia 1991). Summarizing, the capital market is the market in which companies can raise capital coming from investors, who are either individuals or institutions. Analysts function as intermediaries between these two parties. (e.g. Achleitner 2001, Ryan 2007)

In a fast changing economy with globalization on the top, new business challenges and risks appear. Also, the utility industry is facing new risks and challenges, also in the field of CSR, such as climate change (Chapter 2.2.2 Corporate Social Responsibility Topics in the Utility Industry).

In literature, CSR is seen as a trend and as well as a characteristic for good management (Chapter 1.2 Literature Review). Specific CSR criteria are assumed to have a material influence on companies' licenses to operate. Hence, CSR can function as risk management and mitigation if companies are capable of implementing processes to deal with material CSR issues, like climate change (Chapter 2.2.2 Corporate Social Responsibility Topics in the Utility Industry). Assuming that CSR is seen as good management and as risk management and mitigation, it is likely that capital market participants factor it in. It is further assumed, that analysts and investors, as a seismograph for future economic developments, integrate only the criteria with strategic implications into their decision-making process. Arguing from the RBV, the criteria with no strategic influence on the future value of a company are most likely not to be part of investment decisions, as they do not lead to an SCA (e.g. Husted/ Salazar, 2006).

Because of the seismographic abilities of the capital markets, this research takes the perception of analysts and investors, as capital market participants, into account while investigating the CSP/CFP link to ascertain if strategic and non-strategic criteria can be derived from it.

The most appropriate method to first investigate the perception of analysts and investors and to secondly derive strategic and non-strategic CSR is a survey. The main advantage of the survey method in this particular research is that the survey is capable to reach a large population and therefore generate a large sample size. The investment world is very diverse and analysts and investors are often highly specialized on one particular topic (e.g. sell-side analysts, for utilities large caps). With a survey, it is possible to also integrate the niches of the investment world.

Two methods of quantifying specific CSP variables like strategic versus non-strategic CSP are used in research. First, quantifying CSP on beliefs, e.g. by using survey methodology, secondly on firm performance by using commonly used performance measures (Hillmann/ Keim, 2001). This research is trying to first use the first method, the quantification of CSP on beliefs, by using survey methodology and in a second step CSP performance measures are used as well for the quantitative analysis (Chapter 5 Empirical Analyses).

For these reasons, the survey method has been chosen to picture the perception of analysts and investors on specific CSR measures.

It is aim of the survey to examine how analysts and investors value certain CSR criteria and in which way they integrate them into their investment decision. Besides that, the results of the survey are used to aggregate strategic and non-strategic CSP dimensions based on the RBV (Chapter 4.2.2 Operationalizing Strategic and Non-Strategic CSP).

4.2.2 Operationalizing Strategic and Non-Strategic CSP

To take into account the multidimensional nature of CSR is considered a significant theoretical breakthrough in this research area (McWilliams/Siegel/ Wright, 2006). As discussed in Chapter 3 (Theoretical Foundation), a more fine-grained approach to the field of CSP/CFP research emerged in recent years. These approaches take the multidimensional nature of CSR into account. Based on the RBV a distinction between strategic and non-strategic resources (e.g. Baron, 2001; Hillman/Keim 2001; Husted/ Salazar, 2006) can be made. It is assumed that the strategic use of CSR can lead to a sustainable competitive advantage, whereas the non-strategic use or altruistic CSR has no effects or negative effects on the financial performance of firm.
As already mentioned above, in this research, CSP is first quantified based on beliefs, by using survey methodology. Though,

strategic and non-strategic CSP has been rarely quantified yet. However, literature using the RBV and the VRIN-criteria as theoretical background offer an appropriate method. In table 8 (Quantification of Strategic and Non-strategic CSR) an overview of the RBV literature is given, including a summary of which of the researches quantified CSR. This overview shows that only Hillman and Keim (2001) quantified CSR by using the KLD rating scheme.

Quantification of Strategic and Non-Strategic CSR

	CSR typologies	Strategic vs. Non-Strategic CSR	CSR Quantified Yes/ No
Baron (2001)	Strategic CSR = profit maximizing	Strategic	no
	Altrustic CSR = not expecting benefits	Non-strategic	
Hilman/ Keim (2001)	stakeholder management = building better relations with primary stakeholder	Strategic	yes (using KLD rating)
	social issue participation = is not referred to the firm's direct relationship with primary stakeholders = altruistic/ philanthropic CSR	Non-strategic	
Husted/ Salazar (2006)	Altrusitic = CSR engagement without expecting benefits	Non-strategic	no
	coerced egoist = forced CSR activities like regulation	Non (coereced)	
	Strategist = the use of CSR to generate profits	Strategic	

Table 8: Quantification of Strategic and Non-Strategic CSR

The latest research proposing an approach to distinguish between different types of CSP is that of Husted and Salazar (2006). As already discussed (Chapter 3.3.4 Resource-based View and Corporate Social Responsibility), they distinguish between strategic, coerced and altruistic CSR, but did not empirically investigate their prepositions nor did they quantify CSR. However, in comparison for example, to the CSP measures, Hillman and Keim (2001) used, a distinction between these three types (strategic, coerced and altruistic) of CSP is more convincing. Hillman and Keim (2001) screened the KLD items for a direct stakeholder relation (variable: stakeholder management) and all other items were grouped into the variable social issue participation. This attempt of operationalizing the two CSP types, stakeholder management and social issues participation, seems very broad and vulnerable to mismatches, or at least vague measures. Hillman and Keim also admit, that "none of these measures captures the full range of relations (...)" Hillman/ Keim, 2001, 131).

Therefore, this research tries to operationalize CSP differently, by using the proposed typologies, strategic, coerced and altruistic CSP, presented by Husted and Salazar (2006). The advantage of this typology is first, that the theoretical reasoning behind the three types is more profound than that of Hillman and Keim (2001). Secondly, although in general the measurement of CSP is challenging the distinction and measurement of strategic and especially coerced CSP is clearly defined and can therefore be measured. However, especially the distinction between strategic and altruistic CSR is difficult, as they can "coincide at times" (Husted/ Salazar, 2006, 87). The major challenge nevertheless is that the three measures have not been operationalized yet. This research is the first that tries to operationalize the proposed measures of strategic, altruistic and coerced CSR. Moreover this research attempts to empirically investigate the theoretical prepositions in regard to distinguishing between CSP-typologies.

In this research, CSP will be operationalized according to the above given distinction between strategic, coerced and altruistic CSR measures using, in a first step, the RBV with its VRIN-criteria to construct the scales and secondly, validate this distinction with survey methodology. The measures used in the survey will be classified into these three dimensions.

Measures with a long-term orientation, such as policies, programs, strategies and existing management systems, will be grouped to strategic CSP. Coerced CSP measures will be the measures on level of compliance, referring to existing or upcoming regulations. As already mentioned, especially altruistic CSP will be challenging to operationalize, because altruistic refers to a motivation that can not be sorted out exactly. In this research, altruistic CSP refers to the measures that are more or less on the basis of voluntary engagement, and at the same time do not refer to programs or strategies.

This theoretical construct of strategic, coerced and altruistic CSP will be translated into concrete measures in Chapter 5.2.1.5 (Factor Analysis – Constructing Strategic and Non-Strategic CSR) by using the survey data.

4.3 Modeling the Relationship between Corporate Social Responsibility, Firm Performance and Risk for the Empirical Analyses

4.3.1 Introduction

It is aim of this section to model the relation between CSP, CFP and risk as a basis for the empirical analysis. First, the different methods of measuring CSP, CFP and risk are introduced and afterwards the relation between CSP and CFP and between CSP and risk is discussed. Further, other factors influencing these relations are introduced (Chapter 4.3.5 Further Influencing Factors). This section is the foundation for the hypotheses and the research framework (Chapter 4.4 Hypotheses and Research Framework).

4.3.2 Constructing and Operationalizing CSP

As already discussed in the previous chapters (Chapter 1.2 Literature Review), the measurement of CSP remains a main problem in the CSP/CFP research and it is very likely that this is a major reason for the heterogeneity of findings. According to Schreck (2009, 30), the fact that "the studies (…) use so many different ways of operationalizing the construct of CSP, other than ambiguous results as the CSP/CFP link would have been surprising". There is the need to use more fine-grained methods to investigate the link (see Section 3.3.4 Resource-based View and Corporate Social Responsibility). Using only a single aggregated measure to describe CSR does not meet the needs of this research field. The phenomenon of CSR is too complex to describe it with a single composite CSR variable. Therefore, this research is, besides using the composite CSR measures, developing CSR typologies based on the RBV.

In the following a short insight of how the measurement of CSP is designed in this study is given. CSP is modeled from the RBV, taking into account the complexity of CSR to achieve a more differentiated picture of the CSP/CFP link.

To overcome the heterogeneity of research results, most of the recent studies investigating the CSP/CFP link use "more consistent and comparable across-study-measures (...)" (Garcia-Castro, 2009, 108). This section mainly compares two different cross-study measures with each other, the KLD and the Oekom rating, to determine the most appropriate rating scheme for this research.

In most of the studies, the KLD cross-study measure is used. KLD is a rating provided by the rating agency Kinder, Lydenberg & Domini. The main advantage of the KLD rating in contrast to other ratings is the fact that it is the most frequently used rating in CSP/CFP research. This leads to a better comparability of the research results and counter the problem of heterogeneity of CSP data. However, the KLD rating also faces shortcomings, especially concerning the use of it for scientific purposes. Schreck (2009), for example, identified three major shortcomings of the KLD rating scheme when used as a proxy for CSP in research. These shortcomings are: (1) the weighting of single issues, (2) the subtracting concerns from strength and (3) the use of dummy variables (Schreck, 2009, 46ff.). A further critique, coming from UNEP Finance Initiative (2009), is that it could empirically be shown that "KLD ratings don't optimally use available data" (UNEP FI, 2009, 1) and further, that the KLD environmental rating "do not optimally summarize or predict corporate environmental performance (…)" (UNEP FI, 2009, 4). In consequence, this implies that the KLD ratings do not optimally measure CSP, which is, on the one hand, due to the rating methodology used and, on the other hand, the fact that the available data are not optimally used and translated to a profound rating.

Given these limitations of the widely-used KLD rating for CSP/CFP research, it is advisable to have a closer look at alternatives that are more suitable for scientific research. A very appropriate cross-study measure seems to be the Oekom rating provided by the Oekom research AG. Oekom is an independent rating agency as well, providing corporate responsibility ratings for institutional investors and other groups of more than 3000 companies in 50 countries. (Oekom research, 2010)

With regard to the three limitations identified by Schreck (2009) and introduced above, "oekom data is arguably more suitable for such analyzes due to differences in its specific structure" (Schreck, 2009, 47). In the following (Table 9: Comparison KLD and Oekom Rating), a short overview is given in what way Oekom's rating methodology is different from the KLD limitations. Oekom, for example, is using industry-specific weighting schemes, and it is not the absence or presence of certain measures that is assessed but the quality of these measures. This results in a more detailed rating in comparison to KLD.

	KLD Rating	Oekom Rating
Weighting Schemes	All dimensions are treated as equally important	Industry-specific weighting schemes
Strength/ Weakness Concern Scheme	Companies are assessed based on the absence or presence of certain strengths and weaknesses	Companies are not assessed based on the absence or presence of certain strengths and weaknesses
Dummy Variables	Use of dummy variables	No use of dummy variables

Table 9: Comparison KLD and Oekom Rating (based on Schreck, 2009, 46ff)

A further argument to the more detailed assessment methods, which is especially important for the underlying research, is the fact that Oekom is the only rating agency providing specific utility reports for the years before and during the financial market crisis. This is, besides the methodological arguments, the reason why the Oekom rating is used for the cross-sectional regression analysis with CFP and risk data.

However, the Oekom rating is, as the KLD rating, not "designed for the purpose of scientific studies" (Schreck, 2009, 47). The main disadvantage of using the Oekom rating for measuring CSP is the fact that it is not often used in CSP/CFP research. Only two scientific studies investigating the CSP/CFP link have yet been published using Oekom data for assessing CSP[11]. Still, the advantages of the Oekom rating outweigh the advantages of using the KLD rating with regard to investigating the CSP/CFP link. Accordingly, in this research the Oekom company rating is used to measure the corporate social performance of utilities.

CSP is therefore structured according to the Oekom rating methodology. Within the Oekom rating, CSP is measured by a multitude of single components. This multitude of CSP components renders the possibility for a differentiated picture of the CSP/CFP link. However, for reasons of comparability and completeness, this research also uses the regression analysis with the CSR composite ratings.

4.3.3 Constructing CFP

As already discussed in previous chapters (Chapter 1.2. Literature Review, Chapter 3.3.4 Resource-Based View and Corporate Social Responsibility), researchers used various measures to proxy CFP. Margolis and Walsh (2001), for instance, identified more than seventy CFP measures in 95 CSP/CFP studies. The problem of this plurality is that each measure has its specific theoretical implication and therefore the combustibility is not always given. In the following, the main discussion will be displayed and finally the CFP-measures used in this study are presented and integrated in the framework for analyzing the CSP/CFP link.

---

[11] Glaser, J. / Hornung, S. / Labes, M. (2007): Indikatoren für die Humanressourcenförderung, Humankapital messen, fördern und wertschöpfend einsetzen, Berlin 2007.

4.3.3.1 Operationalizing CFP

CFP measures can generally be classified into accounting-based and market-based measures. In Chapter 1.2.5 (Measuring Corporate Financial Performance) this basic distinction has already been discussed with the conclusion that especially the long-term value of a firm is more accurately captured by market measures.

In a meta-analytical review of board compensation, Dalton et al. (1998) discussed the nature of performance measures. They mention that, despite the many advantages of market-based measures, the only shortcoming is "that market-based performance indicators are often subject to forces beyond management's control" (Dalton, et al. 1998, 275). Further, in most of the CSP/CFP literature accounting, measures like ROE and ROA are used as complementary measures. But as already mentioned, these measure are more short-term orientated and might be subject to manipulation (McGuire et al. 1988).

Resuming previous work on this topic, *"there happens to be no consensus regarding the efficacy of reliance on one set of indicators (accounting-based) or another (market-based)"* (Dalton, et al. 1998, 275).

Consequently, for this research both accounting and market-based measures will be used. However, it is expected that the different natures of measures react differently under the influence of CSP. In the following, the effects of CSP on CFP will be discussed shortly and integrated into the research framework.

4.3.3.2 Measurable Effects of CSP on CFP

As discussed above, market-based measures tend to capture shareholder value creation best in comparison to accounting-based measures. The main advantage of market-based measures is that they have the "ability to capture the future value of income streams more appropriately (...)" (Hillman/ Keim, 2001, 130). It is assumed that market-based measure fit best into the CSP/CFP research, because CSR is a concept with a long-term orientation. Accordingly, the long-term orientation of CSR will best be mapped with a CFP measure mapping the future value. Therefore, one expects more consistent results between the relation of CSP to CFP when using market-based measures. Most of the CFP/CFP studies apply Tobin's Q as a market measure. Tobin's Q is calculated as the market value of a company divided by the replacement value of the firm's assets. This ratio was introduced by James Tobin, with the ambition to construct a ratio with macroeconomic significance (Tobin/ Brainard, 1977). Since then, various attempts have been undertaken to adequately compute this ratio. A common approach is to calculate the ratio of the market to the book value (MTBV). In this research MTBV is used as a market measure, which is computed by Datastream and defined as follows: "The market value of the ordinary (common) equity divided by the balance sheet value of the ordinary (common) equity in the company." (Datastream 2010)

Contrary to market measures, accounting measures are less reliable in capturing the long-term value of a company. However, since the short-term value adds up to the long-term value, they still might be an appropriate measure in the CSP/CFP context. Nevertheless, it is expected that the regression analysis with CSP components and accounting-based performance measures does deliver results that are more inconsistent. The most often used accounting measures are the two ratios ROE and ROA. These two measures will also be used in this research. With the advancing deregulation of the utility market in most countries the debt level of energy firms has risen. Therefore, ROA will be the most appropriate accounting measure for CFP.

CSP-Typologies	CSP measurement method		Expected relation between CSP and CFP	Hypotheses	CFP Measures
strategic	1. Perception based with survey methodology	2. for the emperirical analysis with oekom rating scheme	positive relation	H1a: There is a positive link between strategic CSP and CFP (especially market-based measures)	Accounting-based (ROE, ROA) Market-based (MTBV)
coerced (non-strategic)			neutral relation/ no clear results	H1b: There is a neutral to negative link between non-strategic CSP and CFP	Accounting-based (ROE, ROA) Market-based (MTBV)
altrusitc (non - strategic)			neutral relation/ no clear results		

Table 10: Overview Hypothesis: Expected results between CSP-typologies and CFP

Table 10 summarizes the used measures for CSP and CFP and is further formulating the expected result in two hypothesis:

H1a: There is a positive link between strategic CSP and CFP (especially market-based measures).

H1b: There is a neutral to negative link between non-strategic CSP and CFP.

As already mentioned above, this research, like most CSP/CFP research uses also the CSR composite ratings for reasons of comparability and completeness although there is no direct link to RBV (Table 11).

CSP-Typologies	CSP measurement method	Expected relation between CSP and CFP	Hypotheses	CFP Measures
CSR composite rating (all, environmental, social)	with oekom rating scheme	neutral relation/ no clear results	H1c: There is no clear, measurable link between the copmposite CSP measures and CFP	accounting-based (ROE, ROA) Market-based (MTBV)

Table 11: Overview Hypothesis: Expected results between CSP composite rating and CFP

However, hypothesis H1c summarizes the expected result.

H1c: There is no clear, measurable link between the composite CSP measures and CFP

In the following chapter, the CSP risk relation is operationalized and hypotheses are formulated.

4.3.4 Constructing Risk

As discussed in Section 3.3.4.4 (CSR, Crises and Risk Management) it is assumed that CSR can function as a form of risk management, which is referred to as the risk management hypothesis. Investors reward firms with a good reputation for CSR because they face a lower level of risk, and further CSR can act as a 'reservoir of goodwill' during crises. In other words, CSR has the function of an insurance-like protection (Schnietz/ Epstein 2005, Godfrey et al. 2009). In the following, these theory-based assumptions will be translated into the research framework, first by introducing two different approaches of operationalizing risk and secondly by modeling the effects of CSP on risk.

4.3.4.1 Operationalizing Risk

Previous research has focused mainly on the relationship between CSP and CFP rather than between CSP and risk. In most of the studies, risk is only incorporated as control variable like size and industry (Margolis/ Elfenbein Walsh, 2009). However, a few researches investigated the relation between CSP and risk (e.g. Spencer, 1978; McGuire, 1988; Herremans et al. 1993; Godfrey 2005; Godfrey/ Merrill/ Hansen, 2009, Orlitzky/ Benjamin, 2001, Schnietz/ Epstein, 2005). Although it is difficult to compare these studies, because they all had a different focus and set of measures, they all concluded that good CSP is tendentiously related to lower risk. In the following, the different measures and methods are recapped.

Most of the studies investigating the CSP/risk relation use the beta coefficient (systematic risk) as a risk measure. "Systematic risk is typically considered the appropriate risk measure for shareholders of diversified portfolios." (Orlitzky/ Benjamin, 2001, 383) The beta coefficient measures the sensitivity of a given security to the market risk. If a security is more volatile than the market the value of the beta is greater than one and if it is less responsive to market shocks then the average the beta is below one (Ryan 2007, 99). The beta coefficient is theoretical based on the *capital asset pricing model* (CAPM). The CAPM was introduced by William F. Sharpe. *"The CAPM is an equilibrium asset pricing theory that shows that equilibrium rates of expected return on all risky assets are a function of their covariance with the market portfolio."* (Lee/ Lee 2006, 35)

In this work the beta coefficient according to the CAPM is used as a proxy for risk: $\beta_i = \text{Cov}(R_i, R_M) / \text{Var}(R_M)$ [12]

The underlying assumption for this approach, using the beta coefficient, is that CSR has the capacity to lower company risk. This assumption, which has already been investigated by a few scholars ((e.g. Spencer, 1978; McGuire, 1988; Herremans et al. 1993; Orlitzky/ Benjamin, 2001), will also be further investigated in this research for electric utilities.

A second assumption in the CSP/risk research filed is that CSR acts as a reservoir of goodwill. This assumption has already been discussed in Chapter 3.3.4.4 CSR, Crises and Risk Management. The key finding is that CSR may function as a form of risk management during crises (risk management hypothesis), or in other words, is an insurance-like protection reducing risk and this risk

---

[12] Sharpe, 1964

reduction adds value to shareholders (Schnietz and Epstein, 2005; Godfrey, Merrill and Hansen; Godfrey et al., 2009).

The insurance-like protection of CSR during crises is investigated by a different methodological approach, event study methodology. Especially two recent studies based on the RBV apply this methodological approach (Schnietz/Epstein 2005; Godfrey/ Merrill/ Hansen, 2009).

Concerning the second assumption that CSR acts as an insurance-like protection during crises, the CSP/CFP link is analyzed before and during the financial market crises. It will be investigated if companies with a good CSP perform better financially during the crises than companies with a poor CSP before the crisis.

In the following, the possible relation between CSP and risk will be translated into the research framework.

4.3.4.2 Relation between CSP and Risk

Beta, representing the systematic non-diversifiable risk, is a market-based measure. According to the argumentation in the previous chapter (4.3.3.2 Measurable Effects of CSP on CFP), it is assumed that market-based measures fit best into the CSP research, because CSR is a concept with a long-term orientation and market-based measures capture the long-term values of firms best. Accordingly, consistent results between the relation of CSP and the beta coefficient are expected. It is assumed that companies with a good CSP have a lower risk. This expectation is displayed in Table 12.

CSP-Typologies	CSP measurement method		Expected relation between CSP and risk	Hypotheses	Risk Measure
strategic	1. Perception based with survey methodology	2. for the emprirical analysis with oekom rating scheme	positive relation	H2a: There is a positive link between strategic CSP and risk – strategic CSP lowers firm risk	beta coefficient
coerced (non-strategic)			neutral relation/ no clear results	H2 b: There is a neutral link between non-strategic CSP and risk – Non-strategic CSP has a neutral influence on firm risk	beta coefficient
altrusitc (non-strategic)			neutral relation/ no clear results		
CSR composite rating	with oekom rating scheme		Positive / neutral relation	H2c: There is no clear, measurable link between the composite CSP measures and firm risk	beta coefficient

Table 12: Overview Hypothesis: Expected results between CSP and firm risk (beta coefficient)

The hypotheses for the CSP/ risk relation are as follows:

> H2a: There is a positive link between strategic CSP and risk – strategic CSP lowers firm risk.
>
> H2b: There is a neutral link between non-strategic CSP and risk – non-strategic CSP has a neutral influence on firm risk.
>
> H2c: There is no clear, measurable link between the composite CSP measures and firm risk.

The last hypothesis focuses on the insurance-effect CSR can have (Chapter 3.3.4.4 CSR, Crises and Risk Management). Resource-based theory hypothesizes, that CSR in general acts as an insurance during crisis. Companies with good CSP will perform better after a crisis than companies with a poor CSP. Concerning the insurance-effect, the assumed outcome is formulated in hypothesis H3:

> H3: CSP (especially the composite rating) functions as an insurance-like protection during the financial market crisis.

However, it will be difficult to find evidence for this hypothesis, because there are three factors biasing the results.

1. The crisis it too recent

The financial market crisis, which began in 2007, is still not overcome completely; therefore, it is difficult to measure the effects, especially on CSP.

2. Financial market crises is an extreme event affecting the world economy

The crisis is not an event that only affects single companies or industries. The financial market crisis is such an extreme event, influencing the world economy tremendously. Financial measures during this time may not be as reliable as during non-critical times.

3. Measurement methods

A further bias can be the measurement method. The measurement of the expected insurance effect is challenging. Generally, such effects are measured with event study methodology, which is not part of this research paper. Therefore, a simplified method will be used to display this potential effect. Via regression analysis, it will be investigated if companies with a good CSP perform better financially after the crisis than companies with a poor CSP before the crisis. Because of the stated potential biases, the results of the regression analysis between CSP measures before the crises, and CFP measures after the crises, the results are expected to be inconsistent.

Accordingly, the insurance effect can probably not be displayed, yet. However, it is assumed that especially after the crisis the theorized insurance effect could be measured. However, the crisis is still not resolved and therefore this part of the analysis cannot be a central analysis of this study.

In the following paragraph, further factors influencing the research framework are discussed.

4.3.5 Further Influencing Factors

4.3.5.1 The Lagged Effect Between CSP and CFP

It is assumed that CSP leads to better CFP and therefore the model is constructed with a lagged effect between the independent and dependent variable. Hillman and Keim (2001) already found evidence that "effective stakeholder management leads to improved financial performance" (Hillman/ Keim, 2001,133) (Chapter1.2 Literature Review). This indicates that there is no immediate effect from CSR engagement to shareholder value. In this research, the lagged effect is constructed using CSP data of year x and CFP data of year x +1, which is a lagged effect of one year.

4.3.5.2 The Influence of the Market Structure

A further aspect important for this research is in which way the market structure, where companies act, has an influence on CSR. As discussed in the previous chapters, electric utilities operate in a rather oligopolistic market structure, with limited competition, whereas most of the research in the CSP-CFP field investigates the link under the premise of perfect competition. Only a few studies discussed in what way the dynamics of CSR in perfect competition can be translated to oligopolistic market structures, or to companies on their way from imperfect competition to free competition, like the utility industry. Only a few scholars, like Baron (2001) and McWilliams et al. (2006) have investigated or considered this topic in their studies.

According to Baron (2001), the effects of CSP and CFP are diminished by the intensity of competition. Baron (2001) e.g. remarks that the market structure influences the effects of CSP. As cited in McWilliams et al. (2006), *"It is difficult for oligopolistic firms to achieve a competitive advantage through the strategic use of CSR"* (McWilliams/ Siegel/ Wright, 2006, 6). Thus, the possibility to influence a firm through consumer boycotts is limited in oligopolistic markets or industries. A company operating in such a market structure has less possibilities to diversify through CSR, hence the competitive advantage a company can gain is limited as well (Baron, 2001).

Although the possibilities to gain competitive advantage through CSR are limited in oligopolistic industries, there is still room for companies operating in such a market structure to diversify through CSR. It is assumed that, especially companies, like electric utilities, which are in the process of liberalization, have a great chance to diversify and minimize risk through establishing CSR (Chapter 2.2.1.1 Liberalization, Unbundling and Market Regulation).

4.4 Hypotheses and Research Framework

It is aim of this section to recap the introduced hypotheses and integrate them into the research framework. The main assumption underlying this research is that CSR can lead, under certain conditions, to profit maximization and can as well minimize risk. In the previous sections of this chapter, the conditions under which CSR may lead to a better CFP or minimize risk have been presented, and the respective hypotheses were formulated (H1-H3). The fundamental hypothesis of this research is:

Ho: CSR can, under certain conditions, lead to a better CFP.

With the two underlying theories, neoclassical economics and the dynamic resource-based view, the hypotheses Ho - H3 were derived in the previous section. The graph below (Figure 7), pictures the approach of the underlying research. After the theoretical foundation (Chapter 3) and the aggregation of the hypotheses (Chapter 4), the survey is used to derive the CSP typologies and aggregate the strategic and non-strategic (coerced and altruistic) CSP measures. These measures derive into the regression analysis of the CSP/CFP link, before and during the financial market crisis.

```
┌─────────────────┐
│   Theoretical   │   Neoclassical Econmics
│   Foundation    │   Resource-based View
└────────┬────────┘
         │
┌────────┴────────┐
│   Hypotheses    │
└────────┬────────┘
         │
┌────────┴────────┐
│     Survey      │   Before and during the
│                 │   financial market crisis
└────────┬────────┘
    ┌────┴────┐
┌───┴───┐ ┌───┴──────┐
│Strate-│ │Non-Strate│
│gic CSP│ │gic CSP   │
└───┬───┘ └───┬──────┘
    └────┬────┘
┌────────┴────────┐
│   Quantitative  │   Measurement
│   Analysis of the│  before and
│   CSP/ CFP-link │   during the fi-
│                 │   nancial market
│                 │   crisis
└─────────────────┘
```

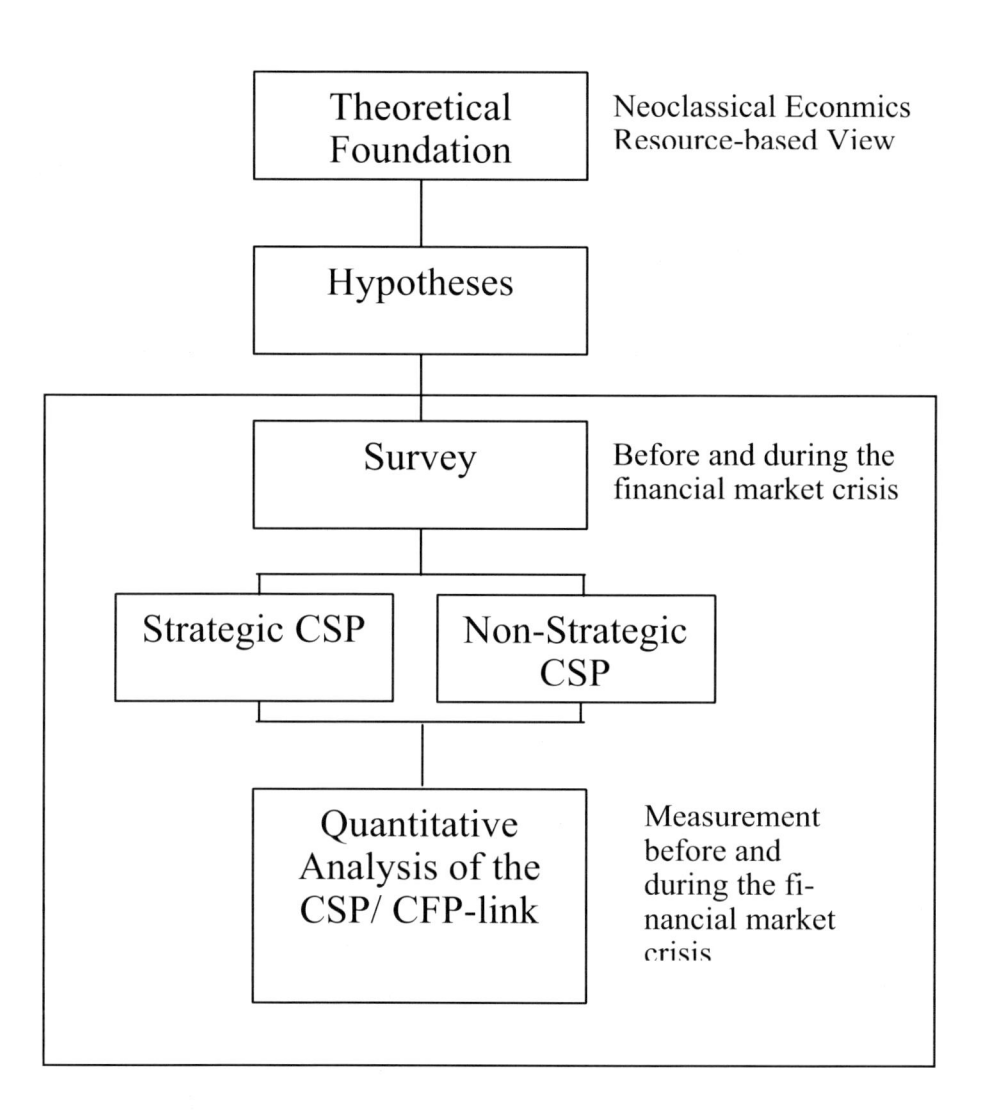

Figure 7: Research Framework

The following list summarizes the hypotheses H0 - H3.

Ho: CSR can, under certain conditions, lead to a better CFP.

H1a: There is a positive link between strategic CSP and CFP (especially market-based measures).

H1b: There is a neutral to negative link between non-strategic CSP and CFP.

H1c: There is no clear, measurable link between the composite CSP measures and CFP.

H2a: There is a positive link between strategic CSP and risk – strategic CSP lowers firm risk.

H2b: There is a neutral link between non-strategic CSP and risk – Non-strategic CSP has a neutral influence on firm risk.

H2c: There is no clear, measurable link between the composite CSP measures and firm risk.

H3: CSP (especially the composite rating) functions as an insurance-like protection during the financial market crisis.

As already argued above (Chapter 4.3.4.2 Relation between CSP and Risk), it will be difficult to measure already the influence the financial market crisis has on the hypothesized insurance effect. Therefore, the focus of the empirical investigation is on the CSP/CFP link (H1) and the CSP/ risk link (H2).

A comprehensive list of the hypotheses, including the used variables (dependent, independent and control variables) is summarized in Chapter 5 (Table 38: Summary of Regression Models and Equations (OLS) before and during the crisis).

5 Empirical Analyses

This chapter presents the results of the empirical analyses of this research. First, the sample of the survey and the sample for the CSP/CFP research will be introduced and discussed (Chapter 5.1 Sample Description). Then the descriptive and bivariate analysis follows, with a comprehensive analysis of the survey results and first bivariate analysis of the CSP/CFP link. A major part of the descriptive analysis is also the factor analysis of the survey data to group the CSR measures into strategic and non-strategic CSR. The Oekom CSP data will be grouped accordingly (Chapter 5.2. Descriptive Statistics and Bivariate Analysis).

After having mapped the strategic and non-strategic CSP dimensions, the cross-sectional regression analysis is presented in the next section. First, the results are presented with a short discussion, and then an in-depth interpretation with further statistical calculation is given (Chapter 5.3 Cross-sectional Regression Analysis). The chapter closes with further testing the OLS-models and a discussion of it (Chapter 5.4 Discussion of OLS-Models).

5.1 Sample Description

The sample for the analysis consists out of primary data for the survey and secondary data for the CSP/CFP regression analysis. In the following, first of all the sample of the survey will be described. This includes a description of the survey structure and the methodology of the data collection (Chapter 5.1.1 Survey Sample). Afterwards the sample for the CSP/CFP analysis will be introduced, starting with the Oekom CSP data and then the CFP data and risk data (Chapter 5.1.2. Sample for CSP/CFP Analysis), followed by the sample description of the electric utilities (Chapter 5.1.3 Sample for Electric Utilities). Included in the sample description is also an analysis of the data limitations (Chapter 5.1.4 Discussion and Limitations).

5.1.1 Survey Sample

Because the sample of the survey consists of self-collected primary data, the following section includes, besides the sample description itself, also a description of the structure of the survey. After presenting the structure of the survey, the data for the CSR measures that are used to aggregate strategic and non-strategic CSR are presented (Chapter 5.1.1.1 Structure of the Survey). Finally, the survey methodology and the selection of participants are introduced (Chapter 5.1.1.2 Survey Methodology and Participant Selection) and the response rate is analyzed (Chapter 5.1.1.3 Response Rate).

5.1.1.1 Structure of the Survey

The survey is structured into three parts; the first part is an introduction in which first general data of the participant are requested. The second part, the main part, consists out of the aggregated CSR criteria, and the third part makes up additional questions that focus on trends in CSR.

Introduction General Data of participants Introductory questions on CSR
Main Part of Questionnaire Likert scaled questions 31 CSR-criteria
Additional Questions Trends on CSR Personal View on CSR

Figure 8: Structure of the Questionnaire

The main part of the survey consists out of 31 Likert scale questions. Investors and analysts were asked to rate each of the criteria from 1 "not important" to 5 "very important" when coming to an investment decision. As discussed in the previous chapter (Chapter 4.2 Survey Framework), the results will be used to derive strategic and non-strategic CSP measures for the analysis of the CSP/CFP link (see Figure 9).

| Introduction |
| General Data of participants |
| Introductory questions on CSR |

| Main Part of Questionnaire |
| Likert scaled (1= not important; 5 = important) questions |
| 31 CSR-criteria |

| Additional Questions |
| Trends on CSR |
| Personal View on CSR |

Strategic CSP → Analysis of the CSP/CFP-link
Non-Strategic CSP →

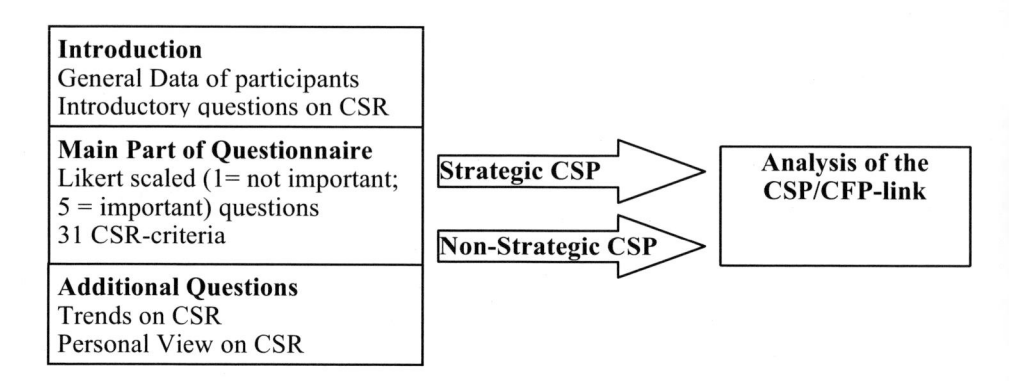

Figure 9: The relation between the survey and the CSP/CFP-link analysis.

The objective was to take a maximum of CSR criteria, especially industry specific criteria, into account. Therefore, the rating catalogs of 11 renowned rating agencies were used to aggregate each of the 31 questions. The used methodology is introduced in Section 5.1.1.2 (Survey Methodology and Participation Selection).

The third part of the questionnaire contains two additional questions and a comment box. The first additional question aims to find out if investors are willing to pay more for a company with good CSP or if CSP does not influence their investment decision. The question is: How much more would you spend for a company with good CSR?

Because this survey has also been conducted during the financial crisis in 2009, it is also interesting to know what investment professionals think about how the financial market crisis may affect CSR. The second additional question asks if the CSR will be strengthened, weakened or will there be no effect at all throughout the crisis.

Lastly, the comment box gives the participants the opportunity to reflect on CSR in general and the chance to give a rather personal view on CSR. These comments may give a hint of which position CSR really has in mainstream investment before and during the financial market crisis. The whole questionnaire is displayed in the appendix (7.2 Survey Questionnaire). In the following paragraph, the methodology used to develop the questionnaire is introduced.

5.1.1.2 Survey Methodology and Participant Selection

As already mentioned above, the main part of the questionnaire consists of 31 questions, in which the participants are asked to rate the different CSR measures. For the aggregate of 31 questions, the rating schemes of renowned CSR-rating agencies were analyzed and evaluated.

The scope contains all rating agencies that send out questionnaires with CSR focus to electric utilities, which are in total 11 rating agencies[13]. Some agencies use industry-specific questionnaires to rate the CSP of utilities and others use standard questionnaires. In addition, the standard of the Global Reporting Initiative (G1) has also been included.

All criteria requested by the 11 rating agencies and the GRI were gathered and listed. After identifying more than 900 CSR criteria in total, the core CSR criteria were identified. These criteria were

---

[13] AccountAbility, Business in the Community, Core Rating, Eiris, Fortis Investment, Imug, Innovest, Oekom, Sustainable Asset Management, SiRi, Vigeo, Global Reporting Initiative

grouped thematically. The most often asked criteria were used for the questionnaire of this study. Only the criteria mentioned in at least nine of the 11 rating catalogs are used for this survey. This process of aggregating the data led to the 31 core CSR criteria.

The fact that the aggregation methodology employed starts with 900 criteria in total and finishes with 31 core criteria, leads to the problem that not every single criteria can be integrated in the study and therefore the results may already be biased. However, it was necessary to read out and aggregate the data and the weighting more than 900 criteria would overcharge the survey participants, especially in terms of time. To be able to reach out to a high number of survey participants, the only option is to aggregate the information.

The 31 criteria are clustered thematically into five main dimensions, following the triple bottom line model, in order to have a clear structure for the survey questionnaire:

1. Economic Responsibility (ER) – consists out of 6 items
2. Environmental Management (EM) – consists out of 14 items
3. Social Responsibility (SR) – consists out of 5 items
4. Corporate Citizenship (CC) – consists out of 2 items
5. Stakeholder Management (SM) – consists out of 3 items

This thematic structure is also the order of the questionnaire (Annex 7.2 Survey Questionnaire).

In the following, the used survey methodology is discussed, including the selection of survey participants, with an overview of the used methodologies.

The survey was conducted in the years 2005 and 2009, which implies that there are two points in time for analysis. To be able to compare the results, the participant selection and the survey itself are created analogically. Therefore, in both years the same methods and criteria of participant selection have been used.

The source of data for the participant addresses is the Thomson Reuters database. The criteria for choosing the participants have been, despite small adjustments, in both years the same. In general, the selection criteria for analysts and investors aim at addressing mainstream capital market participants, with a focus on electric utilities all over the world, who trade large as well as small caps. The following criteria have been chosen:

Focus	Buy-side Analyst	Sell-side Analyst
Job Function	Associate Analyst. Chief Investment Officer. Director of Research. Equity Investment Head. FI - Investment Head. Fixed Income Associate Analyst. Fixed Income Chief Investment. Fixed Income Dir. of Research. Fixed Income Portfolio Manager. Fixed Income Security Analyst. Investment Committee Member. Portfolio Manager. Security Analyst. Strategist/Asset Allocation	
Sector	Utilities	Utilities
Market Cap	All	All
Investment Style	All	All
Global	All	All
N (2005)	1220	843
N (2009)	1534	1095

Table 13: Selection criteria analysts

For investors the search criteria are the following:

Region	Australasia	Japan	Europe	North America
Global Sector	All Utilities	All Utilities	All Utilities	All Utilities
Type	Insurance Company, Mutual Fund, Pension Fund	Insurance Company, Mutual Fund, Pension Fund	Insurance Company, Mutual Fund, Pension Fund	Insurance Company, Mutual Fund, Pension Fund
Trunover	All	All	All	All
N (2005)	251	129	578	846
N (2009)	303	146	502	653

Table 14: Selection criteria Investors

The two tables (Table 13 and 14) above summarize the employed search criteria of the Thomson Reuters financial database and the number of potential participants. The sector focus is for analysts as well as for investors in utilities. A further subordinated focus for analysts is, irrespective of the job function, on buy- and sell-side analysts. The market capitalization, the investment style and the regional focus was set on "all", to integrate a maximum number of potential participants and, more importantly, to avoid a bias of size (market capitalization), investment style and region. For investors, the turnover (size) and the regional focus are as well set on "all", for the same reasons mentioned above. Although they invest globally, the investors are based in the 4 major regions: Australasia, Japan, Europe and North America. This selection is due to the necessity to reduce the total amount of participants. Therefore, only the most important financial regions have been selected.

The total number of potential participants is 3.867 for 2005 and 4.233 in 2009 (Table 15).

Potential Participants

Year of Survey	Investor/Analyst	N
2005	Investor	2063
	Analyst	1804
	Total	3867
2009	Investor	2629
	Analyst	1604
	Total	4233

Table 15: Total number of potential participants

This above-pictured survey design is the foundation for the upcoming descriptive analysis in which the results of the survey are presented, analyzed and the two years are compared with each other.

5.1.1.3 Response Rate

In the previous section, the selection of potential participants has been explained. In this section, the actual participants, and accordingly the response rate, will be displayed.

Table 16 below summarizes the respondents of the survey in 2005 and 2009. The column "Reached Potentials" indicates the number of invitations received by the potential participants. Not all invitations via email could be delivered to the potential participants. Probably, due to the fast employee rotation in the financial industry, not every email invitation arrived at the destined participant. The column "Participants" shows the actual respondents of the survey. In total, 133 investment professionals participated in 2005 and 102 in 2009. This results in an average rate of response of 4.25% in 2005 and 3.45% in 2009.

Respondents to the Survey

Year of Survey	Investor/ Analyst	Reached Potentials	Participants	Response Rate (%)
2005	Investor	1630	39	2,39
	Analyst	1497	94	6,28
	Total	3127	133	4,25
2009	Investor	1656	32	1,93
	Analyst	1299	70	5,39
	Total	2956	102	3,45

Table 16: Respondents to the Survey

The response rate with an average below 5% is low. However, in such surveys, it is rather common to have a response rate in the 5% area and below. However, it can be argued that the low response rate damages the credibility of the results. The fact that the response rate is even lower in 2009 shows that, due to the financial market crisis, less investment professionals are willing to answer the questionnaire.

5.1.2 Sample for CSP/CFP Analysis

In this section the sample for the CSP, as well as the CFP data are presented. As already mentioned the CSP data are based on the Oekom 2004 and 2008 utility rating. The CFP data are provided by the Thomson Reuters database.

5.1.2.1 Oekom CSP Data

The Oekom rating consists of a multitude of single CSP items. In total, 83 items add up to the Oekom Corporate Responsibility Rating 2008, whereas the Oekom utility rating of 2004 measures CSP with only 54 single items. Accordingly, the CSP measures are not entirely the same and congruent for 2004 and 2008. To be able to compare the CSP rating of 2004 with the 2008 rating, the CSP measures need to be harmonized and adjusted. In the following, the process and methodology of adjustment are explained.

The CSP measures of 2008 are more detailed than the measures of 2004. To achieve a high degree of comparability, the measures of 2008 need to be cut down to the measures of 2004. This means that a number of single measures of 2008 cannot be taken into account for this study, because they are not part of the 2004 rating (Annex 7.3 Example Oekom Rating 2004 and 7.4 Example Oekom Rating 2008).

The following example illustrates the structure of the rating scheme and the differences between the years 2004 and 2008. In the years 2004 and 2008, the Oekom rating "Corporate Governance" is a part of the "Social Rating" (Level 2) but is measured on different levels and with different items. The list below demonstrates the difference in measurement between the two years.

Oekom Rating 2004

Level 1: - Corporate Responsibility Rating

Level 2: - Social Cultural Rating

Level 3: - Relation with External Stakeholders

Level 4: - Shareholders/ Corporate Governance

Level 5: - Separation of power between CEO and Chairman of the Board

- Board Committees

- Assignation of Voting Rights

- Size of Shareholding Necessary to Raise Resolutions

- Transparency of Shareholder Structure

Oekom Rating 2008

Level 1: - Corporate Responsibility Rating

Level 2: - Social Rating

Level 3: - Corporate Governance and Business Ethics

Level 4: - Independence and effectiveness of the board

Level 5: - Separation of power between CEO and chair of the board,

   - Existence of different board committees independent of executive managers

The example given above shows the rating differences, starting already on Level 2 between the two ratings. In 2008, Corporate Governance is measured with two items, whereas in 2004 it is measured with four items as part of a subordinated category: Relation with External Stakeholders. However, on the last level (Level 5) one item (Separation of power between CEO and chair of the board) is identical in both years. A further item (Board Committee) used in 2004 is similar to the second item of 2008 (Existence of different board committees independent of executive managers). It is therefore evident that first, not all items can be used and compared and secondly, that the items on the lowest level (Level 5) need to be matched for comparing the ratings of 2004 and 2008. For the analysis in this research paper, the CSP components will be aggregated on all five levels and only identical and in terms of content similar items will be used to measure

CSP. Consequently, some items will fall apart in the aggregation process.

The aggregate results show major changes of the social rating from 2004 to 2008, especially in comparison to the changes in the environmental rating. The rating scheme of the environmental rating stayed more or less stable, only minor changes have been made. For the social rating of 2008, Oekom made major adjustments. First, the social rating of 2008 has a new structure, and secondly, a number of categories and measures were added, such as "work-life balance" and "training and education".

A further limiting factor of the aggregation is the differing depth of information of the two Oekom ratings. For the 2008 rating, all rating results are accessible even on the lowest level, Level 5. The 2004 rating publishes only the subordinated measures of Level 4. In consequence, it means that only a reduced number of CSP measures can be used for 2004.

The survey data have been aggregated from different rating schemes and are therefore not identical with the Oekom rating scheme. This is also a vitiating factor of the study. The strategic and non-strategic CSR measures from the survey cannot be matched one-to-one with the Oekom ratings of 2004 and 2008. This is a possible bias of this research.

The CSP data exist in a classical rating scheme from A+ (the company shows extraordinary performance to D- (the company shows little engagement). This rating scheme needs to be translated into a numeric system, to be able to analyze the CSP results with quantitative methods. Therefore, the rating scheme was translated in a scheme from 1 to 12, with 1 as A+ and 12 as D-. Table 17 pictures the translation of the Oekom rating scheme into the numeric one. Accordingly, this means that the lower the number of CSP is of a company the better is its performance.

Translation of the Oekom Rating into a numeric scheme

A +	1	The company shows extraordinary performance
A	2	•
A -	3	•
B +	4	•
B	5	•
B -	6	•
C +	7	•
C	8	•
C -	9	•
D +	10	•
D	11	•
D -	12	The company shows little engagemnet

Table 17: Translation of the Oekom Rating Scheme into a Numeric Scheme.

5.1.2.2 CFP and Risk Data

In the following, the samples of the CFP and risk data for the regression analysis are described. For analyzing the CSP/CFP link, MTBV, ROE and ROA are used. For investigating the link between CSP and risk, the beta factor (beta) is the used measure.

The first measure is Tobin's Q or MTBV. This is the ratio of the market value to the book value of a company (MTBV). Within the Datastream database, it is defined as: "the market value of the ordinary (common) equity divided by the balance sheet value of the ordinary (common) equity in the company" (Datastream, 2010). The data have been downloaded on a monthly basis, and then converted to a yearly basis by building the mean value (Table 18: List of CFP and Risk Data).

For the calculation of ROE, Datastream uses an index calculation methodology. For this ratio, the output is given in percentage on a yearly basis. ROA could not be provided by Datastream; therefore, it was calculated with the Datastream data of net income and total assets ((net income / total assets)* 100).

In addition, the risk measures beta (β_i) could not be provided by the database for the company sample requested. Therefore, the beta is calculated with the weekly return index (R_i) and the weekly MSCI world index (R_M).

$$\beta_i = Cov\ (R_i, R_M)\ /\ Var\ (R_M)^{14}$$

---

[14] Sharpe, 1964

List of CFP and Risk Data

Company	MTBV 2005	MTBV 2009	ROE 2005	ROE 2009	ROA 2005	ROA 2009	Beta 2005	Beta 2009	Sigma 2005	Sigma 2009
1								0,20		10,91
2			27,04	9,59	14,63					
3	2,660	2,18	30,1	20,15	10,56	6,58	1,77	0,25	31,18	26,34
4	3,670	2,98	58,76	-3,35	7,45	2,9	0,12	0,16	22,36	24,19
5	1,220	1,09	8,33	-5,82	1,65	-0,36	0,24	-0,10	21,18	23,34
6	2,460	1,78	10,93	18,2	1,98	3,03	0,71	0,64	13,25	21,92
7										
8	1,590	0,89	9,06	6,41	4,74	1,89	1,05	0,71	12,21	23,48
9	1,130	1,27	12,93	3,67	3,51	5,62	0,73	0,80	22,76	35,41
10	2,240	3,35	17,89	27,33	6,53		0,24		14,6	
11		1,88	4	5,49	1,69	1,62		0,93		41,74
12	2,820	2,11	16,93	20,48	3,26	5,55	0,84	0,34	15,15	17,11
13	1,720	1,53	14,55	41,97	6,14	5,9	0,61	0,71	24,15	33,33
14	2,310	0,99	13,63	25,95	5,39	3,5	0,49	0,70	12,19	30,27
15	2,100	1,68	11,25	15,32	2,99	3,31	0,74	0,62	13,14	26,34
16	1,110	0,72	7,16	6,2	3,05	2,66	0,14	0,72	25,84	33,5
17	3,620	2,59	19,81	24,78	2,01	5,51	0,86	0,64	13,95	27,58
18	1,640	1,54	10,22	16,2	2,77	2,94	0,82	0,63	13	28,63
19	1,720	1,76	16,59	19,39	5,85	6,63	1,10	1,04	30,96	39,57
20										
21	1,930	1,02	13,65	16,58	5,49	2,7	0,63	0,57	22,91	44,23
22	2,040	1,16	13,51	12,24	4,75	3,36	0,47	0,87	23,75	27,94
23	1,240	1,19	5,5	-4,34	1,07	-0,14	0,46	-0,08	18,14	24,27
24	6,170	3,55	73,49	60,06	3,68	2,1	-0,03	0,37	16,38	21,56
25	1,290	0,67	9,11	1,67	1,58	1,15	0,70	0,96	13,78	30,75
26	1,920	1,41	52,17	13,84	2,7	2,89	0,87	0,34	11,64	20,5
27	2,920	3,11	14,75	21,41	3,83	5,39	0,52	0,48	18,92	21,95
28	2,490	2,59	22,13	22,08	2,16	3,91	0,73	0,79	22,94	26,71
29	3,920	3,36	26	15,92	8,62	0,64	0,26	0,20	16,2	17,69
30	1,860	2,34	12,35	58,73	-2,15		-0,07		19,4	
31	1,720	2,62	6,94	-2,61	2,11	-0,77	0,11	0,43	15,89	23,75
32	-0,010	-6,54						0,02	141,75	241,63
33	1,800	1,05	10,08	8,41	3,9	2,64		0,83	22,9	33,57
34	1,330	1,39	6,34	-11,86	1,69	-0,65	0,14	-0,12	17,66	21,72

35	1,730	1,26	7,48	3,12	5,2	2,43	0,31	0,09	20,53	23,49
36	1,600	1,45	6,88	9,36	2,62	1,9	0,18	0,62	18,8	30,24
37	2,170	1,37	15,72	11,16	5,02	3,14	0,24	0,39	14,63	17,2
38	1,910	1,97	12,15	22,65	4,99		0,42	0,13	**19,3**	**58,27**
39	1,710	3,31	11,23	43,47	3,3	1,85	0,31	0,47	13,49	23,48
40	3,310	1,38	3,82	5,79	1,78	1,03	0,12	0,91	27,99	37,43
41	3,990	3,17	16,13	23,94	5,3	6,23	0,84	1,19	27,41	39,56
Mean Value	2,19	1,65	16,99	15,77	4,1	2,94	0,52	0,48	22,5	32,35
Volatility (Standard Deviation)	1,09	1,62	14,95	16,01	2,94	2,09	0,38	0,35	21,15	36,52
N	39	39	37	37	37	33	34	38	36	38

Table 18: List of CFP and Risk Data.

The table above (Table 18) lists all CFP and risk data used in this research. The marked numbers are outliers. These values might influence the validity of the regression results.

The volatility measured via standard deviation of the CFP and risk data does not show any extreme values. If the results of the regression analysis are not delivering valid results, it is an option to remove the outliers in order to generate results that are more valid.

5.1.3 Sample for Electric Utilities

This section describes in short the sample of the electric utilities. The sample of the utility companies is determined by the Oekom utility ratings of 2004 and 2008, and further by the available CFP and risk data.

The Oekom utility rating 2004 includes 37 utilities; the rating of 2008 includes 30 utilities, of which only 24 are also included in the rating of 2004. The table below shows the utilities, which are part of the Oekom rating and which are included in the CSP/CFP analysis. In total, 41 utility companies are included in the research. However, for only 24 companies the complete CSP data and CFP data are available. This is a very small sample size, which leads to the effect that the analysis might not deliver significant results and furthermore, a small sample size has limited power of prediction and reliability.

Electric Utility List of the Oekom Rating and for the CSP/ CFP-Analysis

2004	2008	CSP/ CFP-Analysis
American Electric Power		American Electric Power
Australian Gas Light	AGL Energy	AGL Energy
CEMIG	CEMIG	CEMIG
Centrica	Centrica	Centrica
Chubu Electric Power		Chubu Electric Power
Dominion Resources	Dominion Resources	Dominion Resources
	DONG Energy	DONG Energy
Duke Energy	Duke Energy	Duke Energy
E.ON	E.ON	E.ON
Electrabel		Electrabel
Electricité de France	Electricité de France	Electricité de France
Elsam		**no CFP data available**
	Enbridge	Enbridge
Endesa		Endesa
Enel	Enel	Enel
Entergy	Entergy	Entergy
EVN	EVN	EVN
Exelon	Exelon	Exelon
FirstEnergy		FirstEnergy
	Fortum	Fortum
FPL Group		FPL Group
Gas Natural	Gas Natural	Gas Natural
Iberdrola	Iberdrola	Iberdrola
Kansai Electric Power		Kansai Electric Power

National Grid Transco	National Grid Transco	National Grid Transco
NiSource		NiSource
PG&E		PG&E
	Red Eléctrica de España	Red Eléctrica de España
RWE	RWE	RWE
Scottish and Southern Energy	Scottish and Southern Energy	Scottish and Southern Energy
Scottish Power		Scottish Power
Severn Trent	Severn Trent	Severn Trent
Southern	Southern	Southern
SUEZ	SUEZ	SUEZ
Terasen		**no CFP data available**
Tokyo Electric Power	Tokyo Electric Power	Tokyo Electric Power
Tokyo Gas		Tokyo Gas
TransAlta	TransAlta	TransAlta
	TransCanada	TransCanada
	Union Fenosa	Union Fenosa
United Utilities	United Utilities	United Utilities
Veolia Environnement	Veolia Environnement	Veolia Environnement
Verbund	Verbund	Verbund

Table 19: Electric Utility List of the Oekom Rating for the CSP/ CFP-Analysis

5.1.4 Discussion and Limitations

Summarizing, for the research, a set of different data is used. These Data can be divided into three different sections, according to the source and the content. The survey data, the Oekom CSP-measures and the CFP and risk measures provided by Thomson Reuters.

The survey aims at reaching a high number of utility analysts and investors. In total 6083 investment professionals have been contacted, of which 3286 are analysts and 2797 investors. The response rate of investors was in both years, 2005 and 2009, lower than the response rate of analysts. This results in a lower number of participants for the group of investors, although more investors were invited to the survey. The total numbers 71 investors, which equals a response rate of 2.16% who participated, and 164 analysts, which equals a response rate of 5.86%. The total sample size is 235 for both years, with 133 for the year 2004 and 102 for 2009. This is a small but very acceptable sample size.

The Oekom CSP data are in general very comprehensive. In the 2004 rating, 54 single CSP-measures are used and in 2008, 83 single items measure CSP. However, the challenge in working with the two Oekom ratings is that the data are not collected with identical measures. This leads to a limited comparability of the data. In consequence, for this research only identical measures are used. This limits the number of potential CSP variables measuring strategic and non-strategic CSP. A further limiting factor is the different sample of companies rated in 2004 and 2008. Only 24 utilities are rated in 2004 and in 2008. However, the total sample of utilities is 41, which is a viable sample size for quantitative analysis.

The CFP data are less affected by limitations, despite the usual possible biases due to the possibility of inaccurate collection and miscalculation. However, these are errors that cannot be resolved if they occur, because the author has to rely on the data provided. However, the Thomson Reuters database is known for a high data-quality. A further limiting factor for the analysis is the outliers in the CFP data. Having said that, if the analysis shows that the results are not valid due to outliers, these data will be removed from the sample.

5.2 Descriptive Statistics and Bivariate Analysis

It is aim of the descriptive and bivariate analysis to give first insights into the results of the research topic, the CSP/CFP link before and during the financial market crisis. The following descriptive statistics are used to describe the main features of the collected data; these encompass the survey data and the CSP, CFP and risk data. This part of descriptive and bivariate analysis starts with the presentation of the survey results (Chapter 5.2.1. Results of the Survey). An essential part of the survey results is the section about the distinction of strategic, and non-strategic CSP by using factor analysis (Chapter 5.2.1.5 Factor Analysis – Constructing Strategic and Non-Strategic CSR).

After having identified strategic and non-strategic CSP from the survey data, the typologies will be adopted to the Oekom CSP data, by using factor analysis as well (Section 5.2.2.1 Factor Analysis – Strategic and Non-Strategic CSP). Afterwards a correlation matrix between CSP and CFP measures is used to derive first insights into the CSP/CFP link.

5.2.1 Results of the Survey

The analysis of the survey results follows the structure of the survey as described above. First, the results of the survey introduction are analyzed (Chapter 5.2.1.1 Results of the Survey – Introduction), secondly, the results of the main part of the survey are presented (Chapter 5.2.1.2 Results of the Survey – Main Part), followed by an analysis of the additional questions of the survey (Chapter 5.2.1.3 Results of the Survey – Additional Questions).

Afterwards, the strategic and non-strategic CSP is derived out of the survey measures.

5.2.1.1 Results of the Survey – Introduction

The following section analyzes the results of the introductory part of the survey. The introduction consists of two questions (Annex 7.2 Survey Questionnaire). The first question asks if the investment professional works as an analyst (sell side or buy side) or investor. It is aim of this question to be able to compare opinions of analysts and investors, in which areas they have equal opinions on CSR, and where the opinions differ. However, the focus of the following analysis is less the differences of opinion between analysts and investor but more the differences of opinion between the two years the survey has been conducted.

The second question of the introduction tries to find out what analysts and investors associate with CSR. They have the option to rate 11 items, from Corporate Citizenship, for example, to a concept with future. This question aims to find out if investment professionals have a common understanding of what CSR is about or if there are any measurable differences, especially between the two years, 2005 and 2009, before and during the financial market crisis. The investment professionals had the option to rate on a scale from 1 (not important) to 5 (very important). The following two tables (Table 20 and Table 21) show the mean value, the standard deviation and the significance[15] of what the investment professionals associate with CSR.

---

[15] The significance is tested with the T-test for the differences between the years 2005 and 2009.

Association with CSR Investors (2005 and 2009)

	2005			2009			Significance
	N	Mean Value	Standard Deviation	N	Mean Value	Standard Deviation	
Corporate Citizenship	37	4,05	1,026	31	3,97	1,016	,730
Causing extra costs	35	2,69	,993	30	2,87	1,167	,502
An essential concept	36	3,92	,937	30	3,87	1,074	,841
An important part of risk management	37	3,76	1,234	30	3,70	1,088	,844
Needs to be included in investment decisions	38	3,63	,970	31	3,42	1,232	,426
Just an over-rated trend	37	2,08	,894	30	2,23	1,040	,522
More research needs to be done on CR	36	4,03	,971	30	3,43	1,194	,029*
A concept with future	37	4,08	,759	31	3,74	1,125	,159
Part of good management	39	4,15	,844	31	4,19	,873	,848
Incorporating economic, environmental and social responsibility	39	4,41	,785	32	4,19	,931	,278
Required from and driven by Non-Governmental-Organisations (NGOs)	32	2,84	,954	30	3,07	1,048	,384

Table 20: Association with CSR Investors (2005 and 2009)

Association with CSR Analysts (2005 and 2009)

	2005			2009			
	N	Mean Value	Standard Deviation	N	Mean Value	Standard Deviation	Significance
Corporate Citizenship	88	3,86	1,074	69	3,68	1,007	,279
Causing extra costs	89	3,06	1,219	70	2,50	1,018	,003*
An essential concept	89	4,01	1,006	69	3,52	1,009	,003*
An important part of risk management	91	4,00	,943	70	3,44	1,085	,001*
Needs to be included in investment decisions	93	3,90	1,084	70	3,51	1,018	,021*
Just an overrated trend	91	2,35	1,224	68	2,44	1,111	,636
More research needs to be done on CR	88	3,52	1,213	70	3,41	,970	,533
A concept with future	89	3,66	1,138	70	3,46	1,059	,245
Part of good management	94	4,31	,843	69	4,06	,784	,055
Incorporating economic, environmental and social responsibility	91	4,35	,835	70	4,33	,775	,858
Required from and driven by Non-Governmental-Organisations (NGOs)	83	3,11	1,126	83	3,11	1,126	,789

Table 21: Association with CSR Analysts (2005 and 2009)

Only looking at the mean values, the results show that analysts and investors have a more or less common understanding of CSR. They define CSR according to the triple bottom line, that it is incorporating economic as well as environmental and social responsibility. Moreover, CSR is seen as "part of good management" and as a form of "risk management" and not as an "overrated trend". This indicates that the investment professionals see CSR as an integral part of today's management, which supports the "good management" hypothesis of CSR (Chapter 1.2 Literature Review and 4.2 Survey Framework). At first glance, these results seem to be a strong support for the good management hypothesis. However, looking a bit more in detail, the results are not significant. Accordingly, no conclusion on the good management hypothesis can be drawn.

Looking at the differences between the two years, a general observation is that not many items are significant. This is probably due to small sample size and the mean value difference. On the investor side, only the item "more research needs to be done" is significant with a decrease of the mean value from 4.03 in 2005 to 3.43 in 2009. This indicates that investors do not see the need for more research in CSR. Especially interesting are the significant results for the item "causing extra costs" for analysts, with a mean value of 3.06 in 2005 and 2.5 in 2009. This argues that through the financial market crisis CSR investments are less seen as a cost-producing and unnecessary tool but more as something that can be effectively used to gain benefits.

To summarize the results of the survey introduction, it can be said that analyst and investors have a common understanding of CSR. This understanding is in line with the most often used definitions, that CSR is incorporating economic, social as well as environmental issues. However, most of the results are not significant and therefore no explanatory power is given.

5.2.1.2 Results of the Survey – Main Part

In the following, the results of the main part of the survey will be analyzed, which reflects the perception of investment professionals on CSR. First, a comparison of the different views of analysts and investors is given. Secondly, the results are analyzed as a comparison between the two years 2005 and 2009. The analysis of results is structured thematically according to the five dimensions presented in: Economic Responsibility, Environmental Management, Social Responsibility, Corporate Citizenship and Stakeholder Management. The results presented in the following are a first indicator in which way the crisis may have affected CSR.

Regarding the differences in the rating of analysts and investors, a general observation is that investors rate CSR higher in 2005 than analysts do (Table 22: Differences between analysts and investors rating for all CSR components). The overall rating of analysts is for both years stable with a mean value of approximately 3.4. In the year 2007, investors rate CSR with a mean value of 3.8 and in the year 2009 they are below the ratings of analysts with 3.2. This shows that investors are prone to trends and the current mood on the financial markets, whereas analysts are more stable in their ratings. This indicates also that analysts are more long-term orientated than investors and that they are not prone to the up- and downturns of the financial markets. Because investors rate lower in 2009 than in 2005, most items are less important when adding the results of analysts and investors. It is further noticed that for analysts specific CSR criteria like energy and climate issues are of importance, whereas for investors an overall good CSR performance is of importance.

Differences between analysts and investors rating for all CSR components

	N	Mean Value	Standard Deviation	Minimum	Maximum
2005 & investor	38	3,773	0,69289	1,97	4,90
2009 & investor	30	3,1962	0,93699	1,69	5,00
2005 & analyst	94	3,3754	0,77601	1,15	5,00
2009 & analyst	70	3,3593	0,74088	1,57	4,75
Total	232	3,4125	0,78886	1,15	5,00

Table 22: Differences between analysts and investors rating for all CSR components

The above analysis of results, by year and investor or analyst, does not allow testing for significance. Therefore, the years 2005 and 2009 have been combined to one group to test for significance between analyst and investor differences (Table 23). The results reflect the above general analysis that investors rate higher than analysts. However, most of the items are not significant. The fact that most of the items are not significant is observable throughout the whole survey. This is, as already mentioned, probably due to the small sample size and the mean value difference. The higher the difference of the mean value the lower is the rate of significance. This reduces the explanatory power of the survey. However, the results should primarily function as a first insight of the perception of investment professionals, the major stakeholder group of electric utilities. However, in the following analysis, the author mainly focuses on the significant results of the survey but also refers to the insignificant results.

Differences between Analysts and Investors perception for the single CSR items (significant values)

	Analyst			Investor			
	N	Mean Value	Standard Deviation	N	Mean Value	Standard Deviation	Significance
Information about energy mix	163	4,07	1,067	64	3,73	1,159	,035*
Health & Safety Programme for employees	161	3,69	1,262	64	4,34	,910	,000*
Existence of a human resources development strategy (demographic development, war for talents etc.)	160	3,45	1,163	63	3,84	1,045	,021*
Endorsement of supra-national organisations like ILO, UNO, OECD, Global Compact	154	2,82	1,382	57	3,34	1,452	,017*
Existence of a Corporate Citizenship Strategy	157	2,97	1,185	61	3,36	1,087	,024*
Policy Statement on community involvement	156	2,88	1,137	61	3,34	1,147	,008*
Details about Corporate Citizenship engagement in reports	158	2,80	1,204	59	3,28	1,244	,009*

Table 23: Differences between Analysts and Investors perception for the single CSR items (significant values)

The table above (Table 23) displays only the significant results. It shows that the differences are mainly significant for social issues like human resources (HR) and corporate citizenship. Only one item falls apart, information about energy mix. This is one of the view items that analysts rate higher than investors. This clearly indicates the high importance for utilities of having a future orientated energy mix, because analysts, who judge primarily with a long-term orientated focus, rate it very high.

Although there are observable differences between analysts' and investors' perceptions, in the following analysis these two groups are summarized to one group, investment professionals. The following analysis focuses on the differences between the two years to find out in which way the financial market crisis may have affected the perception of investment professionals. As already mentioned above, only view item results are significant due to the relatively small sample size and the differences in the mean.

Table 24 (Mean Values and Significance Economic Responsibility) below summarizes the results concerning economic responsibility. First, the results show clearly that all items of economic responsibility are important. Especially the item "good investor relations" has a very high mean value of 3.99 for both years and is highly significant. This indicates that good investor relations is key, but has obviously decreased from 2005 with 4.21 to 2009 with 3.69. The decrease is probably because corporate governance has become essential for corporations to implement. In most countries, either binding law, such as the Sarbanes-Oxley Act in 2002, or comparable codes and guidelines exist, with which a company has to comply. In 2005, these rules were new and therefore were rated higher, whereas nowadays the rules have already been implemented and therefore CG-topics have lost in importance.

The two items, "policy and guidelines for supplier relations" and "monitoring of compliance with policy and guidelines for supplier relations and supplier standards" are the less important in the dimension of economic responsibility and are, therefore, not significant. This indicates that supplier relations in general seem to be less important than taking economic responsibility on the level of good investor relations and customer satisfaction. Investment professionals look primarily on the performance of the company itself and the implementation of standards.

Mean Values and Significance Economic Responsibility (2005 and 2009)

	2005			2009			
	N	Mean Value	Standard Deviation	N	Mean Value	Standard Deviation	**Significance**
Good Investor Relations on CR-Issues (trust, transparency, timeliness, quality)	130	4,21	,994	98	3,69	1,190	0,001*
Compliance with the official Corporate Governance-Codex of a country	129	4,04	1,019	95	3,53	1,129	0,001*
Policy and guidelines for supplier relations and supplier standards	126	3,56	1,070	93	3,31	1,041	,085
Monitoring of compliance with policy and guidelines for supplier relations and supplier standards	125	3,50	1,097	94	3,35	1,130	,334
Monitoring and reporting of customer satisfaction	127	3,93	,953	94	3,61	1,083	0,025*
Existence of Customer-Relationship-Management-System	126	3,80	,996	93	3,47	1,033	0,017*

Table 24: Mean Values and Significance Economic Responsibility

Overall, economic responsibility is important for investment professionals despite supplier issues.

Table 25 (Mean Values and Significance Environmental Management (2005 and 2009)) below summarizes the results of the dimension "environmental management". The item "existence of an environmental policy" is the most important criteria of this dimension, but the importance has decreased slightly from 2005 to 2009. The item "fixed quantitative environmental targets" is the only item that became more important from 2005 to 2009. This indicates that, despite the trend of lower importance, due to the opinion of investors, the importance of fixed quantitative environmental targets has increased. This is in line with the overall trend of the increased quantification of non-financial key performance indicators. In some European countries, like France or Denmark, and in Japan and others, the reporting of non-financial information is already compulsory. The EU is currently working on a directive on disclosure of non-financial information, which is currently in the period of consultation. (European Commission, 2011) These trends show, that some key non-financials e.g. environmental targets are important to quantify. However, these results have to be taken with caution and should not be overinterpreted, as none of the items is significant.

Mean Values and Significance Environmental Management (2005 and 2009)

	N	2005 Mean Value	Standard Deviation	N	2009 Mean Value	Standard Deviation	Significance
Existence of an environmental policy	130	4,06	1,017	92	3,86	1,145	,171
Fixed quantitative environmental targets	127	3,50	1,253	92	3,61	1,131	,525
Certified Environmental-Management-System (ISO 14001, EMAS)	121	3,29	1,221	91	3,20	1,154	,581
Company monitors its environmental impact (risks) without certified Environmental-Management-System (no certificate)	119	3,51	1,080	90	3,33	1,110	,230

Table 25: Mean Values and Significance Environmental Management (2005 and 2009)

Having a closer look at the other items summing up to the dimension Environmental Management the items in regard to certification of the management system are not key. The remarkable result of this section is, that CSP in general may have lost importance but the quantification of non-financial measures seems to be a future topic.

All items summing up the dimension "energy" are part of industry immanent. Especially the two items, "information about the energy mix" and "program for the improvement of energy efficiency" are rated high, with a 4, and are therefore key items for investment professionals. Reporting information about the energy mix are mandatory for utilities and as discussed in Section 2.2.1 (Industry Background) the energy mix itself is a vital factor for the future success of a utility company. The improvement of the energy efficiency is as important as the information about the energy mix. The energy source is not the determining factor; it is more the efficient use of the various energy sources. Accordingly, the item "program for the increasing usage of renewable energy" is less important. Interestingly, the differences between the two years are minor, which indicates that energy issues have not lost in importance through the crisis. But, again, none of the items is significant and therefore, the results only picture a tendency and cannot be generalized.

Mean Values and Significance Energy (2005 and 2009)

		2005			2009		
	N	Mean Value	Standard Deviation	N	Mean Value	Standard Deviation	**Significance**
Information about energy mix	132	3,99	1,059	95	3,94	1,164	,719
Programme for the improvement of the energy efficiency	131	3,99	1,085	96	3,92	1,101	,606
Programme for the increasing usage of renewable energy sources	130	3,61	1,285	96	3,52	1,271	,597
Information on precaution of electricity supply	123	3,62	1,177	91	3,53	1,139	,593

Table 26: Mean Values and Significance Energy (2005 and 2009)

Climate issues are rated high on the agenda of investment professionals. However, it is not the existence of a climate strategy that is the most important but rather the focus on greenhouse gases like CO_2, SO_2 and NO_X. This is probably due to the increasing regulations aiming at reducing greenhouse gas emissions (Chapter 2.2.1 Industry Background). Accordingly, the fact that utility companies focus on the disclosure and reduction of climate gases is of high importance for investment professionals. If companies do not focus on climate gases, they expose themselves to higher regulatory risks and are therefore not as attractive for investors than companies that face these risks. The demand for the existence of a climate strategy increased through the crisis. This might be because climate issues in general are becoming increasingly important and, especially during times of crisis, a company should focus on key issues, like climate change. As most of the other items, none of it is significant and therefore it only reflects a slight tendency.

Mean Values and Significance Climate (2005 and 2009)

	2005			2009			
	N	Mean Value	Standard Deviation	N	Mean Value	Standard Deviation	**Significance**
Existence of a climate strategy	131	3,64	1,209	95	3,75	1,364	,546
Focus on CO2 reduction	127	4,00	1,069	94	3,83	1,154	,247
Focus on SO2 reduction	125	3,92	1,060	92	3,77	1,064	,317
Focus on NOX reduction	124	3,92	1,079	92	3,74	1,069	,224

Table 27: Mean Values and Significance Climate (2005 and 2009)

The items of the dimension "social responsibility" are less important for investment professionals than the environmental dimensions, despite the item "health & safety program for employees". Health and safety issues are crucial for utility companies, because the power industry is prone to fatal accidents. Therefore, it is a key issue for utilities to avoid such accidents in order to e.g. avoid possible payments for workers compensation and negative publicity. Investment professionals rate this item high, because a lower number of incidents means subsequently less costs and a higher reputation. Remarkably low on the scale of importance is the item "endorsement of supranational organizations like ILO, UNO, OECD and the Global Compact". However, against the overall trend, the importance has increased from 2005 to 2009. This indicates that the endorsement is still not crucial for investors and analysts, but the tendency is towards an increasing acceptance of this endorsement by investment professionals. However, the results are as well not significant.

Mean Values and Significance Social Responsibility (2005 and 2009)

	2005			2009			
	N	Mean Value	Standard Deviation	N	Mean Value	Standard Deviation	**Significance**
Diversity-Management/ Equal Opportunities (male/female, minorities)	131	3,19	1,354	94	2,98	1,346	,256
Health & Safety Programme for employees	130	3,96	1,190	95	3,75	1,228	,203
Existence of a human resources development strategy (demographic development, war for talents etc.)	130	3,55	1,155	93	3,57	1,130	,868
Endorsement of supranational organisations like ILO, UNO, OECD, Global Compact	121	2,93	1,427	90	3,01	1,410	,674
Conducting social-impact assessments (e.g. during infrastructure projects)	125	3,52	1,209	93	3,34	1,210	,278

Table 28: Mean Value and Significance Social Responsibility (2005 and 2009)

Corporate citizenship topics are of minor interest and have been consistently from 2005 to 2009. The item "consideration of stakeholder interest" is slightly above average with regard to its importance and is furthermore stable throughout the years. This indicates that incorporating stakeholder interests is not seen as a critical success factor by investment professionals.

Mean Values and Significance Corporate Citizenship und Stakeholdermanagement (2005 and 2009)

	2005			2009			
	N	Mean Value	Standard Deviation	N	Mean Value	Standard Deviation	**Significance**
Existence of a Corporate Citizenship Strategy	127	3,14	1,139	91	2,99	1,212	,336
Policy Statement on community involvement	127	3,12	1,103	90	2,86	1,216	,102
Details about Corporate Citizenship engagement in reports	127	3,04	1,211	90	2,78	1,251	,123
Consideration of stakeholder interests	129	3,69	1,144	95	3,69	,996	,980
Description of stakeholder management in report(s)	129	3,40	1,135	96	3,43	1,088	,801
Stakeholder management in compliance with AA1000 or similar	102	2,98	1,235	72	2,70	1,123	,128

Table 29: Mean Values and Significance Corporate Citizenship and Stakeholder management (2005 and 2009)

5.2.1.3 Results of the Survey – Additional Questions

The results of the additional questions demonstrate once more that the importance of CSR has slightly decreased through the crisis. The first of the two questions is the following: How much more would you spend for a company with good CSR performance? The results demonstrate that the willingness of investors to spend more for good CSR performance has decreased (Table 30). Furthermore, the financial crisis seems to have a neutral to negative effect on CSR from the perspective of investment professionals (Table 31).

Extra Premium for good CSP

	2005	2009	Significance
How much more would you spend for a company with good CSR-performance?	3.7%	3.2%	0,187236215

Table 30: Extra Premium for good CSP

How will the financial crisi affect CSR (in the utility industry)?

	N	%
strengthen	25	26.04
weaken	29	30.21
no effect	41	42.71

Table 31: How will the financial crisis affect CSR?

The decreasing importance might be due to the extreme event of the financial crisis or it might be the emergence of a trend. Nevertheless, the results cannot be generalized as they represent only a small sample of a single industry. If the decrease is a trend or just a temporarily break-in, it can only be investigated by further research after the financial crisis. From the author's point of view, the observed decrease is due to the extreme event of the crisis, because only investors rate CSR lower whereas analysts, who are generally more stable and long-term orientated, rate CSR pretty much the same.

5.2.1.4 Conclusion of Survey Results

Summarizing the main differences between analysts' and investors' perceptions of CSR, the results show that for analysts, specific CSR criteria such as energy and climate issues are of importance, whereas for investors an overall good CSR performance is of importance.

Comparing the results of the two years, the relevance of CSR has decreased from 2005 to 2009, especially for investors. This is probably due to a short-term effect of the financial market crisis. For analysts, the differences between the two years are minor. The results have to be taken with caution, because few of them are significant. This is might be due to the small sample size and the differences of the mean value.

To conclude, the relevance of CSR for investment decisions has decreased. CSR is increasingly seen as "part of good management" and less as a "separated construct" as one participant points out. A further quote of a participant outlines the whole CSR topic as follows: "In summary, CSR has a place, but it's not generally packaged as such." This quote summarizes the whole development of CSR, that it is not a separated construct but more and more an integral part of management, especially because specific CSR issues, like the reduction of climate gases and others are becoming part of regulatory frameworks. Also, reporting on non-financials becomes mandatory for many companies. All these indicators show that CSR has found its way into mainstream business, and should therefore be treated like this. But still, it is assumed that some CSR items are value drivers whereas others may have negative effects on performance. In the following section, the strategic and non-strategic CSR items are determined, based on the assumption that especially strategic CSP has a positive effect on CFP and furthermore minimizes company risk.

5.2.1.5 Factor Analysis – Constructing Strategic and Non-Strategic CSR

In Section 4.2.2 (Operationalizing Strategic and Non-Strategic CSP), the theoretical background for grouping CSR into strategic and non-strategic CSR has been laid. In the following, the 31 CSR criteria of the survey will be grouped according to the theoretical foundation of the RBV using the VRIN-criteria. Afterwards, the three groups of strategic, coerced, and altruistic CSR will be tested statistically with factor analysis and reliability testing. It is the aim of this section to quantify CSP based on beliefs, respectively creating the basis for constructing CSP typologies for the analysis with Oekom rating data.

According to the RBV, the VRIN-criteria (valuable, rare, inimitable, non-substitutable) are those criteria, which are leading to SCA (Barney, 2001). As discussed above, in the following the survey items are judged according to these criteria (Table 32: Grouping into Strategic, Coerced and Altruistic CSR). The items with a high degree of fulfillment of the VRIN criteria are grouped to strategic CSP. The strategic CSR items are those with a long-term orientation, which are valuable, rare and mainly inimitable and non-substitutable. This mainly refers to companies' own policies, programs, strategies and management systems. Coerced CSP are those criteria, which are mainly valuable and non-substitutable. In terms of content, these are items that refer to compliance issues. Lastly, altruistic CSR mainly refers to the measures that are more or less on the basis of voluntary engagement and at the same time do not refer to programs or strategies. The items grouped to altruistic CSR do only fulfill one or none of the VRIN criteria. The grouping into strategic, coerced and altruistic CSR is mainly based on the classification by content. The VRIN criteria are only complementing the content-based classification, because they are only capable of giving a broad orientation, of which the criteria "valuable" has the strongest influence. Items that are rated as "valuable" are therefore either grouped into coerced or strategic CSR, whereas items that do not seem to be valuable are grouped to altruistic CSR.

Identification of Strategic and Non-Strategic CSP

strategic/ coerced/ altruistic	Variable Name	Full Name	Valuable	Rare	In-imitable,	Non-substi-tutable
Economic Responsibility						
coerced	CG_IR	Good Investor Relations on CR-Issues (trust, transparency, timeliness, quality)	X	/	/	X
coerced	CG_compl	Compliance with the official Corporate Governance-Codex of a country	X	/	/	X
strategic	SR_policy	Policy and guidelines for supplier relations and supplier standards	X	X	X	X
altruistic	SR_compl	Monitoring of compliance with policy and guidelines for supplier relations and supplier standards	/	/	/	/
coerced	CR_sat	Monitoring and reporting of customer satisfaction	/	X	/	/
strategic	CR_mgmtsys	Existence of Customer-Relationship-Management-System	X	X	X	X
Environmental Responsibility						
strategic	EM_mgmt	Existence of an environmental policy	X	X	/	X
coerced	EM_fix	Fixed quantitative environmental targets	/	/	/	X
coerced	EM_cert	Certified Environmental-Management-System (ISO 14001, EMAS)	X	X	/	/
coerced	EM_monitor	Company monitors its environmental impact (risks) without certified Environmental-Management-System (no certificate)	X	X	/	/
Energy						
coerced	EGY_info	Information about energy mix	X	/	/	/
strategic	EGY_effi	Programme for the improvement of the energy efficiency	X	X	X	X

strategic	EGY_renew	Programme for the increasing usage of renewable energy sources	X	X	X	X
coerced	EGY_presup	Information on precaution of electricity supply	X	X	/	/
Climate						
strategic	EMS_clim	Existence of a climate strategy	X	X	X	/
strategic	EMS_CO2	Focus on CO2 reduction	X	/	X	X
coerced	EMS_SO2	Focus on SO2 reduction	/	X	X	X
coerced	EMS_nox	Focus on NOX reduction	/	X	X	X
Social Responsibility						
coerced	EMPL_div	Diversity-Management/ Equal Opportunities (male/female, minorities)	X	X	/	/
strategic	EMPL_hs	Health & Safety Programme for employees	X	X	X	X
strategic	EMPL_hr	Existence of a human resources development strategy (demographic development, war for talents etc.)	X	/	X	X
coerced	HR_supra	Endorsement of supranational organisations like ILO, UNO, OECD, Global Compact	X	X	/	/
altruistic	HR_simpac	Conducting social-impact assessments (e.g. during infrastructure projects)				
Corporate Citizenship						
strategic	CC_strat	Existence of a Corporate Citizenship Strategy	X	X	X	X
strategic	CC_poli	Policy Statement on community involvement	X	X	X	X
altruistic	CC_detail	Details about Corporate Citizenship engagement in reports	/	X	/	/
Stakeholder Management						
coerced	STM_consid	Consideration of stakeholder interests	X	/	/	X
altruistic	STM_descipt	Description of stakeholder management in report(s)	/	X	/	/
altruistic	STM_compl	Stakeholder management in compliance with AA1000 or similar	/	X	X	/

Table 32: Grouping into strategic, coerced and altruistic CSR

Because this grouping is based on a theoretical foundation and it is further prone to imprecise classification, it should further be proved statistically via factor analysis. Table 33 (Factor Analysis and Reliability of Strategic, Coerced and Altruistic CSR) shows the results of the factor analysis and the reliability tests. All groups have the KMO test above 0.8 and are significant. Cronbach's Alpha is in all cases above 0.8, which speaks for a good consistency of the factors. These results clearly indicate that it is statistically acceptable to group the items as presented in Table 33 (Factor Analysis and Reliability of Strategic, Coerced and Altruistic CSR).

Factor Analysis and Relaibility of Strategic, Coerced and Altruistic CSR

		Strategic CSR	Coerced CSR	Altruistic CSR
Factor Analysis	Kaiser-Meyer-Olkin	.861	.834	.828
	Bartelt Significance	.000	.000	.000
	Anti-Image-Correlation	All > 0.8	All > 0.76	All > 0.78
	Total Dispersion (Eigen-Value)	2 > 1 (1,339)	2 > 1 (1,147)	1 > 1
	Component-Matrix	All > 0.6	All > 0.53	All > 0.6
Reliability	Cronbachs Alpha	.903	.858	.876
	Cronbachs Alpha (Item Statistic)	All < 0.903	All < 0.858	All < 0.876

Table 33: Factor Analysis and Reliability of Strategic, Coerced and Altruistic CSR

The aggregated dimensions of strategic, coerced and altruistic CSR are the foundation for the further analysis of the CSP/CFP link using the Oekom and Thomson Reuters data.

5.2.2 CSP/CFP Descriptive Data

The following section contains the descriptive analysis of the CSP, based on the Oekom utility ratings of 2004 and 2008 and the CFP data provided by Thomson Reuters. First, the dimensions of strategic, coerced and altruistic CSR will be adapted and applied to the Oekom CSP measures of 2004 and 2008 (5.2.2.1 Factor Analysis – Strategic and Non-Strategic CSP). Secondly, a correlation analysis gives first insights into the relation between CSP and CFP during the two years (5.2.2.2 Correlation Matrix). The chapter closes with a final conclusion (5.2.2.3 Conclusion).

5.2.2.1 Factor Analysis – Strategic and Non-Strategic CSP

It is aim of this section to derive the strategic and non-strategic CSP (coerced and altruistic) measures for this research. For this, the already grouped dimensions of strategic, coerced and altruistic CSR from the survey are used to match them with the Oekom CSP measures of 2004 and 2008. The results will be tested via factor analysis and in a second step verified with reliability testing.

Distinguishing between strategic, coerced and especially altruistic CSP for the Oekom measures is not viable, because the Oekom criteria do only deliver the measures for altruistic CSP in a few cases. Especially for the Oekom utility rating 2004, no measures could be identified that can be clearly classified as altruistic. This observation corresponds with the statements of Baron (2001) and Husted/Salazar (2006) that especially the distinction between strategic and altruistic CSR is difficult. Therefore, the author decided to aggregate only the two dimensions of strategic and non-strategic CSP. Coerced and the few altruistic measures are added up to the dimension of non-strategic CSP. Strategic CSP are the measures that can be clearly identified as strategic.

The tables 34 and 35 (Translating the Oekom 2004/ 2008 CSP measures into strategic and non-strategic CSP) show the results of grouping the Oekom CSP criteria into strategic and non-strategic CSP. The used methods for the classification are similar to the classification of the survey data. First, the Oekom indicators have been matched according to the content of the survey data classification, which is pictured in the column "variable of the survey". Secondly, the classification of the Oekom data according to the survey data has been checked in terms of content. The strategic Oekom CSP items are those with a long-term orientation and mainly refer to company policies, programs and strategies. Whereas the Oekom non-strategic CSP-items are those criteria, which refer mainly to compliance issues.

For 2004 only four single items are considered to be strategic and six as non-strategic. As discussed in previous chapters (Chapter 5.1.2.1 Oekom CSP Data), the Oekom 2004 is not as detailed as the 2008 rating. Accordingly, fewer items can be grouped into these two dimensions. For 2008, seven single items are classified as strategic CSP and nine as non-strategic CSP.

Translating the Oekom 2004 CSP-measures into strategic and non-strategic CSP

	Variables of the Survey	Oekom Indicator	Name	Variable Name
Strategic CSP 2004	EGY_effi	B.3	Eco-Efficiency	CSP_strat_04
	EGY_renew	B.2.5	Strategy on Sustainable Utility Operations	
	EMPL_hs	A.2.3	Health & Safety	
	EMPL_hr	A.2	Staff Relations	
Non-Strategic CSP 2004	CG_ir and CG_compl	A.3.3	Shareholders/ Corporate Governance	CSP_nonstrat_04
	EM_cert	B.1.1	Environmental Management	
	EGY_presup	B.2.1	Energy Generation and Supply	
	EMPL_div	A.2.4	Equal Opportunities	
	CC_strat/ CC_detail	A.3.4	Communiy Involvement	
	STM_consid	A.3	Relations with External Stakeholders	

Table 34: Translating the Oekom 2004 CSP-measures into strategic and non-strategic CSP

Translating the Oekom 2008 CSP-measures into strategic and non-strategic CSP

	Variables of the Survey	Oekom Indicator	Name	Variable Name
Strategic CSP 2008	SR_policy	A.1.2.1	Supplier standards	CSP_strat_08
	EM_mgmt	B.1.1	Corporate Policy covering environmental issues	
	EGY_effi	B.3	Eco-Efficiency	
	EGY_renew	B.2.6	Strategy on Sustainable Utility Operations	
	EMS_clim	B.1.5	Strategy and formal systems for adressing climate change	
	EMPL_hs	A.1.1.4	Health & Safety	
	EMPL_hr	A.1.1	Staff	
Non-Strategic CSP 2008	CG_ir and CG_compl	A.3.1	Corporate Governance	CSP_nonstrat_08
	EM_fix	B.1.4	Environmental performance indicators	
	EM_cert/ EM_monitor	B.1.2.2	Certification to an internal standard	
	EM_cert	B.1.2	Environmental Management	
	EGY_presup	B.2.2	Energy Generation and Supply	
	EMPL_div	A.1.1.5	Equal Opportunities	
	CC_strat/ CC_detail	A.2.1.2	Community	
	STM_consid	A.2.1.5	Stakeholder Dialogue	
	SR_compl	A.1.2.2	Supplier Measures	

Table 35: Translating the Oekom 2008 CSP-measures into strategic and non-strategic CSP

The aggregation of single items to one measure is always prone to biases. First, there will always be a loss in information, which is unavoidable. Secondly, which is specific to this thesis, the attempt to develop CSR typologies on values (the survey) and transfer the value-based typologies on an existing rating scheme is unique, but there is also the possibility of a mismatch between the different methods. Therefore, a factor analysis of the Oekom CSP typologies should prove if the dimension could be grouped into these factors from a static sight. However, due to the above-mentioned possible limitations, the factor analysis might deliver unclear results. Table 36 (Factor Analysis and Reliability Testing of Strategic and Non-Strategic CSP) summarizes the results of the factor analysis and the reliability test.

Factor Analysis and Reliability Testing of Strategic and Non-Strategic CSP

		Strategic CSP 2004	Non-Strategic CSP 2004	Strategic CSP 2008	Non-Strategic CSP 2008
Factor Analysis	Kaiser-Meyer-Olkin	.595	.524	.685	.669
	Bartelt Significance	.000	.000	.073	.000
	Anti-Image-Correlation	All > 0.5	3 > 0.5	All > 0.5	7 > 0.5
	Total Dispersion (Eigen-Value)	1 > 1	2 > 1 (1,228)	2 > 1 (1,095)	2 > 1 (1,728)
	Component-Matrix	3 > 0.6	4 > 0.6	3 > 0.6	5 > 0.6
Reliability	Cronbachs Alpha	.672	.425	.694	.735
	Cronbachs Alpha (Item Statistic)	3< 0.673 Eco-Efficiency (.713)	5< 0.681 Energy Generation and Supply (.632)	6 < 0.694	7 < 0.735 Corporate Governance (.776), Community (.759)

Table 36: Factor Analysis and Reliability Testing of Strategic and Non-Strategic CSP

The results of the KMO test already indicate that the items are not entirely adequate for a factor analysis. The KMO value should be above 0.7. However, for the two dimensions of 2008 this value is nearly reached. The eigenvalue should not be greater than one, but the eigenvalue of strategic CSP 2004 is smaller. The values of the component matrix should ideally be all above 0.6. This is the case for none of the dimensions.

Cronbach's alpha	Internal consistency
α ≥ .9	Excellent
.9 > α ≥ .8	Good
.8 > α ≥ .7	Acceptable
.7 > α ≥ .6	Questionable
.6 > α ≥ .5	Poor
.5 > α	Unacceptable

Table 37: Consistency for Cronbach's alpha

Further, the results of Cronbach's Alpha show that only the dimension of non-strategic CSP 2008 is acceptable. Strategic CSP for 2004 and 2008 can be classified as "questionable", and non-strategic CSP 2004 is "poor". This means that from a statistical point of view the dimensions are not ideal for aggregating them into the proposed dimension. Only the dimension non-strategic CSP 2008 seems to be appropriate from a statistical point of view. However, from a theoretical point of view, it is possible to aggregate the single items of two the proposed dimensions. Although the statistical results are not satisfying, the dimensions strategic CSP 2004/2008 and non-strategic CSP 2004/2008 are used for the further analysis of the relation of CSP and CFP.

5.2.2.2 Correlation Matrix

In the following, the correlation matrices are presented. They describe the degree of relationship between the CSP and the CFP variables. In addition to the strategic and non-strategic CSP dimensions, also the composite CSP measures of the Oekom CSR (CSR-AlL), social (CSR_Soc) and environmental (CSR_Envi) rating are integrated in the correlation matrices. This is done, as discussed above, for reasons of completeness and comparability.

Correlation-Matrix 2004/ 05 (Pearson, two-tailed)

		CSR_ALL_04	CSR_ENVI_04	CSR_SOC_04	CSP_strat_04	CSP_nonstrat_04
CSR Rating	Pearson Correlation	1	,851**	,715**	,811**	,842**
	Significance (2-tailed)		,000	,000	,000	,000
	N	35	35	35	35	35
Environmental Rating	Pearson Correlation	,851**	1	,329	,694**	,592**
	Significance (2-tailed)	,000		,054	,000	,000
	N	35	35	35	35	35
Social Cultural Rating	Pearson Correlation	,715**	,329	1	,669**	,826**
	Significance (2-tailed)	,000	,054		,000	,000
	N	35	35	35	35	35
CSP_strat_04	Pearson Correlation	,811**	,694**	,669**	1	,635**
	Significance (2-tailed)	,000	,000	,000		,000
	N	35	35	35	35	35
CSP_nonstrat_04	Pearson Correlation	,842**	,592**	,826**	,635**	1
	Significance (2-tailed)	,000	,000	,000	,000	
	N	35	35	35	35	35
MTBV_05	Pearson Correlation	-,364*	-,244	-,438*	-,211	-,353
	Significance (2-tailed)	,044	,186	,014	,255	,051
	N	31	31	31	31	31

ROE_05	Pearson Correlation	-,128	-,105	-,247	,084	-,203
	Significance (2-tailed)	,487	,566	,174	,649	,265
	N	32	32	32	32	32
ROA_05	Pearson Correlation	-,056	-,031	-,091	-,029	-,078
	Significance (2-tailed)	,760	,868	,619	,874	,672
	N	32	32	32	32	32
Beta_05	Pearson Correlation	,548*	,410*	,360	,252	,539**
	Significance (2-tailed)	,002	,027	,055	,187	,003
	N	29	29	29	29	29
Market Cap_05	Pearson Correlation	,123	-,194	,669**	,272	,377*
	Significance (2-tailed)	,509	,295	,000	,139	,037
	N	31	31	31	31	31

Table 38: Correlation-Matrix for 2004 (CSP) and 2005 (CFP)

Table 38 gives an overview of the correlations between the CSP and CFP of the years 2004 (CSP) and 2005 (CFP). As the correlation matrix shows, there is no significant dependency between strategic CSP and the CFP and risk variables. This is an unexpected result, because it was assumed that especially strategic CSP is related to a better CFP and lower company risk. But the results of the correlation matrix do not argue for such a relation. Surprisingly, the non-strategic CSP variables correlate significantly with MTBV and beta. The negative correlation between non-strategic CSP and MTBV indicates that lower non-strategic CSP results in higher MTBV. This direction was as well not expected, as a low CSP means a good CSR performance (Table 17: Translation of the Oekom Rating Scheme into a Numeric Scheme). Theory suggested as well that non-strategic CSP rather has no effect or a negative effect on CFP. But the results of the correlation argue for the opposite. Also surprising is the relation between non-strategic CSP and beta. The positive relation between non-strategic CSP and beta illustrates that high non-strategic CSP, which refers to a poor performance, results in a high beta which refers to higher risks. In other words, this correlation indicates that the better a company performs in non-strategic CSR fields the lower is the risk and vice versa the These first results indicate that the dimension strategic CSP is not a good predictor for financial performance in general and further, non-strategic CSP seems to be a better predictor.

The composite CSP variables CSR_ALL_04 and CSR_Social_04 correlate significantly with MTBV. This indicates that social CSR, and CSR in general, are positively linked to firm performance, measured with MTBV, whereas the composite variable for environmental CSP does not deliver any significant results with CFP measures. Environmental performance does not seem to be positively correlated with firm performance in the electric utility industry.

Interestingly all composite CSP variables seem to lower company risk (beta), because they correlate strongly and significantly with beta. Especially CSR_ALL_04 is strongly correlated with beta. These results only count for the correlations between CSP, CFP and risk before the financial market crisis. The following table (Table 39: Correlation Matrix for 2008 (CSP) and 2009 (CFP)) shows the relations during the crisis.

Correlation-Matrix 2008/ 09 (Pearson, two-tailed)		Corporate Responsibility Rating	Environmental Rating	Social Rating	CSP_strat_08	CSP Non-Strategic_08
CSC Rating	Pearson Correlation	1	,920**	,714**	,682**	,789**
	Significance (2-tailed)		,000	,000	,000	,000
	N	30	30	30	30	30
Environmental Rating	Pearson Correlation	,920**	1	,497**	,581**	,758**
	Significance (2-tailed)	,000		,005	,001	,000
	N	30	30	30	30	30
Social Rating	Pearson Correlation	,714**	,497**	1	,612**	,693**
	Significance (2-tailed)	,000	,005		,000	,000
	N	30	30	30	30	30
CSP_strat_08	Pearson Correlation	,682**	,581**	,612**	1	,690**
	Significance (2-tailed)	,000	,001	,000		,000
	N	30	30	30	30	30
CSP Non-Strategic_08	Pearson Correlation	,789**	,758**	,693**	,690**	1
	Significance (2-tailed)	,000	,000	,000	,000	
	N	30	30	30	30	30
MTBV_09	Pearson Correlation	-,417*	-,320	-,276	-,275	-,415*
	Significance (2-tailed)	,027	,097	,155	,156	,028
	N	28	28	28	28	28
ROE_09	Pearson Correlation	-,039	-,060	,211	,077	-,074
	Significance (2-tailed)	,843	,762	,282	,697	,710
	N	28	28	28	28	28
ROA_09	Pearson Correlation	-,083	-,087	-,070	,217	-,091
	Significance (2-tailed)	,688	,672	,735	,287	,657
	N	26	26	26	26	26
Beta_09	Pearson Correlation	-,115	-,027	-,187	-,183	-,234
	Significance (2-tailed)	,560	,891	,341	,352	,231
	N	28	28	28	28	28

Market Cap_09	Pearson Correlation	,128	,105	,325	,087	,339
	Significance (2-tailed)	,533	,609	,105	,673	,091
	N	26	26	26	26	26

Table 39: Correlation Matrix for 2008 (CSP) and 2009 (CFP)

The correlations between CSP and CFP variables for the year 2008/09 deliver less significant results even than for 2004/05. However, it was expected that the results during the financial market crisis are less viable due to the extreme events. Only two strong correlations with significance exist. Like for 2004, the composite variable CSR_ALL_08 is strongly correlated with MTBV. This is a first indicator that good CSR performance is positively correlated with good financial performance, with a lagged effect of one year. Also, the correlation between non-strategic CSP and MTBV is strong and significant, like in 2004. This is a further indicator that non-strategic CSP seems to be a good predicator for future financial performance.

CSP does not correlate with the risk-measure beta for the year 2008/09 like in 2004. This might be a first indicator that good CSP does not lower company risk especially during times of crises.

5.2.2.3 Conclusion

The factor analysis and reliability testing of the survey data resulted in the three dimensions of strategic, coerced and altruistic CSR. While adopting this construct to the Oekom CSP items, it became clear that the dimensions of strategic and non-strategic CSP could not withstand the statistical analysis. However, because theory supports these dimensions they are still used in this research to investigate the CSP/ CFP-link. The fact that the statistical methods of the factor analysis and reliability testing could not support the theoretical approach is a clear limitation of this research.

The correlation analysis gave first insights into the possible relation of CSP and CFP. Especially the measure non-strategic CSP 2004 and 2008 could be correlated with the CFP measure MTBV. This is a first indication that non-strategic CSP seems to be a good predictor for CFP. Moreover, the correlations are positive, which is a first marker that non-strategic CSP leads to a better CFP; whereas the correlations with strategic CSP do not deliver any significant results, which are a first indication that strategic CSP is not a good predictor for future financial performance, like expected. An expected result is, however, the high correlation rate between risk and CSP measures in 2004. This indicates that CSR might be capable of lowering company risks. The results give only a first insight into the CSP/CFP-relation but do not allow conclusions. The following OLS-regression is capable to deliver results that are more concrete.

5.3 Cross-sectional Regression Analysis

To test the hypotheses presented in Chapter 4.4 (Hypotheses), five models are specified with CSP as independent, and CFP and risk as dependent variables. For modeling the relationship between CSP and CFP, the method of ordinary least squares (OLS) is used. OLS is a method for estimating the unknown parameters in a linear regression. The OLS estimator minimizes the average squared difference between the actual values of Y and the predicted value based on the estimated line.

Though the OLS regression results can be affected by unusual results, there are four possibilities by which the OLS regression can be affected by: univariate outliers, regression outliers, leverage and influence. (Andersen, 2008). Univariate outliers are values that stand away from the rest of the distribution. Regression or vertical outliers "stand apart from the general pattern for the bulk of the data." (Andersen, 2008, 31).

Testing the OLS regression models if they are normally distributed is an appropriate method of identifying any unusual observations. However, because the sample size of this research is already small, removing the potential outliers seems not appropriate as this would even smaller the sample size.

In the following section first of all the five models are presented followed by an analysis of the results which are separated

5.3.1 OLS Models

The OLS models are summarized in table 40 (Table 40: Summary of Regression Models and Equations (OLS) before and during the crisis). Models one to three show the regression equations with CFP as dependent variable and model four represents the regressions with the risk-measures beta. The independent variables are strategic and non-strategic CSP and the composite CSP measures CSR_ALL, CSR_ENVI and CSR_SOC. CSR_ALL is the Oekom composite rating, integrating all single measures. CSR_ENVI is the composite rating for the environmental measures and CSR_SOC for the social and cultural measures. The control variables or confounder variables are for all models the company size, represented by the market capitalization. For the OLS model, with CFP (MTBV, ROE, ROA) as dependent variables, risk, measured with beta, is a further confounder. Vice versa, for the OLS model trying to explain risk, the confounding variable is, besides size, the CFP measure MTBV. The hypothesis associated with each equation is written next to the equation.

The four models will be applied for the two years, before and during the financial market crisis. This implies that each model will be calculated twice, for the year 2004 and 2008. The assumed lagged effect CSP has on CFP is expressed by using CFP data one year after the CSP data (year x+1).

Summary of Regression Models and Equations (OLS) before and during the crisis

Model	Dependent Variable (CFP/Risk)	Independent Variables (CSP)	Control Variables	Hypotheses	Equation
1	MTBV	Strategic CSP	Size (Market Capitalization), Risk (Beta)	H1a: There is a positive link between strategic CSP and CFP (especially market-based measures).	$MTBV_{x+1} = \beta_0 + \beta_{strat\_CSP\,x} + \beta_{CO2\_04} + \beta_{risk\_x+1} + \beta_{size\_x+1} + \varepsilon$
		Non-Strategic CSP		H1b: There is a neutral to negative link between non-strategic CSP and CFP.	$MTBV_{x+1} = \beta_0 + \beta_{non\text{-}strat\_CSP\,x} + \beta_{CO2\_04} + \beta_{risk\_x+1} + \beta_{size\_x+1} + \varepsilon$
		CSR_All		H1c: There is no clear, measurable link between the composite CSP measures and CFP	$MTBV_{x+1} = \beta_0 + \beta_{CSR\_all\_x} + \beta_{risk\_x+1} + \beta_{size\_x+1} + \varepsilon$
		CSR_ENVI			$MTBV_{x+1} = \beta_0 + \beta_{CSR\_ENVI\_all\_x} + \beta_{risk\_x+1} + \beta_{size\_x+1} + \varepsilon$
		CSR_SOC			$MTBV_{x+1} = \beta_0 + \beta_{CSR\_SOC\_x} + \beta_{risk\_x+1} + \beta_{size\_x+1} + \varepsilon$
2	ROE	Strategic CSP	Size (Market Capitalization), Risk (Beta)	H1a: There is a positive link between strategic CSP and CFP (especially market-based measures).	$ROE_{x+1} = \beta_0 + \beta_{strat\_CSP\,x} + \beta_{CO2\_04} + \beta_{risk\_x+1} + \beta_{size\_x+1} + \varepsilon$
		Non-Strategic CSP		H1b: There is a neutral to negative link between non-strategic CSP and CFP.	$ROE_{x+1} = \beta_0 + \beta_{non\text{-}strat\_CSP\,x} + \beta_{CO2\_04} + \beta_{risk\_x+1} + \beta_{size\_x+1} + \varepsilon$
		CSR_All		H1c: There is no clear, measurable link between the composite measures and	$ROE_{x+1} = \beta_0 + \beta_{CSR\_all\_x} + \beta_{risk\_x+1} + \beta_{size\_x+1} + \varepsilon$
		CSR_ENVI			$ROE_{x+1} = \beta_0 + \beta_{CSR\_ENVI\_all\_x} +$

				CFP	$\beta_{risk\_x+1} + \beta_{size\_x+1} + \varepsilon$
		CSR_SOC			$ROE_{x+1} = \beta_0 + \beta_{CSR\_SOC\_x} + \beta_{risk\_x+1} + \beta_{size\_x+1} + \varepsilon$
3	ROA	Strategic CSP	Size (Market Capitalization), Risk (Beta)	H1a: There is a positive link between strategic CSP and CFP (especially market-based measures).	$ROA_{x+1} = \beta_0 + \beta_{strat\_CSP\,x} + \beta_{CO2\_04} + \beta_{risk\_x+1} + \beta_{size\_x+1} + \varepsilon$
		Non-Strategic CSP		H1b: There is a neutral to negative link between non-strategic CSP and CFP.	$ROA_{x+1} = \beta_0 + \beta_{non\text{-}strat\_CSP\,x} + \beta_{CO2\_04} + \beta_{risk\_x+1} + \beta_{size\_x+1} + \varepsilon$
		CSR_All		H1c: There is no clear, measurable link between the composite CSP measures and CFP	$ROA_{x+1} = \beta_0 + \beta_{CSR\_all\_x} + \beta_{risk\_x+1} + \beta_{size\_x+1} + \varepsilon$
		CSR_ENVI			$ROA_{x+1} = \beta_0 + \beta_{CSR\_ENVI\_all\_x} + \beta_{risk\_x+1} + \beta_{size\_x+1} + \varepsilon$
		CSR_SOC			$ROA_{x+1} = \beta_0 + \beta_{CSR\_SOC\_x} + \beta_{risk\_x+1} + \beta_{size\_x+1} + \varepsilon$
4	Beta	Strategic CSP	Size (Market Capitalization), CFP (MTBV)	H2a: There is a positive link between strategic CSP and risk – strategic CSP lowers firm risk	$Beta_{x+1} = \beta_0 + \beta_{strat\_CSPx} + \beta_{cfp\_x+1} + \beta_{size\_x+1} + \varepsilon$
		Non-Strategic CSP		H2b: There is a neutral link between non-strategic CSP and risk – Non-strategic CSP has a neutral influence on firm risk	$Beta_{x+1} = \beta_0 + \beta_{strat\_CSPx} + \beta_{cfp\_x+1} + \beta_{size\_x+1} + \varepsilon$
		CSR_All		H2c: There is no clear, measurable link between the composite CSP measures and firm risk	$Beta_{x+1} = \beta_0 + \beta_{CSR\_all\_x} + \beta_{cfp\_x+1} + \beta_{size\_x+1} + \varepsilon$
		CSR_ENVI			$Beta_{x+1} = \beta_0 + \beta_{CSR\_ENVI\_all\_x} + \beta_{cfp\_x+1} + \beta_{size\_x+1} + \varepsilon$

CSR_SOC	$Beta_{x+1} = \beta_0 + \beta_{CSR\_SOC\_x} + \beta_{cfp\_x+1} + \beta_{size\_x+1} + \varepsilon$

Not part of the OLS-models:
H3. : CSP (especially the composite rating) functions as an insurance-like protection during the financial market crisis.

Table 40: Summary of Regression Models and Equations (OLS) before and during the crisis

5.3.2 Results

In the following, the results of the regression models are presented, first for the year 2004 and afterwards for 2008. To avoid an over-specified model, new variables have been calculated for strategic and non-strategic CSP, by generating the mean value of the items used to represent strategic and non-strategic CSP (5.2.2.1 Factor Analysis – Constructing Strategic and Non-Strategic CSP). The problem of over-specification is also the reason why the models are calculated separately from each other. When using too many variables in one model with a too small sample size, the problem of over-specification can occur. This means that the model cannot produce any valid results, because too many variables are taking too much influence on the dependent variable. It is likely that the dependent variable is almost entirely covered by interrelated independent and confounding variables. The results from over-specified models cannot be interpreted, because they produce useless results. Therefore, the variables CSP_strat_04, CSP_nonstrat_04, CSP_strat_08, CSP_nonstrat_08 have been computed. These summarized variables have already been part of the correlation matrices in the previous section.

5.3.2.1 Model 1 to Model 4 for 2004

In the following, the results of Model 1 to 4 for the year 2004 are presented. This section starts with the models for CFP (MTBV, ROE and ROA) followed by risk (beta coefficient).

Table 41 (Regression Model 1: MTBV 2005 with CSP 2004) summarizes the result of the OLS model CFP/ MTBV 2004.

Regression Model 1: MTBV 2005 with CSP 2004

Dependent Variable (CFP/ Risk)	Confounding Variable	R-Square	Sig	Beta		Significance	Pearson-Correlation (zero order)
MTBV	Beta_05	.119	.359	Beta_05	-.152	.466	-.081
	Market Cap_05			Market Cap_05	-.336	.117	-.308
				CSP_strat_04	-.020	.925	-.155
N (29)	Beta_05	.127	.326	Beta_05	-.066	.806	-.081
	Market Cap_05			Market Cap_05	-.269	.282	-.308
				CSP_non strat_04	-.139	.626	-.279
	Beta_05	.158	.223	Beta_05	-.005	.983	-.081
	Market Cap_05			Market Cap_05	-.273	.182	-.308
				CSP_ALL_04	-.251	.289	-.292
	Beta_05	.177	.175	Beta_05	-.055	.788	-.081
	Market Cap_05			Market Cap_05	-.369	.060	-.308
				CSP_ENVI_04	-.266	.195	-.221
	Beta_05	.148	.253	Beta_05	.019	.943	-.081
	Market Cap_05			Market Cap_05	-.082	.810	-.308
				CSP_SOC_04	-.329	.359	-.378

Table 41: Regression Model 1: MTBV 2005 with CSP 2004

All the regressions with MTBV as dependent variable have an r-square below 0.2. (Table 41), which is very low. Furthermore, the model does not deliver any significant results. This indicates that no CSP variables used in this model seem to be a good predictor for MTBV in the year 2005. These rather unexpected results might be due to the small sample size. It is possible that this tendency, of a positive but weak link between CSP and CFP, will be significantly verifiable with a larger sample. The signs of the CSP variables indicate that this might be the case. However, as none of the equations delivers significant results, the hypotheses H1a to H1c can neither be rejected nor confirmed for the year 2004 with MTBV as CFP measure.

The results suggest this positive to neutral relation for all five CSP measures. Interestingly, the regression results of the composite CSP measures and MTBV suggest a stronger relation between CSP and MTBV than the strategic and non-strategic CSP-measures. However, these results are not significant and can only give a hint of a possible relation. For the whole model, no statistically clear conclusion can be drawn, although the correlation matrix suggested a strong relation between MTBV and strategic CSP, CSR_ALL and CSR_SOC. But the CSP variables also correlate strongly with beta. The results of the OLS regression can only be explained with a strong interrelation between beta_05 and the CSP-measures strategic_CSP_04, CSR_ALL_04 and CSR_SOC_04.

The second model with ROE as dependent variable (Table 42: Regression Model 2: ROE 2005 with CSP 2004) has, like the first model with MTBV, no explanatory power, because the values for the r-squares are very low and the results are not significant. Therefore, H1a to H1c can as well not be confirmed nor rejected for the years 2004 and ROE as measure for CFP.

Regression Model 2: ROE 2005 with CSP variables 2004

Dependent Variable (CFP/Risk)	Confounding Variable	R-Square	Sig	Beta		Significance	Pearson-Correlation (zero order)
ROE	Beta_05 Market Cap_05	.092	.482	Beta_05 Market Cap_05 CSP_strat_04	-.121 -.327 .186	.566 .132 .387	.000 -.297 .062
N (29)	Beta_05 Market Cap_05	.068	.615	Beta_05 Market Cap_05 CSP_non strat_04	.006 -.207 -.098	.984 .419 .740	.000 -.246 -.175
	Beta_05 Market Cap_05	.069	.612	Beta_05 Market Cap_05 CSP_SOC_04	.025 -.137 -.155	.930 .702 .677	.000 -.246 -.238
	Beta_05 Market Cap_05	.084	.527	Beta_05 Market Cap_05 CSP_strat_04	-.121 -.327 .186	.566 .132 .387	.000 -.297 .062
	Beta_05 Market Cap_05	.071	.601	Beta_05 Market Cap_05 CSP_non strat_04	.006 -.207 -.098	.984 .419 .740	.000 -.246 -.175

Table 42: Regression Model 2: ROE 2005 with CSP 2004

However, having only a look at the signs that indicate a tendency for the direction of the link, strategic_CSP_04 suggests a rather negative relation with ROE; whereas the other models suggest a positive to neutral relationship between CSP and ROE. Again, the results are not significant, which is probably due to the small sample size, but if they would be significant, the relation is on a very low level and in fact negligible.

Looking at the third regression model for the year 2004 with ROA as the dependent variable (Table 43: Regression Model 3: ROA 2005 with CSP 2004), three equations (non-strategic CSP,

CSR_ALL and CSR_ENVI) deliver significant results with an r-square for the whole model of about 0.3. The model with strategic_CSP_04 as independent variable delivers almost significant results with an r-square of 0.242. Accordingly, this model is rather robust. However, in all equations, the confounding variable beta (risk) has the major influence, followed by the CSP variables.

Regression Model 3: ROA 2005 with CSP variables 2004

Dependent Varible (CFP/ Risk)	Confounding Variable	R-Square	Sig	Beta		Significance	Pearson-Correlation (zero order)
ROA	Beta_05	.242	.070	Beta_05	.437	.030*	.381
	Market Cap_05			Market Cap_05	-.073	.708	-.254
				CSP_strat_04	-.288	.149	-.198
N (29)	Beta_05	.280	.039*	Beta_05	.665	.011*	.381
	Market Cap_05			Market Cap_05	.085	.703	-.254
				CSP_non strat_04	-.490	.067	-.099
	Beta_05	.364	.009*	Beta_05	.676	.003*	.381
	Market Cap_05			Market Cap_05	-.024	.889	-.254
				CSP_ALL_04	-.549	.012*	-.182
	Beta_05	.322	.020*	Beta_05	.505	.011*	.381
	Market Cap_05			Market Cap_05	-.218	.212	-.254
				CSP_ENVI_04	-.422	.028*	-.175
	Beta_05	.211	.109	Beta_05	.537	.048*	.381
	Market Cap_05			Market Cap_05	.111	.734	-.254
				CSP_SOC_04	-.364	.294	-.095

Table 43: Regression Model 3: ROA 2005 with CSP 2004

The calculation of the single r-squares (beta value x correlation) for significant and almost significant (values between 0.05 and 0.1) CSP variables are as follows:

R-square for strategic_CSP_04: (-0.288 x -0.198) x100 = 5.7%

R-square for non-strategic_CSP_04: (-0.490 x -0.099) x100 = 4.85%

R-square for CSR_ALL_04: (-0.549 x -0.182) x100 = 10.0%*

R-square for CSR_ENVI_04: (-0.422 x -0.175) x100 = 7.4%*

This means that 5.7% of the fraction of variance of ROA can be explained by strategic CSP and 4.58% with non-strategic CSP; however, both results are not significant. Therefore, no conclusion can be drawn for strategic and non-strategic CSP. The r-square of CSR_ALL is significant and explains 10% of the variance and 7.4% of the variance is explained with CSR_ENVI_04. A single r-square below 10% shows only a small influence. Only r-square values of above 10% can be seen as a model with an explanatory power on the command variable.

The results show that especially CSP_ALL has an explanatory power on ROA. The hypothesis that especially non-strategic CSP has a neutral influence (H1b) cannot be verified nor rejected. The same is for H2a that especially strategic CSP pays off. The results rather argue that CSP in general (CSR_ALL) has an explanatory power for ROA. The variables CSR_ENVI_04 and CSP_ALL_04, which include measures of strategic and non-strategic CSP, have a higher explanatory power than strategic and non-strategic CSP and are significant.

The fact that the composite CSP variable CSR_ALL_04 has the strongest explanatory power and delivers significant results argues against hypothesis H1c (There is no clear, measurable link between the composite CSP measures and CFP), but the r-square of 10% is very low.

However, the question arises why the models with ROA as CFP measures have at all an explanatory power in contrast to the ROE model. This can be explained with the capital structure of utilities. The deregulation of utilities has an effect on the capital structure of utilities. In the study of Taha (2004), it was shown that utilities increased their level of debt during and after the process deregulation. Because the results of model two with ROE as dependent variable did deliver lower r-squares and insignificant results, it is assumed that especially the level of debt, which is besides equity part of the ROA ratio, is significantly related with CSP.

The fourth model with the beta-coefficient as dependent variable delivers highly significant results for non-strategic CSP and for the composite variables CSR_ALL_04 and CSR_Soc_04 (Table 44: Regression Model 4: Beta 2005 with CSP 2004).

Regression Model 4: Beta 2005 with CSP variables 2004

Dependent Varible (CFP/Risk)	Confounding Variable	R-Square	Sig	Beta		Significance	Pearson-Correlation (zero order)
Beta	MTBV_05 Market Cap_05	.178	.172	MTBV_05 Market Cap_05 CSP_strat_04	-.141 -.365 .335	.466 .076 .090	-.081 -.225 .252
N (29)	MTBV_05 Market Cap_05	.513	.000*	MTBV_05 Market Cap_05 CSP_non strat_04	-.037 -.518 .729	.806 .003* .000*	-.081 -.225 .539
	MTBV_05 Market Cap_05	.393	.005*	MTBV_05 Market Cap_05 CSP_ALL_04	-.004 -.309 .590	.983 .071 .001*	-.081 -.225 .548
	MTBV_05 Market Cap_05	.193	.140	MTBV_05 Market Cap_05 CSP_strat_04	-.054 -.174 .366	.788 .384 .067	-.081 -.225 .410
	MTBV_05 Market Cap_05	.527	.000*	MTBV_05 Market Cap_05 CSP_non strat_04	.011 -.849 .935	.943 .000* .000*	-.081 -.225 .360

Table 44: Regression Model 4: Beta 2005 with CSP 2004

For strategic CSP and CSP_ENVI_04, the overall model, however, does not have a strong r-square and is not significant, but the influence of the CSP variables is still strong and almost significant with 0.67.

Calculating the single r-squares of the model gives insights into the explanatory power of each CSP variable:

R-square for strategic_CSP_04: (0.335 x 0.252) x100 = 8.4%

R-square for non-strategic_CSP_04: (0.729 x 0.539) x100 = 39.3%*

R-square for CSR_ALL_04: (0.590 x 0.548) x100 = 32.3%*

R-square for CSR_ENVI_04: (0.366 x 0.410) x100 = 15.0%*

R-square for CSR_SOC_04: (0.935 x 0.360) x100 = 33.7%*

The results display that the composite variable CSR_SOC_04 has a very strong influence on the risk-measure beta. Through the social performance of a utility, 33.7% of the variance of beta can be explained. This means, for the year 2004, that the better a utility company performs in social issues the lower is its company risk. This result is especially remarkable, because it was assumed that environmental issues count primarily in the utility industry and less in social issues. The model clearly demonstrates that social issues count as well in the utility industry particularly as risk mitigation. The environmental performance however, explains only 15% of the variance of beta. The CSP variable CSR_ALL has also a strong explanatory power of 32.3% of the variance of beta. This implies that a good CSR performance in general lowers company risk. These results are not in line with the hypothesis H2c: (There is no clear, measurable link between the composite CSP measures and firm risk). For the CSR_SOC_04 and CSP_ALL_04 the hypothesis H2c needs to be rejected.

Especially remarkable are the results of the model with non-strategic CSP. This model delivers an r-square of 0.513 and is with 0.000 highly significant. Moreover, non-strategic CSP is the variable with the highest influence on beta of 0.729. In total 39,3% of the variance of beta can be explained with non-strategic CSP. This means that the better a company's performance in non-strategic CSP, which is related to the coerced and altruistic CSR, which refers to the measures that are more or less on the basis of voluntary engagement, the less it is exposed to risk. According to H2b, it is assumed that there is a neutral link between non-strategic CSP and risk. However, the results speak for a positive link between non-strategic CSP and beta as a measure for firm risk. The better a company performance in non-strategic CSR the lower is its firm risk. Hypothesis H2b must be rejected for the year 2004.

5.3.2.2 Summary of Results for the 2004 Models

In summary, as the first regression model for 2004 with MTBV as the dependent variable does not deliver any significant results, therefore the hypotheses H1a to H1c can neither be rejected nor confirmed for the year 2004 and MTBV as CFP measure. The model does not have any explanatory power, although it was assumed that especially the model with MTBV as dependent variable delivers clear results. The same applies to the second model with ROE as dependent variable.

The third regression model with ROA as the dependent variable displays the first significant results. The results show that certain CSP variables are a predictor for ROA. However, the hypothesis that especially non-strategic CSP has a negative to neutral influence (H1b) cannot be verified. The results rather argue that CSP_ALL_04 has an explanatory power for ROA, explaining 10% of the variance of ROA (significance of 0.12). This result is not in line with the hypotheses H1c, that the composite CSP measure does not have any explanatory power. For this model, this hypothesis needs to be rejected.

The hypothesis H1b (There is a neutral to negative link between non-strategic CSP and CFP) needs also be also rejected for the year 2004 and ROA as a measure for CFP, because there is a slight but rather positive relation between the two measures ROA and non-strategic CSP.

The main hypothesis H1a (There is a positive link between strategic CSP and CFP can neither be rejected nor confirmed, because for non-strategic CSP all the results are not significant.

The fourth model with beta as dependent variable delivers highly significant results for non-strategic CSP, CSR_ALL and CSR_SOC. The better a company performance in these CSP variables the lower is the beta coefficient.

Especially the model with non-strategic CSP has a very high r-square of 0.513 and is with 0.000 highly significant.

Table 45 (Table 45: Summary of Results of the OLS Regression Models for 2004) below summarizes the results from the OLS regressions for 2004. It displays that none of the hypotheses could be confirmed. Especially strategic CSP is not a good predictor for CFP and risk at all in the years 2004/05. This might be due to the methods used to measure strategic CSP, or that non-strategic CSP is in general not related to CFP. Before drawing any conclusion on this matter, in the following, the models for the years 2008/09 are calculated and interpreted.

Summary of Results of the OLS Regression Models for 2004

Model	Dependent Varible (CFP/Risk)	Results of the Model	Conclusion in regard to the Hypotheses
1	MTBV	no significant results	Hypothesis H1a-H1c can neither be confirmed nor rejected
2	ROE	no significant results	Hypothesis H1a-H1c can neither be confirmed nor rejected
3	ROA	no significant results	Hypothesis H1a-H1b can neither be confirmed nor rejected
		significant results R-square for CSR_ALL is 10%	Hypothesis H1c must be rejected for 2004 with CSR_ALL as CSP-measure and ROA as CFP-measure
		significant results R-square for CSR_ENVI is 7.4%	Hypothesis H1c must be rejected for 2004 with CSR_ENVI as CSP-measure and ROA as CFP-measure
		no significant results	Hypothesis H1c can neither be confirmed nor rejected for 2004 with CSR_SOC as CSP-measure and ROA as CFP-measure
4	Beta	no significant results	Hypothesis H2a can neither be con-

	firmed nor rejected

significant results
    R-square for non-strategic CSP is 32.3%
significant results – hypothesis is rejected
    R-square for CSR-ALL is 33.6%
	HypothesisH2b must be rejected for 2004
	Hypothesis H2c must be rejected for 2004 with CSR_ALL as CSP-measure

no significant results	HypothesisH2c can neither be confirmed nor rejectedfor 2004 with CSR_ENVI as CSP-measure
significant results – hypothesis is rejected. R-square for CSR_SOC is 39.3%	Hypothesis H2c must be rejected for 2004 with CSR_SOC as CSP-measure

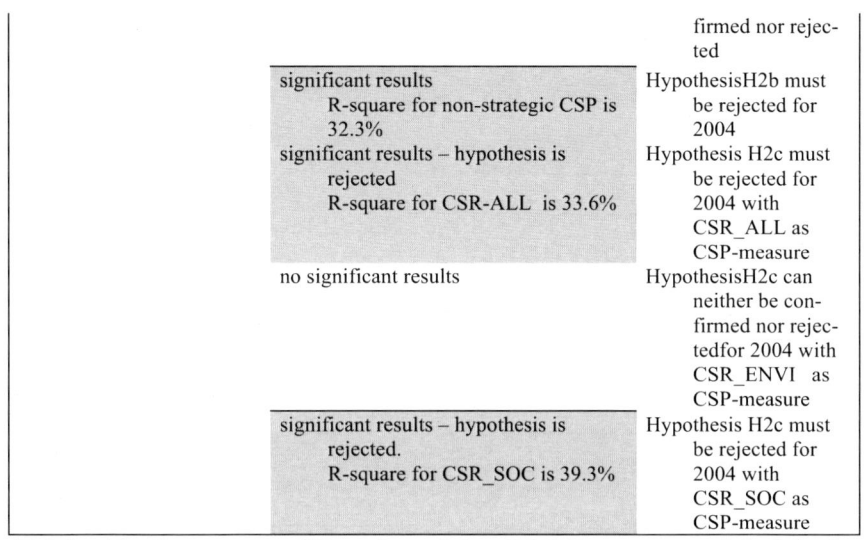

Table 45: Summary of Results of the OLS Regression Models for 2004

5.3.2.3 Model 1 to Model 4 for 2008

In this section, the results of the four OLS regressions for the year 2008 will be introduced and analyzed. The chapter is structured according to the previous chapter, starting with the CFP models, MTBV, ROE and ROA and finishing with the risk model.

Table 46 (Regression Model 1: MTBV 2009 with CSP 2008) summarizes the results of the MTBV_09 model. This model only delivers one significant result, for CSR_ALL_08. However, the main influencing factor is Beta_09 (-0.432) but closely followed by CSR_ALL_08 (-0.403). The variable CSR_ALL_08 explains 17% (-0.403 x – 0.424) x100 = 17%) of the variance of MTBV, which is an acceptable value, especially during times of crisis, in which the CFP data are not as reliable as in times without such extreme downturns. The fact that the results for this model are significant shows that the composite variable CSR_ALL_08 seems to be an acceptable predictor for MTBV. The better a company performs in CSR in general the better it performs also financially. Godfrey, Merrill and Hansen (2009) argued that CSR could create a form of goodwill that acts like an insurance-like protection, especially during times of crisis. This is first evidence, that CSR might function as an insurance-like buffer, which was formulated in H3.

Three other equations of the MTBV model have an acceptable r-square and are close to significance, and therefore will be displayed in the following:

R-square for strategic_CSP_08: (-0.324 x -0.255) x100 = 8.3%

R-square for non-strategic_CSP_08: (-0.299 x -0.300) x100 = 8.9%

R-square for CSR_ALL_08: (-0.403 x -0.424) x100 = 17%*

R-square for CSR_ENVI_08: (-0.250 x -0.288) x100 = 7.2%

R-square for CSR_SOC_08: (-0.293 x -0.329) x100 = 9.6%

The results show that the single values have a rather low explanatory power for MTBV and are not significant, despite CSR_ALL_08. However, a slight tendency is observable that CSP measures have a rather positive influence on MTBV, but due to the insignificant results, no clear conclusion can be drawn.

The only valid conclusion can be made for the model with CSR_ALL, which explains 17% of the variance. This is not a high value but still remarkable, and hypothesis H3 can be confirmed for the model with MTBV as dependent variable.

Regression Model 1: MTBV 2009 with CSP 2008

Dependent Varible (CFP/Risk)	Confounding Variable	R-Square	Sig	Beta		Significance	Pearson-Correlation (zero order)
MTBV_09	Beta_09	.273	.067	Beta_09	-.509	.025*	-.268
	Market Cap_09			Market Cap_09	-.365	.093	-.147
				CSP_strat_08	-.324	.095	-.255
N (26)	Beta_09	.251	.090	Beta_09	-.456	.042*	-.268
	Market Cap_09			Market Cap_09	-.266	.239	-.147
				CSP_non strat_08	-.299	.142	-.300
	Beta_09	.331	.029*	Beta_09	-.432	.041*	-.268
	Market Cap_09			Market Cap_09	-.305	.144	-.147
				CSP_ALL_08	-.403	.032*	-.424
	Beta_09	.233	.113	Beta_09	-.424	.060	-.268
	Market Cap_09			Market Cap_09	-.326	.144	-.147
				CSP_ENVI_08	-.250	.198	-.288
	Beta_09	.248	.093	Beta_09	-.425	.057	-.268
	Market Cap_09			Market Cap_09	-.258	.259	-.147
				CSP_SOC_08	-.293	.149	-.329

Table 46: Regression Model 1: MTBV 2009 with CSP 2008

The next model with ROE as dependent variable (Table 47: Regression Model 2: ROE 2009 with CSP 2008) does not deliver any significant results. Despite the insignificant results, the r-squares of the different equations are very low. This result is not surprising, because it was expected that due to the extreme events of the financial market crisis the link between CSP, CFP and risk would deliver mainly insignificant results.

Regression Model 2: ROE 2009 with CSP 2008

Dependent Varible (CFP/Risk)	Confounding Variable	R-Square	Sig	Beta		Significance	Pearson-Correlation (zero order)
ROE_09	Beta_09 Market Cap_09	.171	.240	Beta_09 Market Cap_09 CSP_strat_08	-.099 -.443 .107	.665 .059 .595	.095 -.386 -.088
N (26)	Beta_09 Market Cap_09	.164	.258	Beta_09 Market Cap_09 CSP_non strat_08	-.188 -.467 .072	.604 .057 .733	.095 -.368 -.063
	Beta_09 Market Cap_09	.160	.271	Beta_09 Market Cap_09 CSP_ALL_08	-.121 -.444 .001	.595 .061 .998	.095 -.368 -.051
	Beta_09 Market Cap_09	.160	.271	Beta_09 Market Cap_09 CSP_ENVI_08	-.120 -.444 .000	.596 .061 .997	.095 -.368 -.049
	Beta_09 Market Cap_09	.271	.069	Beta_09 Market Cap_09 CSP_SOC_08	-.142 -.569 .353	.503 .016 .081	.095 -.368 .184

Table 47: Regression Model 2: ROE 2009 with CSP 2008

The third model with ROA as dependent variable (Table 48: Regression Model 3: ROA 2009 with CSP 2008) has low r-squares and no significant results. The only result worth mentioning is that of strategic_CSP_08. The model is almost significant (0.76) and has an r-square of 0.264. The CSP variable is also the variable with the most influence in the model, with a single r-square of 6.4% (0.297 x 0.217). The positive sign indicates that the higher the CSP value, which is equivalent to poor CSP, the higher is the ROA. Although the r-square is on a low level and the results are not significant, this indicates the tendency that good strategic CSP results in a lower ROA during times of crisis. Because the results are not significant and the r-square is low, it is not possible to generalize this observation. For the whole model no conclusion can be drawn and the hypotheses can neither be rejected nor confirmed.

Regression Model 3: ROA 2009 with CSP 2008

Dependent Varible (CFP/Risk)	Con-founding Variable	R-Square	Sig	Beta		Significance	Pearson-Correlation (zero order)
ROA_09	Beta_09	.264	.076	Beta_09	.293	.182	.358
	Market Cap_09			Market Cap_09	-.255	.236	-.371
				CSP_strat_08	.297	.126	.217
N (26)	Beta_09	.181	.214	Beta_09	.234	.300	.358
	Market Cap_09			Market Cap_09	-.273	.248	-.371
				CSP_non strat_08	.047	.820	-.091
	Beta_09	.180	.215	Beta_09	.234	.301	.358
	Market Cap_09			Market Cap_09	-.252	.269	-.371
				CSP_ALL_08	.041	.836	-.083
	Beta_09	.183	.209	Beta_09	.237	.294	.358
	Market Cap_09			Market Cap_09	-.249	.274	-.371
				CSP_ENVI_08	-.063	.748	-.087
	Beta_09	.181	.214	Beta_09	.230	.310	.358
	Market Cap_09			Market Cap_09	-.274	.251	-.371
				CSP_SOC_08	.045	.829	-.070

Table 48: Regression Model 3: ROA 2009 with CSP 2008

The fourth model with the risk measure beta delivers highly significant results for all CSP variables, like the model for 2004/05. But the main influencing variables are in each equation the confounding variables MTBV_09 and especially the size measured with Market_Cap_09. Further, the CSP variables of the models are not significant. The single r-squares for the CSP variables are as follows:

Strategic CSP: (-0.256 x -0.197) x100 = 5% (not significant)

Non-Strategic CSP: (-0.145 x -0.196) x100 = 2.8% (not significant)

CSR_ALL: (-0.146 x -0.041) x100 = 0.6% (not significant)

CSR_ENVI: (-0.037 x -0.009) x100 = 0.03% (not significant)

CSR_SOC: (-0.063 x -0.111) x100 = 0.69% (not significant)

The results of the single r-squares demonstrate that they do not have any remarkable influence, first because the values are very low and secondly the results are not significant. Accordingly, all the CSP_08 variables have no explanatory power for Beta_09.

The reason why this model delivers significant results is due to the variable Market_Cap_09. The size of a company has a major influence on the risk measure beta in the year 2008/09. In all the equations, Market_Cap_09 accounts for approximately 20% to 25% of the variance of Beta_09 and moreover all the values are highly significant. The smaller a company the higher is its exposure to company risk (measured with the beta-coefficient) in times of crises. The size of a company seems to be a good protection against higher level of risk, especially during times of crisis. It becomes evident that it is less the good CSP, which can protect the company value during times of crisis, but more the size of a company, which functions like an insurance-like buffer. Summarizing, also the models with the beta coefficient seem to have a high explanatory power on the first sight. However, for the year 2008/09 and the utility industry, CSP is not related to company risk.

Regression Model 4: Beta 2009 with CSP variables 2008

Dependent Variable (CFP/Risk)	Confounding Variable	R-Square	Sig	Beta		Significance	Pearson-Correlation (zero order)
Beta_09	MTBV_09 Market Cap_09	.414	.007**	MTBV_09 Market Cap_09 CSP_ALL_08	-.410 -.523 -.256	.025* .005** .143	-.268 -.485 -.197
N (26)	MTBV_09 Market Cap_09	.370	.016*	MTBV_09 Market Cap_09 CSP_ALL_08	-.384 -.492 -.145	.042* .012* .447	-.268 -.485 -.196
	MTBV_09 Market Cap_09	.370	.016*	MTBV_09 Market Cap_09 CSP_ALL_08	-.407 -.526 -.146	.041* .006** .443	-.268 -.485 -.041
	MTBV_09 Market Cap_09	.345	.020*	MTBV_09 Market Cap_09 CSP_ALL_08	-.357 -.533 -.037	.060 .006** .837	-.268 -.485 .009
	MTBV_09 Market Cap_09	.356	.020*	MTBV_09 Market Cap_09 CSP_ALL_08	-.365 -.518 -.063	.057 .009** .744	-.268 -.485 -.111

Table 49: Regression Model 4: Beta 2009 with CSP 2008

5.3.2.4 Summary of Results for the 2008 Models

The OLS regression models for 2008 deliver less significant results than the models of 2004 (Table 50: Summary of Results of the OLS Regression Models for 2008). Due to the extreme events of financial market crisis, the mainly insignificant results were expected, though two results stand out. The only remarkable result is that CSP_ALL_08 has a strong relation to MTBV_09, explaining 17% of the variance. This means that the better a utility company performs in CSP, the higher is its financial performance in the year after. This is a first indication that CSR can really function as a buffer during times of crisis.

Strategic CSP has a rather negative effect on risk. It was assumed that in general and especially during times of crisis, strategic CSP has the capacity to lower company risk. But the results with beta as risk measures demonstrate that if strategic CSP has an influence it is a rather negative influence. However, the results for strategic CSP are in all models not significant.

Table 50 below summarizes the key results of the OLS regression models of 2008. The table demonstrates that for the models with ROE, ROA and beta as dependent variables no clear conclusions can be drawn, because the r-squares are very low and more importantly the results are not significant. The insignificant results are probably due to the small sample size. In 2008, only 26 utility companies were part of the analysis, whereas in 2004 the sample size was 29. The results of the models and its implications will be analyzed in-depth in the upcoming section (Chapter 5.4 Discussion of OLS-Models).

Summary of Results of the OLS Regression Models for 2008

Model	Dependent Variable (CFP/Risk)	Results of the Model	Conclusion in regard to the Hypotheses
1	MTBV	no significant results	Hypothesis H1a-H1b can neither be confirmed nor rejected
		significant results – R-square for CSR_ALL is 17%	Hypothesis H1c must be rejected for 2008 with CSR_ALL as CSP-measure and MTBV as CFP-measure
			First evidence that hypothesis H3 can be confirmed: CSP functions as an insurance-like protection during the financial market crisis. can be confirmed for CSR_ALL as CSP-measure.
		no significant results	HypothesisH1c can neither be confirmed nor rejected
2	ROE	no significant results	HypothesisH1a-H1c can neither be confirmed nor rejected
3	ROA	no significant results	HypothesisH1a-H1c can neither be confirmed nor rejected
4	Beta	no significant results	HypothesisH2a-H2c can neither be confirmed nor rejected

Table 50: Summary of Results of the OLS Regression Models for 2008

5.4 Discussion of OLS Models

In the previous chapter, the results of the OLS-regression models have been presented. In this section, the results will be discussed in-depth.

In the following, the significant as well as insignificant regression models are parts of further investigation. Before drawing further conclusions for the significant models, some assumptions made in OLS regressions will be tested (Chapter 5.4.1 Testing Normal Distribution and Homoscedasticity). After that the single items of the constructed variables strategic and non-strategic CSP will be analyzed (Chapter 5.4.2 Testing the Single Items of Strategic and Non-strategic CSP). The chapter closes with a summary of the main results (Chapter 5.4.3 Summary of OLS-Models).

5.4.1 Testing Normal Distribution and Homoscedasticity

It is possible that the assumptions made in the OLS regressions are biased, which leads to unusual observations. In Section 5.3.1 (OLS Models), the reasons for unusual observations of OLS regressions have already been mentioned. A method of detecting unusual observations is to look at the distribution and the homoscedasticity of data. The normal distribution gives a hint if there are possible outliers that may bias the results. Also, the homoscedasticity will be tested with a scatter plot, because the presence of heteroscedasticity can invalidate the tests of significance.

For all the regressions carried out in this research the normal distribution has been checked with a histogram and the p-p diagram of standardized residuals. In all cases, no abnormalities have been observed. The following graphs stand exemplary for the tests carried out. It shows the histogram and the p-p diagram with a normal distribution. The scatter plot displays no value above three, which speaks for homoscedasticity. The example below shows the graphs of the regression with sigma as dependent variable, the social rating as independent and market capitalization as confounding variable.

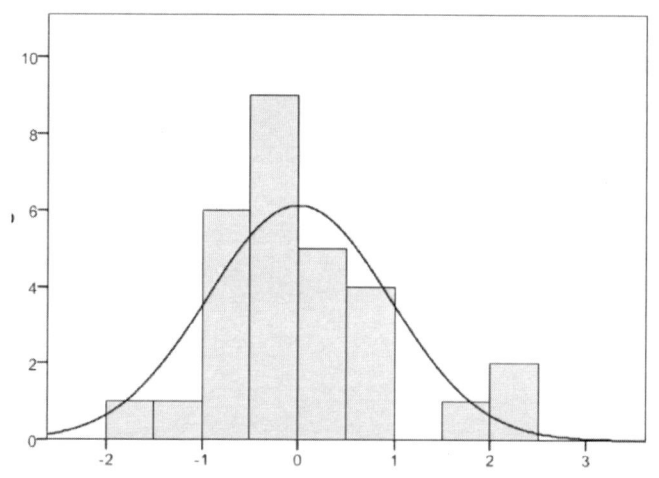

Figure 10: Histogram Beta_05/ Relations with External Stakeholders_04

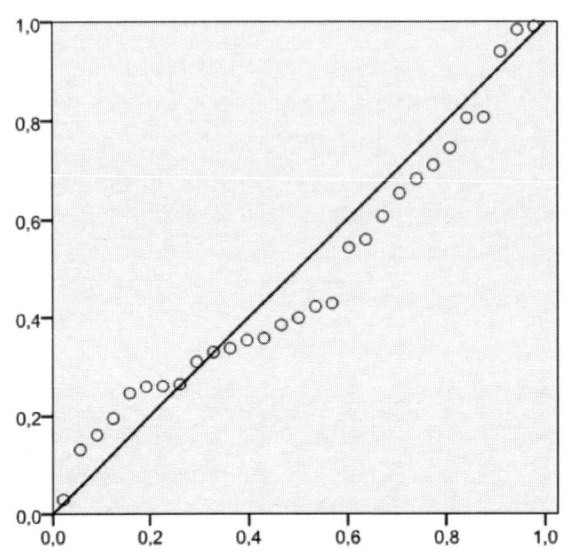

Figure 11: P-P Diagram Beta_05/ Relations with External Stakeholders_04

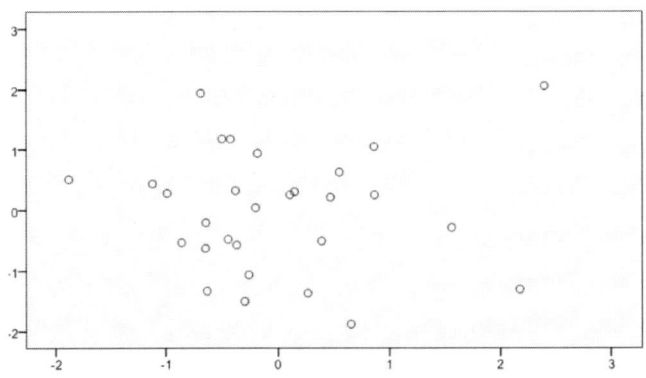

Figure 12: Scatter Plot Beta_05/ Relations with External Stakeholders_04

Summarizing, all the regressions carried out show similar results with regard to the test of normal distribution and homoscedasticity. Therefore the preconditions for OLS-regression analysis are fulfilled and no potential outlier needs to be removed from the sample or can bias the results.

The main question stays, why the constructed variables strategic and non-strategic CSP did only deliver a few significant results. In the following, additional statistical tests will be carried out to investigate the main assumptions of this research.

5.4.2 Testing the Single Items of Strategic and Non-strategic CSP

Only a few of the OLS-regression models with strategic CSP and non-strategic CSP as independent variables delivered significant results. There are two possible reasons for these insignificant results:

1. The sample is too small
2. The link between dependent and independent variable is too weak. Or, in other words, the constructed variables of strategic and non-strategic CSP may have no explanatory power and rather the single items have a higher explanatory power.

The fact that a sample of 29 observations for 2004 and 26 for 2008 is small has already been mentioned, and might be a reason for the high number of insignificant results. The second possible reason for the mainly insignificant results will be tested in the following with correlation analysis. If the single CSP items of a constructed variable correlate stronger with CFP and risk than the constructed CSP variables, this might be first evidence that the constructed variables do not have enough explanatory power. If one of the single items has a higher correlation than the constructed CSP variables and is as well significant, it is possible that this item has also a higher explanatory power than the constructed variable in the regression models, which will also be tested.

In the following, the correlation analysis for each year will be displayed, with the constructed variables, first strategic and then non-strategic CSP and the associated single items. If one of the single items correlates higher with CFP or risk and is also significant, a regression analysis will be carried out to find out if the single item is a better predictor for performance or risk than the constructed variable.

Correlation-Matrix 2004 Strategic CSP versus single CSP-measures (Pearson, two-tailed)

		CSP_strat_04	Staff Relations	Health & Safety	Strategy on Sustainable Utility Operations	Eco-Efficiency
MTBV_05	Pearson Correlation	-,211	-,353	-,200	-,191	-,006
	Significance (2-tailed)	,255	,052	,281	,303	,974
	N	31	31	31	31	31
ROE_05	Pearson Correlation	,084	-,127	,166	-,009	,077
	Significance (2-tailed)	,649	,490	,365	,961	,677
	N	32	32	32	32	32
ROA_05	Pearson Correlation	-,029	-,140	,034	-,141	,018
	Significance (2-tailed)	,874	,443	,856	,441	,923
	N	32	32	32	32	32
Beta_05	Pearson Correlation	,252	,151	,114	,175	,256
	Significance (2-tailed)	,187	,435	,556	,364	,179
	N	29	29	29	29	29
Sigma_05	Pearson Correlation	,014	-,350	-,046	-,096	,282
	Significance (2-tailed)	,943	,062	,814	,620	,138
	N	29	29	29	29	29

Table 51: Correlation-Matrix 2004 Strategic CSP versus single CSP-measures

The correlation matrix for strategic CSP (Table 51: Correlation-Matrix 2004 Strategic CSP versus single CSP-measures) indicates that the variable staff_relations_04 might be a better predictor for MTBV_05 than the variable strategic_CSP_04. The correlation is higher and almost significant with 0.52. Therefore, it will be tested via OLS regression if the item staff Relations_04 is a better predictor for MTBV (Table 52).

Regression Model MTBV: Strategic CSP versus Staff Relations 2004

Dependent Varible (CFP/ Risk)	Beta			Significance	Pearson-Correlation (zero order)
MTBV	Beta_05		-.152	.466	-.081
	Market Cap_05		-.336	.117	-.308
	CSP_strat_04		-.020	.925	-.155
	Beta_05		-.126	.538	-.081
	Market Cap_05		-.278	.245	-.308
	Staff_rel_04		-.114	.626	-.275

Table 52: Regression Model Strategic CSP versus Staff Relations 2004

The results of the OLS regression with staff relations do not deliver better r-squares than with strategic CSP, nor are the results significant. This implies that neither the constructed variable of strategic CSP nor the single item of staff relations has an explanatory power for MTBV. Strategic CSP seems not to be linked with MTBV for the year 2005 in the utility industry.

The next table (Table 53: Correlation-Matrix 2004 Non-strategic CSP versus single CSP-measures) summarizes the correlation of non-strategic CSP 2004 and the single items of non-strategic CSP with the CFP and risk measures.

Correlation-Matrix 2004 Non-Strategic CSP versus single CSP-measures (Pearson, two-tailed)

		CSP_non strat_04	Shareholders/ Corporate Governance	Environmental Management	Energy Generation and Supply	Equal Opportunities	Communiy Involvement	Relations with External Stakeholders
MT BV _05	Pearson Correlation	-,353	-,170	-,181	,044	-,282	-,271	-,482**
	Significance (2-tailed)	,051	,361	,329	,821	,124	,141	,006
	N	31	31	31	29	31	31	31
RO E_05	Pearson Correlation	-,203	-,270	-,110	,210	-,124	-,254	-,331
	Significance (2-tailed)	,265	,136	,549	,266	,497	,161	,064
	N	32	32	32	30	32	32	32
RO A_05	Pearson Correlation	-,078	-,188	,142	-,189	,141	-,162	-,109
	Significance (2-tailed)	,672	,302	,437	,316	,441	,375	,553
	N	32	32	32	30	32	32	32
Beta_05	Pearson Correlation	,539**	,093	,657**	,150	,158	,175	,400*
	Significance (2-tailed)	,003	,633	,000	,454	,414	,365	,031
	N	29	29	29	27	29	29	29
Sigma_05	Pearson Correlation	,123	-,044	,229	,091	-,241	,242	-,024
	Significance (2-tailed)	,524	,820	,231	,653	,209	,206	,900
	N	29	29	29	27	29	29	29

Table 53: Correlation-Matrix 2004 Non-strategic CSP versus single CSP-measures

The correlation matrix shows a strong and significant correlation between the variable "relations with external stakeholders" and the two CFP measures MTBV and ROE. Environmental management correlates stronger with beta than non-strategic CSP does. The following three regression analyses investigate if these single items are a better predictor for the command variables (Table 54: Regression Model Non-Strategic CSP versus single items 2004).

Regression Model: MTBV: Non_ Strategic CSP versus Relations with External Stakeholders 2004

Dependent Varible (CFP/ Risk)	Con- founding Variable	R- Square	Sig	Beta		Signi- fica- nce	Pearson- Correlation (zero order)
MTBV	Beta_05 Market Cap_05	.127	.326	Beta_05 Market Cap_05 CSP_non strat_04	-.066 -.269 -.139	.806 .282 .626	-.081 -.308 -.279
N (29)	Beta_05 Market Cap_05	.244	.068	Beta_05 Market Cap_05 Ext-rel_ 04	.210 -143 -.646	.416 .635 .052	-.081 -.308 -.473

Regression Model: ROE: Non_ Strategic CSP versus Relations with External Stakeholders 2004

Dependent Varible (CFP/ Risk)	Con- founding Variable	R- Square	Sig	Beta		Signi- fica- nce	Pearson- Correlation (zero order)
ROE	Beta_05 Market Cap_05	.068	.615	Beta_05 Market Cap_05 CSP_non strat_04	.006 -.207 -.098	.984 .419 .740	.000 -.246 -.175
N (29)	Beta_05 Market Cap_05	.110	.396	Beta_05 Market Cap_05 Ex_rel_04	.164 .035 -.391	.556 .914 .265	.000 -.246 -.304

Regression Model 4: Beta 2005 with CSP variables 2004

Dependent Varible (CFP/ Risk)	Con-founding Variable	R-Square	Sig	Beta		Significance	Pearson-Correlation (zero order)
Beta	MTBV_05 Market Cap_05	.513	.000*	MTBV_05 Market Cap_05 CSP_non strat_04	-.037 -.518 .729	.806 .003* .000*	-.081 -.225 .539
N (29)	MTBV_05 Market Cap_05	.448	.002*	MTBV_05 Market Cap_05 CSP_non strat_04	-.003 -.130 .637	.987 .426 .000*	-.081 -.225 .657

Table 54: Regression Model Non-Strategic CSP versus single items 2004

The first regression with MTBV as dependent variable illustrates that the single item for external relations with stakeholders has a high explanatory power. The single r-square is with 0.052 almost significant and explains 30.5% of the variance of MTBV. The better a company performs in "relations with external stakeholders", the better it performs financially. It is less the constructed variable of non-strategic CSP that can explain MTBV but more the single item measuring stakeholder relations. Even for ROE, the stakeholder relation variable seems to be a good predictor. The item explains 11.9% of the variance of ROE. However, this value is not significant and therefore no conclusion can be drawn based on these results.

The third regression, with beta as dependent variable, delivered already highly significant results. However, in comparison to 39.3% with non-strategic CSP, environmental management as independent variable accounts for an even higher variance of beta of 41.9%. This implies that non-strategic CSP does not seem to lower company risk but rather a good environmental management. This means, the better a company performance in environmental management, the lower is its level of risk. Especially for electric utilities, this result is not surprising. As discussed in Chapter 2.2 (The Utility Industry), one of the major risks and challenges facing the power industry are environmental issues mainly due to climate change. A utility company must respond to these challenges, e.g. by implementing environmental management systems as a basis for tackling climate change issues.

The correlation matrix (Table 55: Correlation-Matrix 2008 Strategic CSP versus single CSP-measures) for strategic CSP in 2008 shows that only the single item 'health & safety' correlates slightly higher and is with 0.64 almost significant.

Correlation-Matrix 2008 Strategic CSP versus single CSP-measures (Pearson, two-tailed)

		CSP_strat_08	Supplier standards	Corporate Policy covering environmental issues	Eco-Efficiency	Strategy on Sustainable Utility Operations	Strategy and formal systems for adressing climate change	Health & Safety	Staff
MTBV_09	Pearson Correlation	-,275	,084	-,307	-,210	-,069	-,238	-,362	-,235
	Significance (2-tailed)	,156	,671	,111	,285	,728	,224	,064	,228
	N	28	28	28	28	28	28	27	28
ROE_09	Pearson Correlation	,077	-,020	,041	,209	,101	-,022	-,050	-,013
	Significance (2-tailed)	,697	,918	,838	,285	,610	,911	,806	,949
	N	28	28	28	28	28	28	27	28
ROA_09	Pearson Correlation	,217	,128	,097	,312	,117	,183	,088	-,148
	Significance (2-tailed)	,287	,532	,637	,120	,569	,372	,677	,471
	N	26	26	26	26	26	26	25	26
Beta_09	Pearson Correlation	-,183	-,037	,015	-,109	-,189	-,083	-,220	-,240
	Significance (2-tailed)	,352	,851	,942	,579	,335	,675	,270	,218

	N	28	28	28	28	28	28	27	28
Sigma_09	Pearson Correlation	,103	-,213	,255	,103	-,017	,192	,162	,037
	Significance (2-tailed)	,602	,276	,190	,602	,932	,329	,419	,853
	N	28	28	28	28	28	28	27	28

Table 55: Correlation-Matrix 2008 Strategic CSP versus single CSP-measures

The regression model with health & safety is significant and the single r-square is with 29.4% high. Strategic CSP explains only a variance of 8.3% and is not significant. This means that the single item health & safety has, in comparison to strategic CSP, an explanatory power for MTBV. The better a company performs in health & safety during the crises, the higher is its MTBV. Health & safety is key for the electric utility industry (Chapter 2.2.2.2 Major Environmental and Social Concerns). However, the r-square with 8.3% is very low, but it still indicates a relevance of health & safety issues, also during times of crises.

Regression Model: MTBV: Strategic CSP versus Health & Safety 2008

Dependent Variable (CFP/Risk)	Confounding Variable	R-Square	Sig	Beta		Significance	Pearson-Correlation (zero order)
MTBV_09	Beta_09	.273	.067	Beta_09	-.509	.025*	-.268
	Market Cap_09			Market Cap_09	-.365	.093	-.147
				CSP_strat_08	-.324	.095	-.255
N (26)	Beta_09	.497	.002*	Beta_09	-.541	.006*	-.275
	Market Cap_09			Market Cap_09	-.377	.045*	-.143
				H&S_08	-.573	.001	-.513

Table 56: Regression Model Strategic CSP versus single items 2008

The last correlation matrix for 2008 shows that the variable "stakeholder dialog" is higher correlated with MTBV than with non-strategic CSP (Table 57: Correlation-Matrix 2008 Non-strategic CSP versus single CSP-measures). However, the regression analysis (Table 58: Regression Model Non-strategic CSP versus single items 2008) shows that the model with stakeholder dialog as independent variable is not significant and has an even lower r-square than the model with non-strategic CSP. Therefore, the single items, as well as the constructed variable non-strategic CSP, have no explanatory power for MTBV during the crisis.

Correlation-Matrix 2008 Non-Strategic CSP versus single CSP-measures (Pearson, two-tailed)

		CSP Non-Strategic_08	Corporate Governance	Environmental performance indicators	Certification to an internal standard	Environmental Management	Energy Generation and Supply	Equal Opportunities	Community	Stakeholder Dialogue
MTBV_09	Pearson Correlation	,415*	,182	-,282	-,355	-,348	-,175	,110	,177	,453*
	Significance (2-tailed)	,028	,354	,146	,064	,069	,384	,578	,377	,015
	N	28	28	28	28	28	27	28	27	28
ROE_09	Pearson Correlation	-,074	,096	,122	-,238	-,009	-,023	,031	,056	,209
	Significance (2-tailed)	,710	,626	,537	,222	,963	,909	,876	,781	,285
	N	28	28	28	28	28	27	28	27	28
ROA_09	Pearson Correlation	-,091	,015	,078	-,306	,055	-,216	,024	,027	,038
	Significance (2-tailed)	,657	,941	,706	,129	,790	,300	,909	,899	,853
	N	26	26	26	26	26	25	26	25	26
Beta_09	Pearson Correlation	-,234	,172	-,130	-,222	-,190	,067	-,325	,107	-,202
	Significance (2-tailed)	,231	,381	,510	,257	,334	,738	,091	,595	,303
	N	28	28	28	28	28	27	28	27	28
Sigma_09	Pearson Correlation	,249	,202	,206	,238	,204	,153	-,107	,057	,343
	Significance (2-tailed)	,200	,302	,293	,223	,297	,445	,588	,776	,074
	N	28	28	28	28	28	27	28	27	28

Table 57: Correlation Matrix 2008 Non-strategic CSP versus single CSP-measures

Regression Model: MTBV: Non-Strategic CSP versus Stakeholder Dialogue 2008

Dependent Variable (CFP/Risk)	Confounding Variable	R-Square	Sig	Beta		Significance	Pearson-Correlation (zero order)
MTBV_09	Beta_09 Market Cap_09	.251	.090	Beta_09 Market Cap_09 CSP_non strat_08	-.456 -.266 -.299	.042* .239 .142	-.268 -.147 -.300
N (26)	Beta_09 Market Cap_09	.226	.124	Beta_09 Market Cap_09 H&S_08	-.441 -.316 -.237	.052* .160 .228	-.268 -.147 -.259

Table 58: Regression Model Non-strategic CSP versus single items 2008

5.4.3 Summary of OLS-Models

The results show that in some cases the use of single items results in a higher relation between CSP and CFP. Especially the regression models with the variable non-strategic CSP_04 deliver higher r-squares when the single item "relation with external stakeholders" is used. This indicates that the constructed variables are probably not the best predictor for the variance of CFP and risk measures. In most of the cases, the regressions with the single items deliver higher r-squares and are significant. This furthermore shows that it is difficult to measure CSP with composite variables. The use of the composite variables strategic and non-strategic CSP, as suggested by Hillman/Keim (2001) and Husted/Salazar (2006), produced ambiguous results for this sample. This might be due to the small sample size, but a further reason might be that the used CSP dimensions are probably not the best possible predictors of CSP. However, although many of the hypotheses are rejected some of the results clearly show that CSP has an influence especially on the risk measure beta. However, the predicted insurance-like buffer could not be proven. In the next chapter, a final conclusion will be drawn and the limitations of this research pictured.

Table 59 (Summary of Results of the OLS-Models) summarizes the results concerning the hypotheses. The table also contains the conclusions, which can be drawn out of the results and further observations made.

Summary of Results of the OLS Models

Hypotheses	Results 2004	Results 2008	Results Single Items	Conclusion/ Further Observations
Ho: CSR can, under certain conditions, lead to a better CFP.				Some of the models deliver significant results with a high r-sqaure, which is evidence for Ho, that under certain conditions CSR can lead to a better CFP and moreover is related to lower firm risk. However, the results are not in all cases consistent.
H1a: There is a positive link between strategic CSP and CFP (especially market-based measures).	HypothesisH1a can neither be confirmed nor rejected		2004: no differing results through further analysis

2008: the single item 'Health & Safety' has in comparison to strategic CSP an explanatory power for the MTBV(r-square of 8,3%) | For strategic CSP no results could be aggregated. This speakseither for an inadequate measure for CSP or the results are insignificant due to the small sample size. |
| H1b: There is a neutral to negative link between non-strategic CSP and CFP. | HypothesisH1b can neither be confirmed nor rejected | | 2004 and 2008: no differing results through further analysis | For non-strategic CSP no results could be aggregated. This speaks either for an inadequate measure for CSP or the results are insignificant due to the small sample size. |

H1c: There is no clear, measurable link between the composite CSP measures and CFP	Hypothesis H1c must be rejected for 2004 for CSR_ALL (r-square 10%) and CSR_ENVI (r-square 7,4%) as CSP-measure and ROA as CFP-measure	Hypothesis H1c must be rejected for 2008 for CSR_ALL (r-square 17%) as CSP-measure and MTBV as CFP-measure			The models with the composite measures are partially significant and deliver as well consistent results. CSP_ALL is positive related to CFP. The better a company performs in CSP before and during the market crisis the better is also its firm performance. These results speak for the good management hypothesis. (see 1.2.4 Measuring Corporate Social Performance)
H2a: There is a positive link between strategic CSP and risk – strategic CSP lowers firm risk	Hypothesis H2a can neither be confirmed nor rejected	Hypothesis H2a can neither be confirmed nor rejected	2004 and 2008: no differing results through further analysis		The models for strategic CSP and risk delivered no results. This speaks either for an inadequate measure for CSP or the results are insignificant due to the small sample size. However, one result is that the models for the year 2008 are significant due to the variable Market_Cap. This implies, that especially during times of crises the size of a company is protecting it for higher level of risks.
H2 b: There is a neutral link between non-strategic CSP and risk – Non-strategic CSP has a neutral influence on firm risk	Hypothesis H2b must be rejected for 2004 (r-square of 39,3%)	Hypothesis H2b can neither be confirmed nor rejected	2004: The single item 'environmental management' has a higher explanatory power (r-square of 41,9%) for beta than non-strategic CSP 2008: no differing results through further analysis		For the year 2004 non-strategic CSP is a very good predictor for risk, however environmental management as part of the measure non-strategic CSP is an even better predictor. The results show that a good performance in non-strategic CSP and a especially in environmental management is reltated to lower firm risk.
H2c: There is no clear, measurable link between the composite CSP measures and firm risk	Hypothesis H2c must be rejected for 2004 with CSR_ALL (r-square of	Hypothesis H2c can neither be confirmed nor rejected			For the year 2004 the composite CSP measures CSR_ALL and CSR_SOC are a very good predictor for risk.

	32,3%) and CSR_SOC (r-square 33,7%) as CSP-measure		
H3. : CSP functions as an insurance-like protection during the financial market crisis.			The results of the OLS-regression with CSR_ALL as CSP-measure and MTBV as CFP-measure gives first evidence that CSP can function as an insurance -like protection. However, the results are not verified through the other models. As assumed the insurance-effect can not be displayed yet.

Table 59: Summary of Results of the OLS-Models

Overall, it was detected that the results for the main measures, strategic and non-strategic CSP, are not in all cases consistent. However, the results with the composite ratings show clearly that although the theory suggests more fine-grained measures, the composite rating can be a good predictor for CFP and as well for risk. One example are the results of the model with CSP_ALL and ROA in 2004 and MTBV in 2008, showing that the better a company performs in CSP before and during the market crisis the better is also its firm performance. These results speak for the good management hypothesis (see Section 1.2.4 Measuring Corporate Social Performance), assuming that corporate responsibility stems from good management and enhances the firm's competitive advantage.

The results of this research, the limitations and the implications for future research and management will be discussed in the following and final chapter 6 (Conclusion).

6 Conclusion

It was aim of this research to investigate the CSP/CFP link before and during the financial market crisis with a special focus on the question of how investment professionals value CSR.

Building on neoclassical economics and the RBV, the research framework was developed. Based on previous literature of e.g. Baron, 2001; Hillman/Keim 2001 and Husted/Salazar, 2006, this research distinguished between strategic and non-strategic CSP to investigate the CSP/CFP link.

The main hypotheses underlying this research, was that CSR can under certain conditions lead to profit maximization (H0). It was further assumed that especially strategic CSP leads to profit maximization, whereas non-strategic CSP has a neutral to negative influence on CFP (H1). A further assumption was, that good CSP can be risk mitigation (H2), and that a company's good CSP functions as an insurance during times of crisis (H3) (Godfrey/ Merrill/ Hansen, 2009), or acts as a "reservoir of goodwill" during corporate crises. (Schnietz/ Estein, 2005, 327).

Methodologically this research took a classical approach to the field of CSP/CFP research by using OLS regressions. Besides that, it included the opinion of investment professionals by using survey methodology.

This research was further aiming at advancing the existing approaches of CSP/CFP research. This demand was met, by first using a single industry approach. In this research the scope was the electric utility companies as one of the biggest industries worldwide, playing an important role in the future development of economies and facing challenges like liberalization and reducing climate gases.

A unique feature of this research is that it has two points of measurement, before and during the financial market crises. Also unique is using a perception-based (survey) as well as firm performance measures to construct CSP.

In the following, the results of the survey (Chapter 6.1 Survey Results) and the OLS regression (Chapter 6.2 Strategic versus Non-strategic CSR-resources and Chapter 6.3 CSP, Risk and the Insurance effect during the crisis) are presented. Further, the limitations (Chapter 6.4 Limitations) and the implications for future research and management (Chapter 6.5 Implications for Future Research and Management) are finally discussed.

6.1 Survey Results

It was aim of the survey to examine how mainstream analysts and investors who focus on utilities value certain CSR criteria. The results gave a first insight of what CSR criteria rate high on the agenda of investment professionals and therefore can add to value creation. Furthermore, the change in the perception before and during the crisis was displayed.

In total, 133 investment professionals (39 investors and 94 analysts) participated in the survey in 2005 and 102 professionals (32 investors and 70 analysts) in 2009. Through the first question that was posed, it became clear that analysts as well as investors have a clear and common understanding of what is meant with CSR.

They define it according to the triple bottom line, which incorporates economic, social and environmental responsibility.

Investment professionals further see CSR as part of good management and a concept with a future, and not as an overrated trend, which causes extra costs.

A general observation is that the rating of analysts is constant throughout the years, whereas the rating of investors is more volatile. In 2005 investors rated CSR higher than analysts, and in 2009 the rating is lower than that of analysts. This first demonstrates that investors are prone to trends and the current mood on the financial markets, whereas analysts are more stable in their ratings. It is further an indication that analysts tend to be more long-term orientated than investors. A further observation is that, for analysts, specific CSR criteria like energy and climate issues are of importance, whereas for investors an overall good CSR performance is the key.

These first results of the survey indicate that CSR in general has lost importance for investors during the crisis. This tendency of loss in importance is also confirmed by the results of the additional questions of the survey. Investors are still willing to pay an extra premium for a company with good CSP, but in comparison to 2004, the premium has decreased. Investment professionals believe that the crisis has a negative to neutral effect on CSR. This again emphasizes the loss in importance of CSR during the crisis. This decrease might be due to the extreme events of the financial crisis or it can also be the emergence of a trend. However, the results cannot be generalized, as they represent only a small sample of one industry, and most of them are not significant. This is a major limitation of the survey.

Future research should investigate the perceptions of investment professionals after the crisis and try to integrate different industries. The question is whether CSR still has its place after the crisis or if its importance still decreases, so that one can speak of a trend.

A quote by a survey participant summarizes the current status of CSR as follows: "In summary, CSR has a place, but it's not generally packaged as such." This quote summarizes the developments of CSR, that it is less seen as a separated construct but more and more as an integral part of management, especially because specific CSR issues, like the reduction of climate gases, and others are becoming part of regulatory efforts (Chapter 2.2.1 Industry Background). These are all indicators that CSR has found its way into mainstream business and should therefore be treated as such. The decrease in importance is probably due to the extreme events of the crisis and not a general trend. However, future research should further investigate this assumption. If it can be validated through further research, this would be a clear implication for management – treating CSR as an integral part of the company culture, or in other words, allowing CSR to become part of the company DNA.

In the research it was hypothesized that only the use of specific CSR resources is related to higher profits or reduced risk (Chapter 3.3 Resource-based View). In the following section, the results of the OLS regressions trying to investigate the CSP/ CFP link are concluded.

6.2 Strategic versus Non-strategic CSR-resources

The hypotheses H1a/H2a and H1b/H2b mainly build on the RBV, assuming that the strategic use of CSR can lead to a sustainable competitive advantage whereas, non-strategic CSR has a neutral to negative effect on the financial performance and risk of firms (e.g. Baron, 2001; Hillman/Keim 2001; Husted/ Salazar, 2006). These theoretical assumptions have been translated into the hypotheses:

> H1a: There is a positive link between strategic CSP and CFP (especially market-based measures).
>
> H2a: There is a positive link between strategic CSP and risk – strategic CSP lowers firm risk.
>
> H1b: There is a neutral to negative link between non-strategic CSP and CFP.
>
> H2b: There is a neutral link between non-strategic CSP and risk – non-strategic CSP has a neutral influence on firm risk.

Strategic CSP refers to the items that are long-term orientated and are closely related to subordinated strategies and policies of a company. Non-strategic CSP consists of the measure coerced and altruistic CSP. Coerced CSP are items that refer to compliance issues and altruistic CSP are more or less based on voluntary engagement, the execution of CSR.

The hypotheses have been tested with OLS-regression analysis. For H1a, assuming that strategic CSP leads to a positive relation with CSP, no clear results could be derived. All the regressions, with strategic CSP as independent variable trying to explain CFP, delivered insignificant results. Either the results speak for an inadequate measure for CSP or the results are insignificant due to the small sample size. In general, strategic CSP is not a good predictor for future performance.

A better predictor for CFP is non-strategic CSP, but only for the model with the beta coefficient as confounding variable and not CFP. In 2004/05, non-strategic CSP accounts for 39.3% of the variance. The better a company performs in non-strategic CSP, the lower is the company risk. Therefore, H2b was rejected. The regression models for the year 2008/09 were all insignificant and delivered weak r-squares. This means that, for the year during the crisis, non-strategic CSP has no explanatory power at all.

The fact that strategic CSP does not have a relation with CFP or risk, but non-strategic CSP has a relation with the risk measure beta, indicates that especially compliance and the execution and procedures, measured with non-strategic CSP, are rewarded. Not the policies and the strategies a company has in regard to CSR are accounted for but the actual doing. This implies for management that they should follow the motto: Walk your talk! This can prevent higher risks for a company. However, strategies are essential as they give the direction for the procedures and the operative actions.

Further statistical tests, carried out with the single items of the two constructed variables, strategic and non-strategic CSP (Chapter 5.4.2 Testing the Single Items of Strategic and Non-strategic CSP), demonstrated that the single items have in two cases an even stronger explanatory power. One example for this effect is the regression with the single item environmental management as part of non-strategic CSP. The item environmental performance accounts for 41.9% of the variance of beta in 2004/05. Although non-strategic CSP with 39.3% already has a high r-square, the r-square of environmental management is even higher. However, this does not necessarily mean that the constructed variables are not appropriate, but it demonstrates that the aggregation of data results, in this case, in a loss of information. In addition, the regressions with the single items did not deliver a clear picture of the CSP/CFP relation.

Surprisingly, especially models with the composite measure CSR_ALL did deliver significant results with acceptable and high explanatory power, depending on the model. The hypotheses for the composite measures are:

H1c: There is no clear, measurable link between the composite CSP measures and CFP

H2c: There is no clear, measurable link between the composite CSP measures and firm risk

In the cases in which the models with the composite measures (CSR_ALL, CSR_ENVI and CSR_SOC) delivered significant results, they displayed a positive relation with CFP and a negative relation with risk. Accordingly, H1c was rejected for 2004 for the ROA model, with a relevant explanatory power of CSR_ALL (r-square 10%). In addition, for 2008 H1c was rejected for CSR_ALL with an even higher explanatory power (r-square 17%) for the model with MTBV as CFP measure. The results are a clear indication for, first, that the better a company performs in CSP before and during the market crisis, the better is its firm performance. Secondly, these results show, like the results of H2c, that the composite measure CSR_ALL is an appropriate measure for CSR, which is seen as critical in the current CSP/CFP literature (Chapter 1.2 Literature Review). These results, with the composite measures explaining a great share of the variance, speak for the good management hypothesis, assuming that CSR is a form of good management and if incorporated into daily business processes it enhances the firm's competitive advantage (Chapter 1.2.4 Measuring Corporate Social Performance).

The results of H2a to H2c are discussed in the following chapter, which focuses on the question of which way CSP and risk are related.

6.3 CSP, Risk and the Insurance effect during the crisis

The hypothesis H2 assumed that good CSP can lower the company risk. It was further assumed that especially strategic CSP has a strong relation to the company risk measures beta (H2a), whereas non-strategic CSP has a rather neutral relation to the risk measure (H2b).

The OLS models with non-strategic CSP as independent and risk as confounding variable; trying to investigate H2a did not deliver any valuable, significant results. Either this speaks for an inadequate measure for CSP or the results are insignificant due to the small sample size. However, one result is that the models for the year 2008 are significant, due to the variable Market Cap. This implies that, especially during times of crises, the size of a company is protecting it from higher level of risks.

Non-strategic CSP seems to lower the company risk but only in the years before the financial crisis. In 2004/05 non-strategic CSP is a very good predictor for the risk measure beta, accounting for 39.3% of the variance, but as already mentioned, the single item environmental management as part of the measure non-strategic CSP is an even better predictor. The results show that a good performance in non-strategic CSP, and especially in environmental management, is related to lower firm risk. As already discussed in Section 6.2 (Strategic versus Non-strategic CSR-resources) the hypothesis H2b must be rejected for 2004. This result shows that CSP, in this case non-strategic CSP is related to lower risks. More evidently is this relation of a lower risk in the models with the composite CSP measures.

For the year 2004, the composite CSP measures CSR_ALL and CSR_SOC are a very good predictor for risk. Through the social performance (CSR_SOC) of a utility, 33,7 % of the variance of beta can be explained. This means that the better a utility company performs in social issues, the lower is its company risk. This result is especially remarkable, because it was assumed that environmental issues primarily count in the utility industry and less social issues. The model clearly demonstrates that social issues count as well in the utility industry particularly as a risk mitigation. CSR_ALL has also a strong explanatory power of 32,3% of the variance of beta. Accordingly, H2c was rejected for 2004 for CSR_ALL and CSR_SOC. This is more of an indication that the composite measures, not as predicted and proposed by literature, are an appropriate measure for CSP. They seem to be more valid than the constructed variables. This result can also be explained with the good management hypothesis, supported by the survey results. The current status of CSR is that it is has found its way into mainstream business and is seen as part of good management. The results of the models with the composite CSP measures further support this hypothesis. It is more a responsible business conduct in general than in single measures, which can prevent a company from higher risks and lower financial performance. This idea is further discussed in the upcoming Section 6.5 (Implications for Future Research and Management)

Summarizing, the results indicate that good CSP can function as risk mitigation, but not during times of crisis. These results are also in line with the result of the survey, that CSR is part of good management. Investment professionals valued CSR as part of risk management in 2005 as high, whereas during the crisis it lost in importance. These results are probably due to the extreme events of the financial market crisis, which caused lasting confusion.

Comparing the regression results of the two years with each other, it can be summarized that with regard to the proposed insurance effect (H3) no conclusion can be drawn. However, good CSP (CSR_ALL) is rewarded by higher MTBV, explaining 17% of the variance during the crisis. The better a company performs in CSR, measured with the composite variable CSR_ALL, the better it performs also financially. Godfrey, Merrill and Hansen (2009) argued that CSR can create a form of goodwill that acts like an insurance-like protection, especially during times of crisis. This is first evidence that CSR might function as an insurance-like buffer. The loss in trust due to the downturn of the financial markets could not be balanced with a good CSP on the risk level, but much so on the level of financial performance measures (MTBV).

These results are, with regard to the question in which way CSR is influenced by the crisis, not entirely satisfying, as expected. Therefore, further research still needs to be done to investigate exactly how the crisis has affected CSR. The loss of importance observed throughout the survey cannot exactly be validated with the results of the regression. The results rather indicate that measurement during times of crisis is too fragile to produce clear and significant results. This is also a reason to further investigate this topic, for example by comparing the data before, during and after the crisis.

6.4 Limitations

The limitations of this research have already been named in the context of the survey and the regression. Basically, the limitations can be classified into data-based and methodological limitations.

In research, the data and as well the methodology used are always prone to biases and involve the risk of certain limitations. In this research the survey data, the Oekom CSP data and the CFP/risk data are exposed to the following limitations.

The survey data suffer from a relatively low response rate and, accordingly a small sample size. In total 6083 investment professionals have been contacted. Only 71 investors, who equal a response rate of 2.16 %, and 164 analysts, who equal a response rate of 5.86%, participated in the survey. The total sample size of 235 is small and therefore a generalization of results is problematic, as most of the results are not significant. The insignificant results are probably due to the small sample and the differences in the mean. This is a clear bias of this research and accordingly a generalization of results is not possible. But it is still possible to formulate tendencies grounded on the survey data.

A further limitation is the used CSP data. However, all the datasets measuring CSP are exposed to certain limitations and are not developed for scientific research. Although the KLD rating scheme is the most often one used in the field of CSP/CFP research, in this research the Oekom rating was used to measure CSP. The main reason, besides the methodological arguments of e.g. industry-specific weighting schemes, was that Oekom provides comprehensive utility sector ratings, for the relevant years before and during the crisis. Because this research is taking a single-industry approach, the sample size is per se limited to the industry. A further factor limiting the sample size is brought by the Oekom scope. The Oekom utility rating 2004 includes 37 utilities, the rating of 2008 includes 30, from which only 24 are also included in the rating of 2004. In total, 41 utility companies are included in the research. However, only for 24 companies the complete CSP and CFP data are available. This is a very small sample size, which leads to the effect that only a few models delivered significant results and, furthermore, a small sample size has limited power of prediction and reliability. Yet, when using a single-industry approach, the problem of a small sample size always occurs.

A further limiting factor of the CSP data is that the methods of measurement have changed between the two years. In the 2004 rating, 54 single CSP measures are used and summed up to the composite rating, whereas in 2008, 83 single items measure CSR performance of the utilities. Moreover, the data are not collected with identical measures. This means, from 2004 to 2008 not only the total sum of the measures has grown, but also in terms of content the items are not similar anymore. This leads to a limited comparability of the data. Consequently, for this research only identical measures were used, which limits the number of potential CSP variables measuring strategic and non-strategic CSP.

This might explain the poor results of the models using strategic and non-strategic CSP as independent variables. However, as already mentioned above, CSP measures are always prone to limitations, both when using existing rating schemes and when collecting CSP data for research. This is immanent to the whole research field.

The CFP data are less affected by limitations, despite the possibility of inaccurate collection and miscalculation by the data provider. However, these errors cannot be resolved. Datastream provided the CFP and risk data, and is renowned for a high data quality. Accordingly, this is a possible limitation but not seen as a limiting factor in this research.

Despite the used dataset for this research, the used methods are also exposed to certain limitations. First, it had to be ascertained that the derivation of strategic and non-strategic CSP is affected by the limitation that the dimensions of strategic and non-strategic CSP could not withstand the statistical analysis (Chapter 5.2.2.1 Factor Analysis – Strategic and Non-Strategic CSP). However, because theory is supporting the proposed classification, the constructed variables strategic and non-strategic CSP have still been used in this research to investigate the CSP/CFP link. The dimensions of strategic and non-strategic CSP have been constructed as variables by building the mean value. This also has led to a loss in information, but it was necessary in order to avoid an over-specified model.

The usual limitations of OLS regression, the problem of outliers, has been checked with histograms and p-p diagrams, to test for normal distribution, and scatter plots, to test for homoscedasticity. These tests did not display any abnormalities. Therefore, the conditions for solid OLS regressions are given.

Overall, the major limiting factor of this research is the small sample size of the survey, and especially of the utilities, and the inconsistency in measuring CSP due to the methodological change of Oekom between the two years. Future research should try to avoid these problems.

6.5 Implications for Future Research and Management

Future research should try to avoid the pitfalls of past research. This research took a single-industry approach and classified CSR into different dimensions, arguing that some CSR resources lead to a competitive advantage and others not. This research, like previous research, failed to prove a clear relation between CSP and CFP. The idea of using more fine-grained methods to investigate the CSP/ CFP-link did not lead to the expected results. Rather the models with the composite ratings (CSR_ALL) display a relation with CFP and risk. This indicates the following:

1. CSR composite measures are appropriate to display a relation between CSP and CFP/risk measures.
2. The fine-grained measures used in this research are either not appropriate or fine-grained measures are in general not appropriate to picture the CSP/CFP relation.

The question if the fine-grained measures are in general not appropriate for CSP/CFP-research or if only the used measures of strategic and non-strategic CSP are not appropriate cannot be answered through this research. Neither did the research validate a generic link between CSP and CFP. This research rather proposes two general implications, which can be drawn out of the results of this research for future research:

1. Future research should further investigate the CSP/CFP link by using fine-grained CSP measures.
2. Also, the question concerning a generic CSP/CFP link should be followed further and not be neglected by future research.

Measuring CSP remains critical and, up to now, fine-grained measures are only used rarely. However, this is exactly what future research should further improve, methods investigating the CSP/CFP link with specified CSP measures. In the past, it was not possible to use specified measures for CSP as the whole "CSR industry" was not developed like it is nowadays. Today it is possible to collect highly-specified CSP measures, like measures that try to operationalize the climate performance of a company. Here future research is called for, using the possible fine-grained measures in order to build a clear picture of the CSP/CFP link and determining which measures are especially valuable and which are neutral or maybe negative with regard to CFP. In addition, interdependencies between various CSP measures should further be investigated. This is also the trend in current literature. Current literature is rather proposing fine-grained measures (Chapter 1.2 Literature Review) to picture the CSP/CFP relation and is assuming that a generic CSP/ CFP link cannot be displayed. The main argument, which can be found in literature, why a generic link cannot be displayed is the fact that more than 40 years of research failed to find this generic link. However, from the author's point of view, it is reasonable to investigate the generic link further, especially because of this research. It seems to be that CSR has found its way into mainstream business and is nowadays a more-or-less integral part of the way business is conducted. In former times, CSR was not integrated into business as it is today, accordingly it was difficult to find proof for a generic link. Based on the good management hypothesis it is assumed that an overall responsible manner to conduct business pays off and can also reduce company risk. If this is the case, it should be possible to find evidence for the generic link or, in other words, validate the good management hypothesis. Therefore, it is legitimate to explore for further proof of a generic link.

From the authors point of view, and based on the results of this research, future research should therefore focus on both, the search for a generic link in regard to the good management hypothesis and at the same time the search for interdependencies between fine-grained CSP measures and financial performance measures.

Specifically in the CSP/CFP research field, it means also taking a single industries approach, like in this thesis. Because CSR is manifold, it cannot be generalized for all industries. There is no "one size fits all" solution for CSR. CSR depends on the stakeholder needs and they vary, depending e.g. on the industry, the country and other factors. All these influencing factors should be taken into account in future research, investigating the link between CSP and CFP. This results in research that could also display specific segments of the big picture. Moreover, the single-industry approach will always suffer from the problem of small sample sizes.

Research is indispensable when coming to the question in which way the crisis may have affected the future of CSR. The results of this research give only a first glimpse into this complex topic. On the one hand, the results indicate that CSR can function as an insurance-like buffer. On the other hand, they indicate a loss of importance through the crisis via the results of the survey. The future development of CSR and its connection to the state of the financial markets should be further investigated, for example by comparing the data before, during and after the crisis. It should also be investigated empirically, as proposed by Fernández-Feijóo Souto (2009), if a constant CSR performance on medium to superior level has the capacity to build trust and, therefore, better overcome the turbulences brought by the financial market crisis.

Especially the survey results provide valuable implications for management. They demonstrate that CSR has found its way into mainstream business and that it is seen and valued as part of good management. Accordingly, CSR should also be treated as mainstream in management and should constantly be integrated into the DNA of a company.

A central implication for management can be summarized with the motto: Walk your talk – otherwise CSR does not pay off. The fact that strategic CSP does not have a relation with CFP, but non-strategic has this relation, shows that the execution and proper procedures are essential. It is not enough to have strategies and policies; the implementation and execution of CSR procedures is a key. However, good and profound strategies are the foundation for good operational CSR.

7 Annex

7.1 Summary and Assessment of Critiques to the RBV

Critique	Assessment
1. The RBV has no managerial implications.	Not all theories should have direct management implications.
	Through its wide dissemination, the RDV has evident impact.
2. The RBV implies infinite regress.	Applies only to abstract mathematical theories. In an applied theory such as the RBV levels are qualitatively different.
	It may be fruitful to focus on the interactions between levels rather than to consider higher levels prior as a source of SCA.
3. The RBV's applicability is too limited.	Generalizing about uniqueness is not impossible by definition.
	The RBV applies to small firms and startups as well, as long as they strive for an SCA.
	Path dependency is not problematic when not taken to the extreme.
	The RBV only applies to firms in predictable environments.
4. SCA is not achievable.	By including dynamic capabilities, the RBV is not purely static. Though, it only explains *ex post,* not *ex ante* sources of SCA.
	While no CA can last forever, a focus on SCA remains useful.
5. The RBV is not a theory of the firm.	The RBV does not suffiently explain why firms exist.
	Rather than requiring it to do so, it should further develop as a theory of SCA and leave additional explanations of firm existence to TCE.
6. VRIN/O is neither necessary nor sufficient for SCA.	The VRIN/O criteria are not always necessary and not always sufficient to explain a firm's SCA.
	The RBV does not sufficiently consider the synergy within resource bundles as a source of SCA.
	The RBV does not sufficiently recognize the role that judgement and mental models of individuals play in value assessment and creation.
7. The value of a resource is too indeterminate to provide for useful theory.	The current conceptualization of value turns the RBV into a trivial heuristic, an incomplete theory, or a tautology.
	A more subjective and creative notion of value is needed.
8. The definition of resource is unworkable.	Definitons of resources are all-inclusive.
	The RV does not recognize differences between resources as inputs and resources that enable the organization of such inputs.
	There is no recognition of how different types of resources may contribute to SCA in a different manner.

7.2 Survey Questionnaire 2009

Questionnaire 2009

Dear Sir or Madam,

Corporate Social Responsibility (CSR) is "an approach to business that embodies transparency and ethical behaviour, respect for stakeholder groups and a commitment to add economic, social and environmental value". (UN Global Compact 2004) The project's objective is to analyse the impact of CSR on capital market financing. We would be very grateful, if you could take the time (approximately 15 minutes) to fill in the Online-questionnaire. The data will be treated confidentially and we will inform you on the anonymized results. If you have any question, please do not hesitate to contact us.

Do you work as an:

- Investor
- Buy side Analyst
- Sell side Analyst
- Other

Introduction What do you associate with Corporate Responsibility?

- Corporate Citizenship
- Causing extra costs
- An essential concept
- An important part of risk management
- Needs to be included in investment decisions
- Just an overrated trend
- More research needs to be done on CSR
- A concept with future
- Part of good management
- Incorporating economic, environmental and social responsibility
- Required from and driven by Non-Governmental-Organisations (NGOs)

Strategy & Organisation Please rate the following CSR-criteria in terms of their importance for making an investment decision/company analysis.

- Existence of a person responsible for CSR-issues on management board level
- Existence and description of CSR-strategy
- Quantification of CSR-target
- Consideration of CSR-issues in Risk-Management-System
- Existence of Managementsystem for Non-Financial Risks (e.g. Issue Management)

Quality of CSR Reporting Please rate the following CSR-criteria in terms of their importance for making an investment decision/ company analysis.

- CSR-Reporting in accordance with GRI (Global Reporting Initiative)
- External certification of CSR-Report

Corporate Governance Please rate the following CSR-criteria in terms of their importance for making an investment decision/ company analysis.

- Good Investor Relations on CSR-Issues (trust, transparency, timeliness, quality)
- Compliance with the official Corporate Governance-Codex of a country

Supplier Relations Please rate the following CSR-criteria in terms of their importance for making an investment decision/ company analysis.

- Policy and guidelines for supplier relations and supplier standards
- Monitoring of compliance with policy and guidelines for supplier relations and supplier standards

Customer Relations Please rate the following CSR-criteria in terms of their importance for making an investment decision/ company analysis.

- Monitoring and reporting of customer satisfaction
- Existence of Customer-Relationship-Management-System

Environmental Management Please rate the following CSR-criteria in terms of their importance for making an investment decision/ company analysis.

- Existence of an environmental policy
- Fixed quantitative environmental targets
- Certified Environmental-Management-System (ISO 14001, EMAS)
- Company monitors its environmental impact (risks) without certified Environmental-Management-System (no certificate)

Energy Please rate the following CSR-criteria in terms of their importance for making an investment decision/ company analysis.

- Information about energy mix
- Programme for the improvement of the energy efficiency
- Programme for the increasing usage of renewable energy sources
- Information on precaution of electricity supply
- Operation of nuclear power plants (sero emission of climate gases)

Emission Strategy Please rate the following CSR-criteria in terms of their importance for making an investment decision/ company analysis.

- Existence of a climate strategy
- Focus on CO2 reduction
- Focus on SO2 reduction
- Focus on NOX reduction
- Is emission trading an appropriate and important instrument for you?

Employees Please rate the following CSR-criteria in terms of their importance for making an investment decision/ company analysis.

- Diversity-Management/ Equal Opportunities (male/female, minorities)
- Health & Safety Programme for employees
- Existence of a human resources development strategy (demographic development, war for talents etc.)

Human Rights Please rate the following CSR-criteria in terms of their importance for making an investment decision/ company analysis.

- Endorsement of supranational organisations like ILO, UNO, OECD, Global Compact
- Conducting social-impact assessments (e.g. during infrastructure projects)
- Existence of a human resources development strategy (demographic development, war for talents etc.)

Corporate Citizenship Please rate the following CSR-criteria in terms of their importance for making an investment decision/ company analysis.

- Existence of a Corporate Citizenship Strategy
- Policy Statement on community involvement
- Details about Corporate Citizenship engagement in reports

Stakeholder Management All stakeholders (in particular NGO's, employees, public authorities, etc.) except shareholders. Please rate the following CSR-criteria in terms of their importance for making an investment decision/ company analysis.

- Consideration of stakeholder interests
- Description of stakeholder management in report(s)
- Stakeholder management in compliance with AA1000 or similar

Added Value through CSR-Management

- How much more would you spend for a company with good CSR-performance?

CSR and the financial crisis:

How will the financial crisis affect CSR (in the utility industry)?

- Strengthen
- Weaken
- No effect

Your comments on CSR

8 Bibliography

Achleitner, A.-K. (2001): Handbuch Investment Banking, 2. Auflage, April 2001, Gabler, Wiesbaden 2001.

Allouche, J. / Laroche, P. (2005): A Meta-Analytcal Investigation of the Relationship Between Corporate Social and Financial Performance, Cahier de Recherche Gregor, Cahrier 03-2005.

Andersen, R. (2008): Modern methods for robust regression, University of Toronto, Sage Publications, 2008.

Atienza Serna, L. (2009): Unbundling – Strategic and Organizational Challenges for Power and Supply Companies. In: Handbook Utility Management, Springer 2009.

Aupperle, K. E/ Carroll, A. B./ J. D. Hatfield.,H.D.(1985): An empirical examination of the relationship between corporate social responsibility and profitability, The Academy of Management Journal 28(2): 446-463, 1985.

Bamberger, I., Wrona, T. (1996): Der Ressourcenansatz und seine Bedeutung für die Strategische Unternehmensführung, ZfbF, 48. Jg., Heft 2, S. 130-153, 1996.

Barney, J. B. (1986a). Strategic factor markets: Expectations, luck and business strategy." Management Science, 32, pp. 1512-1514, 1986.

Barney, J. B. (1986b). "Organizational culture: Can it be a source of sustained competitive advantage?" Academy of Management Review, 11, pp. 656-665.

Barney, J. B. (1991): Firm Resources and Sustained Competitive Advantage, Journal of Management, 17(1), 99-120, 1991.

Barney, J. B. / Arikan, A.M. (2001): The Resource-based View: Origins and Implications, In: The Blackwell Handbook of Strategic Management, Hitt, M.A./ Freeman, E.R./ Harrison, J.S., Blackwell publishers, Oxford, 2001.

Barney, J./ Wright, M./ Ketchen, Jr. (2001): The resource-based view of the firm: Ten years after 1991, Journal of Management, 27 (2001), 625-641, 2001.

Bassen, A./ Kovacs, M. (2008): Environmental, Social and Governance Key Performance Indicators from a Capital Market Perspective (September 11, 2008). Zeitschrift für Wirtschafts- und Unternehmensethik, No. 9/2, pp. 182-192, 2008.

Bassen, A./ Meyer, K./ Schlange, J. (2006): The influence of Corporate Responsibility on the Cost of Capital. SSRN Paper No. 984406, 2006.

Bauer, R./ Hann, D. (2010): Corporate Environmental Management and Credit Risk, SSRN Paper No.1660470, 2010.

Blacconiere, W./ Northcut, W. (1997): Environmental Information and Market Reactions to Environmental Legislation, Journal of Accounting, Auditing, and Finance Vol. 12, (Spring), 149-178, 1997.

Blaug , M. (1996): Economic theory in retrospect, 5th Edition, Cambridge University Press, Cambridge 1996.

Boettke, P.J./ Luther, W.J.(2010): The ordinary economics of an extraordinary crisis. In: Kates, S. (2010): Macroeconomic Theory and Its Failings – Alternative Perspectives on the Global Financial Crisis, Edward Elgar Publishing, 2010.

Bowen, H.R. (1953): Social responsibilities of the businessman, 1. Auflage, New York: Harper & Row, 1953

Bowie, N.E./ Werhane, P.H. (2005): Management Ethics 105, Wiley-Blackwell, 2005.

Bragdon, J./ Marlin, J (1972): Is Pollution Profitable? Risk Management Risk Management, April 1972: 9-18, 1972.

Branco, M.C./ Rodrigues, L.L. (2006): Corporate Social Responsibility and Resource-Based Perspectives, Journal of Business Ethics, 69:111–132, 2006.

Bulan, L.T./ Sanyal, P. (2008): Leverage, Growth Opportunities and The Deregulation of U.S. Electric Utilities, Brandeis University, 2008.

Byrne J. and Mun Y. (2003) "Rethinking Reform in the Electricity Sector: Power Liberalization or Energy Transformation?", Center for Energy and Environmental Policy, University of Delaware, 2003.

Carroll, A.B. (1979): A three dimensional conceptual model of corporate performance, Academy of Management Review, 4: 497-505.

Carroll; A.B. / Shabana, K.M. (2010): The Business Case for Corporate Social Responsibility: A Review of Concepts, Research and Practice, Volume 12, Issue 1, 85–105, March 2010.

Carr, A. (1968) : Is Business Bluffing Ethical?, Harvard Business Review, Vol. 46, p. 143-153, 1968.

Center of Financial Market Integrity - CFA Institute (2008): Environmental, Social, and Governance Factors at Listed Companies - A Manual for Investors, London, 2008.

Ceres (2010): Electric Utilities: Global Climate Disclosure Framework, Ceres 2010.

Cochran, P.L./ Wood, R.A. (1984): Corporate Social Responsibility and Financial Performance, The Academy of Management Journal, Vol. 27, No. 1, pp. 42-56, Mar., 1984.

Colander, D. (2002): The Death of Neoclassical Economics, Middlebury College Economics Discussion Paper No. 02-37, Middlebury, Vermont, 2002.

Cox, P. / Brammer, S./ Millington, A. (2004): An Empirical Examination of Institutional Investor Preferences for Corporate Social Performance, Journal of Business Ethics, Volume 52, Number 1, 27-43, 2004.

Crowther, D./ Rayman-Bacchus, L. (2004): Introduction: Perspectives on Corporate Social Responsibility,in: Crowther, D./ Rayman-Bacchus, L. (Eds.): Perspectives on Corporate Social Responsibility, Aldershot u. a.: Ashgate, 1-17, 2004.

Daily, C.M./ Dalton, D.R./ Cannella, A.A. (2003): Corporate Governance: Decades of Dialogue and Data, The Academy of Management Review, Vol. 28, No. 3 (Jul., 2003), pp. 371-382, 2003.

Dalton, D.R./ Daily, C.M./ Ellstrand, A.E./ Johnson, J.L. (1998): Meta Analytic Reviews of Board Compensation, Leadership Structure, and finnacial Performance. In: Strategic Management Journal, Vol. 19, 269-290, 1998.

Davis, K. (1960): Can Business Afford to Ignore Corporate Social Responsibilities? California Management Review, Spring 1960, Vol. 2, Issue 3, p70.

Davis, K. (1967): Understanding the social responsibility puzzle, Business Horizons, 1967, Vol. 10, Issue 4, p 45-50.

Delmas, M.A./ Russo, M.V./ Montes-Sancho, M.J./ Tokat, Y (2009): Deregulation, efficiency and environmental performance: evidence from the electric utility industry. In: Regulation, Deregulation, Reregulation – Institutional Perspectives, 2009.

Derwall, J., N. Guenster, R. Bauer and K. Koedijk (2005), "The Eco-Efficiency Premium Puzzle," Financial Analysts Journal, Vol. 61, March/April. pp. 51-63, 2005.

Derwall, J.M.M. (2007): The Economic Virtues of SRI and CSR, ERIM Ph.D. Series Research in Management, Rotterdam 2007.

Diamond, D.W./ Verrecchia, R.E. (1991): Disclosure, Liquidity, and the Cost of Capital; The Journal of Finance, Vol.46, No. 4 (Sep., 1991), pp. 1325-1359, Blackwell Publishing, 1991.

Diltz, D.J. (1995): "Does Social Screening Affect Portfolio Performance", Journal of Investing, Vol. 4, p. 64-69, 1995.

Donaldson, T. (1982): Corporations and Morality, Loyola University, Chicago Prentice-Hall, Englewood Cliffs, New Jersey, 1982.

Donaldson, T. / Preston, L. (1995): The Stakeholder Theory of the Corporation: Concepts, Evidence, and Implications, Academy of Management Review, Vol. 20, No. 1: 65-91, 1995.

Edison Electric Institute (2010): Statistical Yearbook of the Electric Power Industry, 2009 Data, December 2010.

Edwards, S./ Allen, A.J./ Shaik, S. (2006): Market Structure Conduct Performance (SCP) Hypothesis Revisited using Stochastic Frontier Efficiency Analysis, Selected Paper prepared for presentation at the American Agricultural Economics Association Annual Meeting, Long Beach, California, July 23-26, 2006.

Evan, W.M./ Freeman, R.E. (1993): A Stakeholder Theory of the Modern Corporation: Kantian Capitalism", Beauchamp, T. L. and N. E. Bowie (eds.), Ethical Theory and Business, 4th edition, Prentice Hall, Englewood Cliffs NJ 1993.

Fernández-Feijóo Souto, B. (2009): Crisis and Corporate Social Responsibility: Threat or Opportunity?, International Journal of Economic Sciences and Applied Research 2 (1): 36-50, 2009.

Fraser, P. (2003): Power Generation Investment In Electricity Markets, International Energy Agency/ OECD, Paris, 2003.

Freeman, R.E. (1984): Strategic Management: A Stakeholder Approach. 1. Auflage, Boston: Pitman, 1984.

Freeman, R.E./ Ramakrishna Velamuri, S./ Moriarty, B. (2006): Company Stakeholder Responsibility: A New Approach to CSR, Business Roundtable Institute for Corporate Ethics, Bridge Papers 2006.

Freeman, R.E./ McVea, J.A. (2001): Stakeholder Approach to Strategic Management, Darden Business School Working Paper No. 01-02, SSRN: 263511, 2001.

Friedman, M. (1970): The Social Responsibility of Business is to increase its Profits,The New York Times Magazine, September 13, 1970.

Gablers Volkswirtschaftslexikon (1996): Neoklassik, In: Gablers Volkswirtschaftslexikon, Bd. 2, L-Z, 1996, Gabler, Wiesbaden 1996.

Garcia, G./ Fink, W. (2009): What Next for European Power Utilities?, In: Handbook Utility Management, Springer 2009.

Garriga, E. / Melé, D. (2004): Corporate Social Responsibility Theories: Mapping the Territory, Journal of Business Ethics 53: 51-71, 2004.

Giannarakis, G./ Theotokas, I. (2011): The Effect of Financial Crisis in Corporate Social Responsibility Performance, International Journal of Marketing Studies, Vol. 3, No. 1; February 2011.

Godfrey, P.C. (2005): The relationship between corporate philanthropy and shareholder wealth: a risk management perspective, Academy of Management Review;Oct2005, Vol. 30 Issue 4, p777, October 2005.

Godfrey, P. C./ C. B. Merrill/ J. M. Hansen. (2009) "The relationship between corporate social responsibility and shareholder value: An empirical test of the risk management hypothesis." Strategic Management Journal, 30 (4): 425-445, 2009.

Hart, S.L. (1995): A Natural-Resource-Based View of the Firm, The Academy of Management Review, Vol. 20, No.4, 968-1014, 1995.

Heise, M. (2011): The stock markets – a handy seismograph?, Börse Online, June, January 2011.

Henderson, D. (2001): Misguided Virtue: False Notions of Corporate Responssibility, New Zealand Business Roundtable, 2001.

Henning, R. (1991): Nachhaltswirtschaft. Der Schlüssel für Naturerhaltung und menschliches Überleben, Quickborn 1991.

Herremans, I. M. / Akathaporn, P. / McInnes, M (1993): An Investigation of Corporate SocialResponsibility Reputation and Economic Performance Accounting, Organizations and Society, 18: 587–604, 1993.

Hoffmann , N.P. (2000): An Examination of the "Sustainable Competitive Advantage" Concept: Past, Present, future, Academy of Marketing and Science Review, Volume 4, 2000.

International Energy Agency/ OECD (2007): Energy Security and Climate Policy - Assessing Interactions, Paris, 2007.

International Energy Agency/ OECD (2005): Lessons from Liberalised Energy Markets, Paris 2005.

Joskow, P.J. (2008): Lessons Learned From Electricity Market Liberalization, The Energy Journal, Special Issue, The Future of Electricity, IAEE 2008.

Kasthofer, K.A. (1818): Bemerkungen über Wälder und Auen des Bernischen Hochgebirges, Aarau 1818.

Kor, Y.Y./ Mahoney, J.T. (2004): Edith Penrose's (1959) Contributions to the Resource-based View of Strategic Management, Journal of Management Studies, 41:1, p. 182-191, Blackwell Puplishing, January 2004.

Kraaijenbrink, J./ Spender, J.-C./ Groen, A.J. (2010): The Resource-Based View: A Review and Assessment of Its Critiques, Journal of Mangement, Vol. 36, No. 1, p. 349-372, 2010.

Kramer, S. (2009): Strategic Sustainability: The case of the New Zealand energy sector, thesissubmitted to the Victoria University of Wellington, 2009.

Lee, C.F. / Lee, A.C. (2006): Encyclopedia of Finance, Springer Science + Business Media, 2006.

Lélé, S.M. (1991): Sustainable development: A critical review, In: World Development, Volume 19, Issue 6, p. 607-621, June 1991.

Levitt, T. (1958): The Dangers of Social Responsibility," Harvard Business Review, 1985, 36(5), p.41-50.

Levitt, T. (1960): Busines Should Stay out of Politics, Business Horizons, 1960, Vo. 3 No.2, p. 45-51.

Maaß, F./ Clemens, R. (2002): Corporate Citizenship: Das Unternehmen als 'guter Bürger', In: Schriften zur Mittelstandsforschung, Nr 94 NF, Institut für Mittelstandsforschung, Deutscher Universitätsverlag, Wiesbaden 2002.

Macharzina, K. (1999): Unternehmensführung: das internationale Managementwissen, Konzepte - Methoden – Praxis, 3. Aufl. Wiesbaden, Gabler, 1999.

Madhani, M.P. (2010): Resource Based View of Competitive Advantage: An Overview, SSRN: http://ssrn.com/abstract=1578704, 2010.

Mäkinen, S./ Seppänen, M. (2006): Strategic Management of Exploiting Technological Opportunities: Integrating Strategy to Operations with Business Model Concept, Proceedings of 15th International Conference on Management of Technology, "East Meets West: Challenges and Opportunities in the Era of Globalization", IAMOT 2006, Beijing, China, May 22-26, 2006.

Margolis, J.D./ Walsh, J.P. (2001): People and Profits: The Search for a Link Between a Company's Social and Financial Performance, Psycology Press, 2001.

Margolis, J.D./ Walsh, J.P (2003): "Misery Loves Companies: Rethinking Social Initiatives by Business", Administrative Science Quarterly, 48, 268-305, June 2003.

Margolis, J.D./ Elfenbein, H.A./ Walsh, J.P. (2009): Does it pay to be good ... And does it matter? A meta-analysis of the relationship between Corporate Social and Financial Performance, SSRN Article Number 1866371, March 2009.

Marshall, A. (1920): Principles of economics, 8th Edition, Macmillan and Company, London, 1920.

Matten, D./Crane, A. (2005): Corporate Citizenship: Toward an Extended Theoretical Conceptualization, in: Academy of Management Review, Volume 30, No. 1, S. 166 -179. Cambridge Univ. Press, 2005.

McGuire, J.B./ Sundgren, A./ Schneeweis, T. (1988): Corporate Social Responsibility and Firm Financial Performance, The Academy of Management Journal Vol. 31, No. 4, pp. 854-872, Dec., 1988.

McIntosh, M./ Thomas, R.; Leipziger, D. / Coleman, G. (2003): Living Corporate Citizenship. Strategic routes to socially responsible business. Edinburgh: Pearson 2003.

McWilliams, A./ Siegel, D. (1997): Event Studies in Management Research: Theoretical and Empirical Issues, The Academy of Management Journal, Vol. 40, No. 3, pp. 626-657, Jun., 1997.

McWilliams, A./ Siegel, D. (2000): Corporate social responsibility and financial performance: correlation or misspecification?, Strategic Management Journal, Vol. 21, Issue 5, 603–609, May 2000.

McWilliams, A./ Siegel, D./ Wright, P.M. (2006): Corporate Social Responsibility: Strategic Implications, Rensselaer Working Papers in Economics, Number 0506, 2005.

Milgate, M. (1987): Equilibrium (Development of the Concept), p. 21-25, In: The New Palgrave Dictionary of Economics, Volume 5, Second Edition (2008), Palgrave MacMillan.

Moskowitz, M (1972): Choosing Socially Responsible Stocks, Business and Society Review (1), S. 71-75, 1975.

Newbert, S.L. (2007): Empirical Research on the Resource-Based View of the Firm, An Assessment and Suggestion for Future Research, In: Strategic Management Journal, 28: 121–146, 2007.

Norman, W./ Mac Donald, C. (2003): Getting to the bottom of the triple bottom line, In Press, Business Ethics Quarterly, 2003.

Oekom (2004): Corporate Responsibility Industry Report, oekom-research, Munich 2004.

Oekom (2008): Corporate Responsibility Industry Report, oekom-research, Munich 2008.

Orlitzky, M./ Benjamin, J.D. (2001): Corporate Social Performance and Firm Risk: A Meta-Analytical Review, Business Society 2001, 40: 369-396, 2001.

Orlitzky, M. F., Schmidt, L., Rynes, S.L. (2003): "Corporate social and financial performance: A meta-analysis." Organization Studies, 24, 2003.

Paladino, A./ Widing, R. / Whitwell, G. (1998): "Synthesising the resource based view and market orientation to understand organizational performance" (Work in Progress), The University of Melbourne, 1779-1784, 1998.

Porter, M. E. (1985): The Competitive Advantage: Creating and Sustaining Superior Performance, N.Y.: Free Press, 1985.

Penrose, E.T. (1959): The theory of the growth of the firm, 2nd edition (1995), Oxford University press, New York, 1995.

Peteraf, M.A. 1993: The Cornerstones of Competitive Advantage: A Resource-Based View, Strategic Management Journal, 14, 179-191, 1993.

Preston, L.E./ Post, J.E. (1975): Private management and public policy: The principle of public responsibility. Englewood Cliffs, NJ: Prentice Hall, 1975.

Preston, O'Bannon (1997): The Corporate Social-Financial Performance Relationship: A Typology and Analysis, In: Business Society, Volume 36, Issue: 4, 419-429, 1997.

Priem, R.L./ Butler, J.E. (2001): Is the Resource-Based „View" a useful Perspective for Strategic Management Research?, Academy of Management Review, Vol 26, No. 1, 22-40, 2001.

Rauscher, M. (1996): Sustainable Development and Complex Ecosystems: An Economist's View. Working Paper No.2, Thünen-Series of Applied Economic Theory, Universität Rostock, CEPR London, 1996.

Rao, S.M. (1996), "The Effect of Published Reports of Environmental Pollution on Stock Prices", Journal of Financial and Strategic Decisions, Vol. 9, pp. 25-32, 1996.

Rennings, K./ Schröder, M./ Ziegler, A. (2003): The Economic Performance of European Stock Corporations. Does Sustainability Matter?, Greener Management International 44, 33-43.

Rutherford, D. (1992): Routledge Dicitionary of Economics, Routledge, London, New York, 1992.

Ryan, B. (2007): Corporate Finance and Valuation, Thomson Learning, London 2007.

Searcy, C./ McCartney, D. / Karapetrovic, S. (2006): Sustainable Development Indicators for the Transmission System of an Electric Utility, In: Corporate Social Responsibility and Environmental Management 14, 135–151 (2007), published online 25 August 2006 in Wiley InterScience.

Sharpe, W.F. (1964): Capital Asset Prices: A Theory of Market Equilibrium under conditions of risk, The Journal of Finance, Vol. 19, No. 3, p.425-442.

Shleifer, A./ Vishny, R. W.(1997): A Survey of Corporate Governance, Journal of Finance Volume 52, No. 2, 1997.

Shotter, M. (2006): The influence of Marshallian neo-classical economics on management accounting in South Africa. Faculty of Economic and Management Sciences at the University of Pretoria, Pretoria, 2006.

Simon, HA (1959): Theories of decision-making in economics and behavioural sciences, In: The American Economic Review, 49 (3): 253-283.

Smith, A. (1776): The Wealth of Nations, Cannan Edition, Modern Library, New York, 1937

Smith, N.C. (2003): Corporate Social Responsibility: Whether or How?, California Management Review, Vol. 45, No. 4, 52-76, 2003.

Spicer, B.H. (1978): Investors, corporate social performance and information disclosure: An empirical study, Accounting Review 53(1): 94–111, 1978.

Starace, F. (2009): The Utility Industry in 2020, In: Handbook Utility Management, Springer 2009.

Sternberg, E. (1999): The Stakeholder Concept: A Mistaken Doctrine, Centre of Business and Professional Ethics, University of Leeds and Analytical Solutions, Foundation of Business Reponsibilities UK), 1999.

Stigler, G.J. (1989): Competition, p. 51-56, In: The New Palgrave Dictionary of Economics, Volume 2, Second Edition (2008), Palgrave MacMillan.

Stiglitz, J.E. (2010): Homoeconomicus: The Impact of the Economic Crisis on Economic Theory, Applied Social Science Associations, January 2-5, 2010, Session E3, Economics for the Good Society, 2010

Sun, W. / Stewart, J./ Pollard, D. (ed.) (2010): Reframing Corporate Social Responsibility: Lessons from the Global Financial Crisis (Critical Studies on Corporate Responsibility, Governance and Sustainability, Volume 1, Emerald Group Publishing Limited, 2010.

Taha, O. (2004): Utility Deregulation on Capital Structure, Leonard N. Stern School of Business, New York University, May 2004.

The Economist (2008): January 17th, 2008: Special report: Corporate social Responsibility, Just good business, 2008.

Tywoniak, S. (2007): Making sense of the resource-based view? In: Proceedings Academy of Management, Philadelphia, USA. paper presented at the 2007 Academy of Management Conference, Philadelphia, 2007.

Tobin, J./ Brainard, W.C. (1977): Assets Markets and the Cost of Capital, In: Essays in Honor of William Fellner, North-Holland, 1977.

Ullmann, A.A. (1985): Data in Search of a Theory: A Critical Examination of the Relationships among Social Performance, Social Disclosure, and Economic Performance of U.S. Firms. Academy of Management Review, Vol. 10: 540-557, 1985.

UNEP Finance Initiative (2009):RI Digest, ESG rating services: How well do they assess corporate performance?, December 2009.

United Nations Environmental Programme (UNEP) Finance Initiative (2005): A legal framework for the integration of environmental, social and governance issues into institutional investment, New York 2005.

Vance, S (1975): Are socially responsible firms good investment Risks. Management Review, Vol. 64: 18-24, 1975.

Varadarajan, P.R./ Menon, A. (1988): Cause-Related Marketing: A Coalignment of Marketing Strategy and Corporate Philanthropy, The Journal of Marketing, Vol. 52, No. 3 (Jul., 1988), pp. 58-74.

Vahrenholt, F. 2009: Renewable Resources for Electric Power: Prospects and Chllenges, In: Handbook Utility Management, Springer 2009.

Waddock S.A./ Graves, S.B. (1997): The corporate social performance-financial performance link. Strategic Management Journal, Vol. 18(4): 303-319, 1997.

Waddock, S.A./ Graves, S. B. (2000): Beyond Built to Last... Stakeholder Relations in 'Built to Last' Companies, In: Business and Society Review 105 (4), S. 393-418, 2000.

Waddock, S. (2008): Corporate Responsibility -Corporate Citizenship: The Development of a Construct, In: Scherer, A.G./ Palazzo, G.:

(Eds.): Handbook of Research on Global Corporate Citizenship, Cheltenham, 25 – 49, 2008.

Waddock, S. (2004): Parallel Universes: Companies, Academics, and the Progress of Corporate Citizenship. In: Business and Society Review, 109 (1), 5-42, 2004.

Wagner, M./ Schaltegger, S. (2003): How does Sustainability Performance Relate to Business Competitiveness?, Greener Management International (GMI), Issue 44, Special Edition on: Sustainability Performance and Business Competitiveness, 5-16, 2003.

Wernerfelt, B (1984).: A Resource-Based View of the Firm, Strategic Management Journal 5 (1984), Vol. 2, 171–180, 1984.

Womack, K.L./ Zhang, Y. (2003): Understanding Risk and Return, the CAPM, and the Fama-French Three-Factor Model, Tuck Case No. 03-111, Tuck School of Business at Dartmouth, 2003.

World Business Council for Sustainable Development (WBCSD) (1999): Corporate Social Responsibility, Meeting Changing Expectations, Genf: WBCSD, 1999.

Online

Centrica (2012): Materiality, http://www.centrica.com/index.asp?pageid=1073 (10.04.2012).

EDF (2012): Stakeholder Engagement, http://www.edfenergy.com/sustainability/our-commitments/stakeholders/stakeholder-engagement.shtml (10.04.2012).

Elkington, J. (2004): Enter the Triple Bottom Line, http://www.johnelkington.com/TBL-elkington-chapter.pdf, (26.1.2009).

Electricity Storage Association (2012): Technology Description of Electricitiy Storage, http://www.electricitystorage.org/technology/storage_technologies/technology_comparison (01.04.2012).

Energy Storage Council (2007): Storage – Value Chain, http://www.energystoragecouncil.org/storage_valuechain.html (01.04.2012).

European Commission (2001): Green Paper - Promoting a European framework for corporate social responsibility, COM (2001) 366 final, Brussels, 18.7.2001, http://eurlex.europa.eu/LexUriServ/LexUriServ.do?uri=COM:2001:0366:FIN:EN:PDF (10.02.2009).

European Commission (2008): Citizen's summary – EU climate and energy package, Brussels 2008, http://ec.europa.eu/climateaction/docs/climate-energy_summary_en.pdf, (18.01.2009).

European Commission (2011): Public consultation on disclosure of non-financial information by companies, http://ec.europa.eu/internal_market/consultations/2010/non-financial_reporting_en.htm. (25.09.2011).

Fonseca, G.L. (2010): The History of Economic Thought, http://homepage.newschool.edu/het//thought.htm#neoclassical, (11.2.2010).

International Energy Agency for electricity supply statistics, http://www.iea.org (12.06.2006).

International Energy Agency (2012), http://www.iea.org/subjectqueries/keyresult.asp?KEYWORD_ID =4103, (1.5.2012).

IPCC (2007): Climate Change 2007 – Synthesis Report, An Assessment of the Intergovernmental Panel on Climate Change, http://www.ipcc.ch/pdf/assessment-report/ar4/syr/ar4_syr.pdf (18.01.2009).

Linde (2009): Our Responsibility, http://www.linde.de/international/web/linde/like35lindecom.nsf/docbyalias/nav_cr_strategy (26.01.2009).

National Grid (2012): Responsibility: Our Investors, http://www.nationalgrid.com/corporate/Our+Responsibility/Our+Stakeholders/Investors/ (10.04.2012).

Oekom Research, 2010, http://www.oekom-research.de/index.php?content=ratings-assessments, (6.7.2010)

PricewaterhouseCoopers (2008): Utilities Global Survey 2008, A world of difference, Tomorrow's power utilities industry, http://www.pwc.com/at/pdf/presse/pwc_pa_080509.pdf (18.01.2009).

Siemens (2009): Corporate Responsibility Framework, http://w1.siemens.com/responsibility/en/framework/index.htm. (26.01.2009).

SustainAbility/ UN Global Compact (2004): *Gearing up: From Corporate Social Responsibility to Governance and Scaleable solutions.* Sustainability, London, 2004, http://www.unglobalcompact.org/docs/news_events/8.1/gearing-up.pdf (10.02.2009).

The New York Times (2011): Led by Demand in China, Energy Use Is Projected to Rise 53% by 2035, September 19, 2011, http://www.nytimes.com/2011/09/20/business/energy-environment/energy-demand-is-expected-to-rise-53-by-2035.html, (30.3.2012)

Weintraub, E. R. (2002): Neoclassical Economics, The Concise Encyclopaedia of Economics, Economic Library, http://www.econlib.org/library/Enc1/NeoclassicalEconomics.html (19.06.2009).

Wikipedia (2009): Corporate Responsibility, http://de.wikipedia.org/wiki/Corporate_Responsibility (26.01.2009).